CW00524241

Contents

BARTLETT

**SUMMER
2021**

Introduction

Over the past 18 months, architecture students around the world have been challenged like no other generation before, constrained by limited resources and restricted social contact. Many have had to adapt to new modes of study and engagement with their schools and peers. Many have had to pilot new platforms for the production and representation of their work and have had to perform on screen to communicate and engage with others. To all first-year students, some abroad from home for the first time, and those in later academic stages who have had to recalibrate their rhythm and momentum, we wish to express our deepest admiration and respect for you.

The Covid-19 pandemic has been a profoundly difficult experience, yet the knowledge gained during this period marks a vital opportunity for a turning point in our discipline and the part we play in shaping it. As one of many schools of architecture in the world, and regarded as one of the best, we must perpetually reflect upon and develop our progression, seeking out every dimension where we can improve, do better, listen and learn. We are always on this journey, and there are times like now when its direction takes on a heightened significance. In this regard, The Bartlett Faculty's recent Athena Swan Silver Award is an encouraging sign that we are on the right track.

This year's Summer Show book offers a glimpse into the work of students on five of our taught programmes: Architecture BSc, Architectural & Interdisciplinary Studies BSc, Engineering & Architectural Design MEng, Architecture MSci and Architecture MArch. It celebrates the students' creativity, activism, inspiration and ingenuity, and reflects the evolution of individual pursuits increasingly motivated by sharing and collaborating on collective goals. The book also conveys an overwhelming motivation to contribute to the evolution of our discipline in ways that are critical, ethical, opposed, constructive, visionary, insightful, innovative and open. It is upon these trajectories that we build our reputation for radical thinking, utilising the collective intelligence and creative and critical abilities of the diverse and talented individuals that make up our school.

The book accompanies our virtual Summer Show, which provides more information, context, analysis and representation for each project. For the second year running, we are missing the presence of a physical show and the buzz of curious and excited crowds. These memorable experiences will soon return, yet we must not diminish the achievement and value of the digital exhibition environment that shares our students' work with more visitors than ever before. Over the past year, more than 90,000 users have visited our virtual exhibitions; more than twice as many as our physical shows would typically attract in a year. This speaks to us in many ways, not least to the accessibility that this resource offers to those who could not visit before. Many people deserve thanks for this achievement and special praise indeed to our Bartlett Show website team, comprised of staff from our B-made, Education and Communications departments.

Amongst the vanguard of initiatives recently launched at The Bartlett School of Architecture, 2020/21 marks the first graduating year for Engineering & Architectural Design MEng: our four-year programme developed and delivered in collaboration with the UCL Institute for Environmental Design and Engineering and UCL Department of Civil, Environmental and Geomatic Engineering. Congratulations to the graduating students, of whom 50% gained first-class degrees. We also welcome another pioneering cohort onto our Architecture MSci programme, the school's new and innovative alternative route to RIBA/ARB Parts 1 and 2, with a novel fifth year based in practice.

Before you advance to the book's core content, we wish to express our sincere thanks to the full community of academic and professional services staff within The Bartlett School of Architecture, The Bartlett Faculty and across the UCL campus, including tutors, administrators, technicians, librarians, professors and security staff, amongst others. Your response to the pandemic, including your volunteering efforts, has been immense and has propelled us towards greater inclusivity, exchange and collaboration. Thank you also to our many guests and supporters, including alumni, invited practitioners, researchers and critics. Your invaluable contributions have guided and informed us and have vividly illustrated how dependent we are on these generous relationships, which care for and invest in our students' futures.

Finally, an open call. The 26th UN Climate Change Conference (COP 26) will be held in Glasgow in October 2021. Researchers from across UCL and The Bartlett will be taking part and helping to shape the urgent need for a coherent and focussed outcome. Building upon The Bartlett's legacy of critical and visionary work, and looking forward to the academic year ahead, we encourage our entire school community and graduates to channel their many collective talents and abilities towards the ongoing climate emergency and all associated forms of social injustice. It is our collaborative strength that will resolve the greatest environmental challenge of our time.

Professor Bob Sheil
Director of The Bartlett School of Architecture
Barbara-Ann Campbell-Lange
Deputy Director of The Bartlett School of Architecture
Professor Frédéric Migayrou
Chair, Bartlett Professor of Architecture, The Bartlett School of Architecture

Working from home. Photo by Will Hodges, UG12

Architecture BSc
(ARB/RIBA Part 1)

Architecture BSc (ARB/RIBA Part 1)

Programme Directors:
Ana Monrabal-Cook, Luke Pearson

The boundaries of the architectural profession have been tested more than ever in recent times, not only by technological and cultural shifts but also environmental, political and human crises. In this context, Architecture BSc continues to establish primary knowledge and understanding about the core principles of the discipline, providing a platform from which experimental and challenging design work can emerge.

The programme teaches students the fundamentals of architecture, developing their critical ability to think about what it means to synthesise architectural designs and what methods they can utilise to do so. This year the programme accommodated a wider set of methods and research themes than ever before, with social projects for community groups and participatory practices sitting alongside explorations in advanced digital simulations, experimental drawing practice, filmmaking and virtual reality. Experimentation is tied to a rigorous approach to design, not only in spatial planning but also in technology, social engagement, environmental design and computation, allowing our students to produce complex and layered buildings.

Our Year 1 cohort is organised as a single group before a design unit system begins in Year 2. The first year is contextual through which architectural expertise is developed using diverse experimentation and exploration. Several modules, including 'The History of Cities and their Architecture' and 'Making Cities', meld ideas from different programmes and areas of research within The Bartlett, allowing students to develop an understanding of the historical and social role of the architect.

In Years 2 and 3, our design units offer unique expertise and a broad range of approaches, allowing students to connect their studies to their developing interests. The 14 units explore diverse themes and agendas, including the relationship between architecture and landscape; digital simulation and fabrication; and the role of narrative and the political context of design, from working with housing associations in the UK to the study of the development gap between the Global North and South. Each unit establishes a methodology that builds core skills and expands students' work in new directions.

Following tailored research briefs, students are encouraged to contextualise their projects by carrying out in-depth studies into urban and rural conditions to understand the complexities of producing architecture in radically different environments. This year, restrictions relating to the global pandemic impacted our ability to carry out field trip activities and physically visit sites, other architecture schools and studios. Instead, each design unit organised online masterclasses, workshops, talks and virtual tours, allowing students to connect with a community of experts and professionals.

Throughout the degree, students relate their design projects to all other taught modules. This culminates in Year 3, where design and technology are developed in synthesis, complemented by self-selected thematic interests in history and theory. By the end of their undergraduate studies, our students are equipped to engage with the design of architecture in a sophisticated manner, placing their own practice and research into wider socio-political, historical and environmental contexts.

This year, the varied and ambitious design projects all showed a desire to tackle the complexities of our built environment and the pressing issues it faces. Students addressed ecology through bioreceptive materials, analysis of sites through deep time and new ways of understanding natural processes through advanced computation. The social potential of architecture was explored in projects examining programmes for community groups, the vernacular architecture of South America and the impact of failed and re-purposed developments in Asian cities. Architecture as spatial storytelling assumed a renewed purpose as a way of connecting people, with students exploring innovative techniques in drawing and animation to propose buildings that communicate alternative futures and suggest new ways of living. Many students draw from their own personal experiences and geographical location, demonstrating a broad range of backgrounds and influences. The work this year is therefore both uniquely diverse and culturally specific.

The Covid-19 pandemic continues to challenge our studio culture. Students and tutors have adjusted to working online, using digital platforms to communicate ideas. From digital pinboards to overhead cameras, we have used all tools available to maintain the visual communication necessary to develop creative and inventive proposals. Even in this adversity, the students have produced projects that are imaginative, rigorous and sensitive. The sheer range of approaches and the daring acts of design that have emerged demonstrate that, as our undergraduate students carefully study the fundamentals of architecture, whatever circumstances arise, they continue to push the ever-shifting boundaries of the profession.

Many thanks to our Programme Senior Administrator, Kim van Poeteren, and our Postgraduate Teaching Assistants Stephannie Contreras-Fell, Zoe Diakaki, Hannah Lewis, Dan Pope, Arinjoy Sen and William Sheng-Yang for all your positive energy and hard work.

Year 1 Students

Sara Abbod, David Abi Ghanem, Fatemeh Abkhou, Dimitrios Andritsog, Lorenzo Angoli, Shujian (Bob) Bao, Eirini Bargiotak, Amy Bass, Ellen Baxter, Ani Begaj, Ayisha Belgore, Sarah Bibby, Jack Bowers, Marcus Busby, Adam Butcher, Maria Bystrons, Zeynep Cam, Marco Carraro, Fasai Chainuvati, Sharukan Chandrar, Zhun Lyn Chang, Ibrahim Charafi, Nan-Hao Chen, Jaeho (Leo) Cho, Yongjun Choi, Daniel Cioara, Ilia Cleanthous, Rebecca Criste, Amy Daja, Sophie Du Ry Van Beest Holle, Josiah Elleston-Burell, Chuhan (Paris) Feng, Scarlet Fernandes, Sofia Forni, Maria Gasparinatou, Magdalena Gauden, Luke Gifford, Myles Green, Edmund (Flurry) Grierson, Esin Gumus, Shuhao Guo, Phoebe Hampson, Magdalena Herman, Ioi (Nicole) Ho, Shing (Bertha) Ho, Sophie Hoet, Claudiu-Liciniu Horsia, Rabiyya Huseynova, Maria Hussiani, Zubair Ibrahim, Ina-Stefana Ioan, Fahad Janjua, Zuzanna Jastrzebska, Marike Jungk, Fatim Kamara, Katie Kamara, Shouryan Kapoor, Fardous Khalafalla, Adam Klestil, Archie Koe, Mikaella Konia, Emmanouil Konstantinou, Arushi Kulshreshtha, James Kumagai, Shiwei Lai, Tran Lai, Chin (Shirley) Lam, Hoi Lee, Chanya (Miu) Leosivikul, Jinyi (Athena) Li, Yutong (Sabrina) Li, Hannah Lingard, Zofia Lipowska, Maisy Liu, Sze (Christopher) Liu, Hui-Shan Low, Mayling Ly, Riya Mamtora, Max Messer, Natalia Michalowska, Po (Tate) Mok, Giulia Mombello Perez, Jihoon Moon, Peter Moore, Rohini Mundey, Iga Najdeker, Jatin Naru, Barbara Nohr, Ciaran O'Donnell, Zeynep Okur, Ioana Oprescu, Charize Orio, Luiza-Elisabeta Oruc, Roland Paczolay, Sneha Parashar, Alexandria Pattison, Gabriella Peixouto Bandeira Da Silva, George Perks, Keeleigh Pham, Maria Pop, Milen Purewal, Gautham Puthenpurackal, Eden Robertson, Adriana Rodriguez-Villa Lario, Julia Rzaca, Luke Saito Koper, George Sanger, Gabriela Sawicka, Nora Seferi, Oyku Sekelu, Teshan Seneviratne, Elina Seyed Nikkhou, Rauf Sharifov, Yingqi (Isabella) Shen, Annika Siamwalla, Yong (Benedict) Siow, Kateryna Skiba, Besim Smakiq, Skylar Smith, Julia Specht, Ilinca-Maria Stanescu, Layla Stevens, Teodora-Georgiana Strugariu, Pasut Sudlabha, Sidre Sulevani, Scott Tan, Alara Taskin, Ilya Tchevela, Amelia Teigen, Cosmin Ticus, William Tindall, Emily To, James Tyler, Amelia (Lettie) Vera-Sanso Talbot, An Vu, Eloise Joanne Walders Searle, Chi (Matthew) Wang, Haodi (Hardy) Wang, Caitlin Wong, Jade Wong, Kwong (Christine) Wong, Tsz (Vivian) Wong, Zaynah Younus, Nicole Zhao, Ziyan Zhao, Deqing (Rachel) Zhou, Yanyu (Cici) Zhou, Shiyan Zhu, Mateusz Zwijacz

Distantly Close

Year 1

Directors: Max Dewdney, Frosso Pimenides

This unprecedented year started with a project entitled 'Rear Window', which asked students to examine their immediate physical space – objects, thresholds and interfaces – and explore their windows and the world beyond them. Through this drawing study of proximity, perspective and perception they discovered a different form of imagining, inventing extraordinary versions of the ordinary.

The Year 1 installation, a collective project, had to occur virtually for the first time. Collaboration is a skill used to cultivate at all levels; as we learned to collaborate remotely across the globe, this extraordinary year saw fiction become reality. The installation was based on an examination of the students' own daily rituals, as well as those of others, and what was both near and far. These examinations were then translated into ten spaces of wonder. Each group of 15 students was given one well-known personality, including the astronaut Mae Carol Jemison, artists Ai Weiwei and Marina Abramović and the musicians Patti Smith and Björk, amongst others. Working with physical modelling and stop-frame animation, the students produced ten short films that translated their characters' everyday rituals and routines into spatial events.

As an alternative field trip, we embarked on a new way of learning and familiarising ourselves with the world. We collaborated with five international architectural museums/archives: RIBA/V&A (London, UK), Drawing Matter (Somerset, UK), CCA (Montreal, Canada), M+ (Hong Kong) and Norman Foster Foundation (Madrid, Spain), in order to understand drawing as a fundamental tool of communication.

This year's main building project was called 'Proximity City: Looking back to go forward', which operated on two scales: the first addressed the students' local areas and identified what was special about them and what was missing from a civic point of view; the second located a site for students to design a building that addressed their reading of the area. In particular, students drew ideas from the concept of the '15-minute city' – a city of proximity – and identified an immediate social programme of living, working, supplying, caring, learning and enjoying.

Through a small building design we encouraged students to develop a critical understanding of what immediately surrounds them, creating a future vision for that which is missing and to visualise what it could become in a post-pandemic world. Year 1 Architecture BSc became a global studio, endeavouring to understand the cultural heritage and personal interests of each student in their unique first year of architectural education.

Associates: Stefan Lengen, Gavin Robotham, Manolis Stavrakakis

Tutors: Alastair Browning, Joel Cady, Ivan Tsz Long Chan, Zachary Fluker, Maria Fulford, Alicia Gonzalez-Lafita Perez, Ashley Hinchcliffe, Vasilis Ilchuk, Fergus Knox, Stefan Lengen, Matt Lucraft, Laura Mark, Alicia Pivaro, Lucy Read, Isaac Simpson, Colin Smith, Manolis Stavrakakis, Gabriel Warshafsky

Thank you to our media studies coordinators Joel Cady and Stefan Lengen, and tutors Zachary Fluker, Niamh Grace, Jack Hardy, Matt Lucraft

Y1.1 Ellen Baxter, Ibrahim Charafi, Nan-Hao Chen, Daniel Cioara, Rebecca Criste, Chuhan (Paris) Feng, Maria Hussiani, Yutong (Sabrina) Li, Zofia Lipowska, Jatin Naru, Ciaran O'Donnell, Charize Orio, Gabriela Sawicka, Yingqi (Isabella) Shen, Tsz (Vivian) Wong 'Wunderkammer'. The project is composed of 15 tapestries all inspired by the life, work and daily rituals of Italian fashion designer Elsa Schiaparelli (1890–1973).

Y1.2, Y1.26 Maisy Liu 'The Fish Hut'. The project is located in the rural district of Shunyi in Beijing, China. Because the area is primarily private and residential, there are minimal facilities for entertainment and leisure activities. Situated along an existing bridge and dam, it provides a space for fishermen and other members of the community to prepare, cook, smoke and eat fish.

Y1.3 Cosmin Ticus 'Rear Window'. Inspired by Alfred Hitchcock's 1954 film, the project represents a reading of a room through light and the surfaces it interacts with.

Y1.4 Po (Tate) Mok 'In Celebration of Children's Literature'. The project develops the ethos of The Foundling Hospital in London and the Coram foundation through the construction of a reading pod and a set of climbing frames that act as an interchangeable façade.

Y1.5 Mateusz Zwijacz 'The Fire-Prevention Centre in the Canopy'. The proposed building is located in Tatra National Park, southern Poland. It is designed as part of a building complex that aims to raise awareness among tourists about forest fires.

Y1.6 Chuhan (Paris) Feng 'Rear Window: Emotion Islands'. Inspired by Alfred Hitchcock's 1954 film, the project explores the relationship between inside and outside, and brings them together.

Y1.7 Zeynep Cam, Scarlet Fernandes, Ina-Stefana Ioan, Archie Koe, Chanya (Miu) Leosivikul, Sze (Christopher) Liu, Mayling Ly, Luiza-Elisabeta Oruc, Skylar Smith, Ilya Tchevela, Cosmin Ticus, Zaynah Younus, Shiyan Zhu, Mateusz Zwijacz 'Wunderkammer'. A project composed of a series of sound installations inspired by the life, work and daily rituals of the Icelandic singer Björk.

Y1.8 Julia Rzaca 'Community Centre for the Strzeszyn Literacki Area'. Located in Strzeszyn Literacki, Poland, the proposal consists of two main buildings, the smallest of which is a quiet space for the elderly. The building's shape is tightly knit and features a significant amount of greenery.

Y1.9 Rauf Sharifov 'Tea House'. The project is located in the city of Baku, Azerbaijan, in one of the Narimanov neighbourhoods. The building consists of two indoor tea huts and an outdoor courtyard that acts as a communal space for the residents of the neighbourhood.

Y1.10 Adam Butcher 'The Tree Pod Loop'. A building on a footbridge that crosses over Bloodmoor Road in Lowestoft, Suffolk that blends distant views with the immediate landscape to create a place that brings the human experience into context through contemplation and the juxtaposition of near and far.

Y1.11 Myles Green 'Rear Window'. The project investigates a leak in the ceiling of a bay window and explores surveying as a method to measure and investigate the transformative power of rainwater.

Y1.12 Zofia Lipowska 'Rear Window'. The project explores how everyday objects – in this instance a sink – can become evidence of our actions.

Y1.13 Yutong (Sabrina) Li 'Horse Chestnut Launderette for Canal and Land Lifestyles'. Situated by the Regent's Canal in Kings Cross, London, is a launderette that is accessible for people who live on the canal and those living on the land. A horse chestnut tree is planted in the middle of the courtyard and symbolises the ecologically friendly system that substitutes the chemical detergent used in the launderette.

Y1.14 Julia Rzaca 'Rear Window'. The project focusses on voyeurism, self-awareness, the observation of habits and the avoidance of others because of the Covid-19 rules.

Y1.15, Y1.18 Barbara Nohr 'The Home for the Collective Memory of 'Ox Town's' Displaced Commun.' The project is situated in the Polish town of Wołów. The building is composed of a timber-frame structure and thatched roof native to the Eastern Borderlands, and was originally constructed by the community.

Y1.16, Y1.17 Cosmin Ticus 'Marshalsea Bouldering Centre'. An outdoors and semi-outdoors bouldering facility in the centre of London. The building anchors itself to the last remaining wall of the Marshalsea Prison, extending into the courtyard of St George the Martyr. It activates both a deserted garden and a seemingly unsafe and dark alley.

Y1.19 Claudiu-Liciniu Horsia 'The Bird Watching Tower'. The project is located in the heart of Transylvania, in central Romania, at the edge of a forest near the small village of Cornești. The building is a tower dedicated to bird watching.

Y1.20 Rohini Mundey 'Mushroom Cave'. The project is situated in St Chad's Place, a quiet alleyway in Kings Cross, London. The alleyway is used as a space to sell homeopathic mushrooms for the Royal London Hospital for Integrated Medicine on Great Ormond Street.

Y1.21 Maisy Liu 'Rear Window'. Inspired by Roy Andersson's film sets and David Hockney's collages, the project explores how multiple picture planes can be combined to create the illusion of a complete space.

Y1.22 Katie Kamara 'Rear Window'. The project attempts to observe and codify interactions with changing states and obstacles that cause displacement while walking on Dartmoor in Devon.

Y1.23 Sophie Du Ry Van Beest Holle 'Rear Window'. A transportable duvet that inflates. The inside space is designed to induce the same feeling of comfort one might feel at home.

Y1.24 Chuhan (Paris) Feng 'A Composing Studio for Travel Composers, within a Botanic Garden'. A house and studio, located on Lützowplatz in Berlin, designed to bring back the site's vitality and keep the spirit of its history alive. The main feature of the house is a garden for composers, which also acts as an open-air recital space in the summer months.

Y1.25 Sophie Du Ry Van Beest Holle 'Papier-mâché 'After School' Club'. Located in the heart of Camden, London, on the corner where the high street and Regent's Canal intersect. The building hosts after-school papier-mâché furniture-making classes for local primary school children.

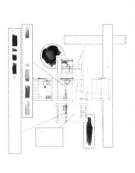

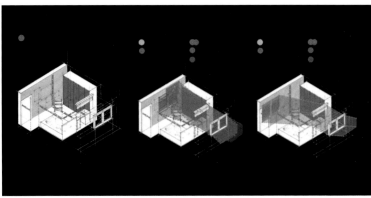

Y1.3

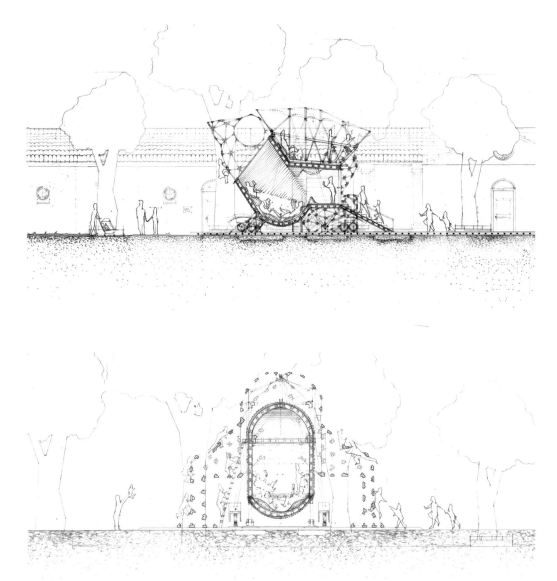

Y1.4

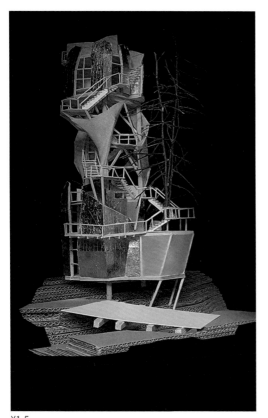

Y1.5

Y1.6

Y1.7

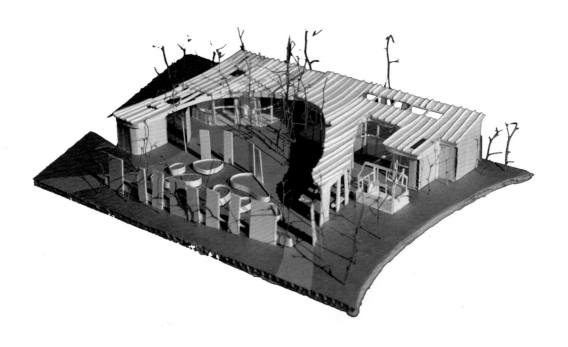

Y1.8

Y1.9

Y1.10

Y1.11

Y1.12

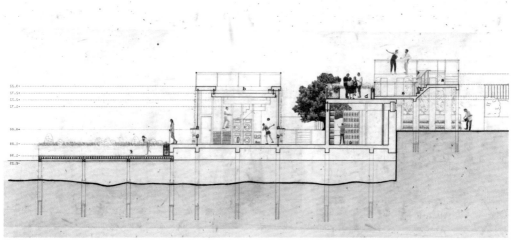

Y1.13

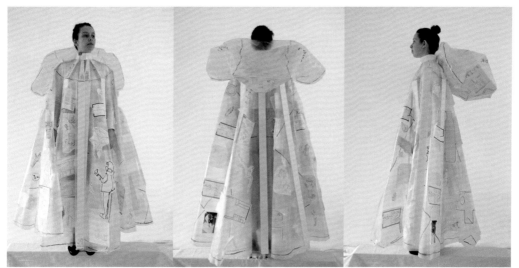

Y1.14

Y1.15

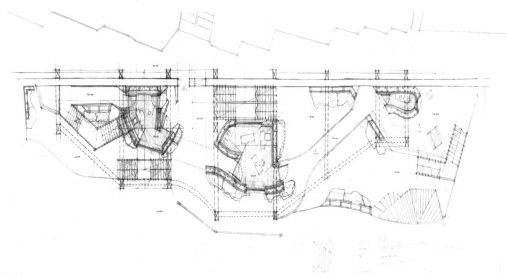

Y1.16

Y1.17

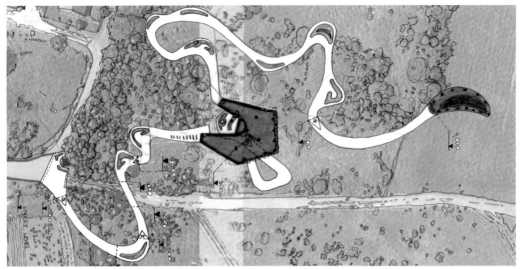

Y1.18

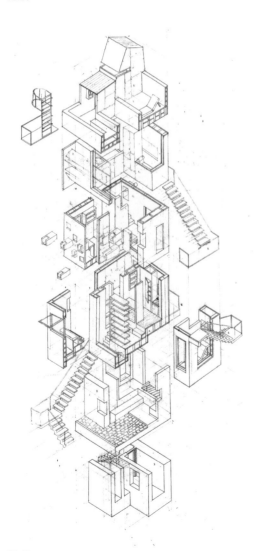

Y1.19

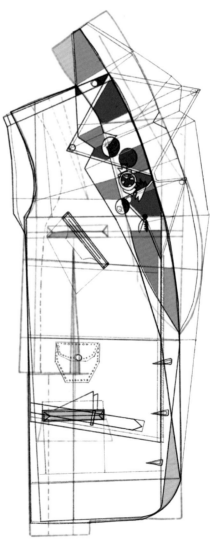

Y1.20

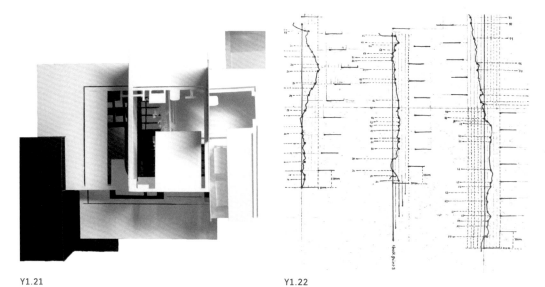

Y1.21   Y1.22

Y1.23

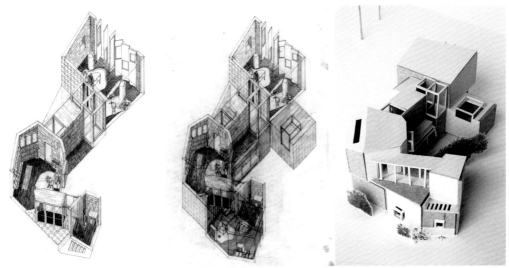

Y1.24

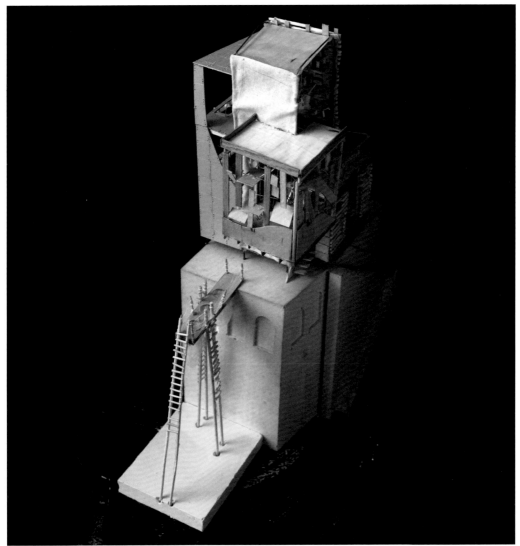

Y1.25

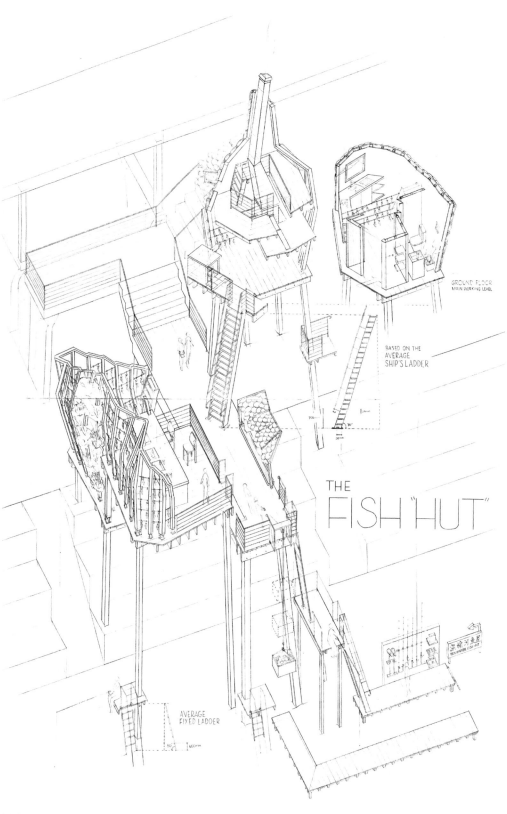

GROUND FLOOR
MAIN WORKING LEVEL

BASED ON THE
AVERAGE
SHIP'S LADDER

THE
FISH "HUT"

AVERAGE
FIXED LADDER

Y1.26

Stealth Ecology

Murray Fraser, Michiko Sumi

This year students were asked to think about social and environmental sustainability in an inventive and sensuous manner. A collective approach to building cities is vital if we are to reduce energy consumption and subsequent environmental damage, even if free-market capitalism challenges such aspirations. To do so, radical thinking about the relationship between humans and nature, and how we organise society, is required. Increasingly, in ecological terms, the modern metropolis is both the cause and effect of this struggle encompassing power, economics, culture and nature.

Why is ecological thinking such a crucial challenge today? The shift towards the East, notably China and India, in terms of capital and power, is one obvious consequence of globalisation. This can be viewed positively, e.g. our growing understanding of global networks and their relationship to the planet as a complex ecosystem, and negatively, e.g. the severity of the Covid-19 pandemic.

Biodiversity is the subject of the moment; the biodiversity of cities is essential for social, cultural and economic life. Cities must not be seen in opposition to nature; rather, they exist within a sophisticated system where the preservation of animal and plant life is equally as important as reducing carbon emissions and energy consumption, possibly even more so.

UG0 examined many aspects of biodiversity and social and environmental sustainability in relation to building programme, construction, theory and architectural meaning. We designed novel and captivating proposals using interventions that seek to improve urban biodiversity for birds, mammals, reptiles, insects, fish, trees, flowers and plants. As ever, the aim was for students to carry out a process of intensive research into contemporary architectural ideas, urban conditions, cultural relations and practices of everyday life, and learn how to use these findings to create innovative and challenging forms of architecture for the contemporary city. Since there was no field trip, students spent time testing their designs by inserting 3D digital models into a real-time model of London.

Year 2
Marius Balan, Alannah Fowler, Jack Powell, Rupert Rochford, Luke Sturgeon, Karla Torio Rivera, Isobel Watson

Year 3
Eudon Gray Desai, Megan Irwin, Angharad James, Ye Ha Kim, Rebecca Miller, Sirikarn (Preaw) Paopongthong, Konrad Pawlaczyk, Jiayi (Silver) Wang

Technical tutors and consultants: Thomas Bush, Ewa Hazla, Nick Jewell, John I'Anson

Critics: Sabina Andron, Julia Backhaus, Johan Berglund, Anthony Boulanger, Eva Branscome, Malina Dabrowska, Pedro Font-Alba, Millie Green, Ben Hayes, Jonathan Hill, Kaowen Ho, Becci Honey, Bruce Irwin, Anja Kempa, Yeoryia Manolopoulou, Hazel McGregor, Ana Monrabal-Cook, Oliver Morris, Aggie Parker, Luke Pearson, Theo Games Petrohilos, Stuart Piercy, Joshua Scott, Ben Stringer, Mika Zacharias

Sponsors: Bean Buro, KPF, VU City

0.1, 0.3–0.4 **Ye Ha Kim, Y3** 'Digital Grotesque/Liquid Gold, W1'. The scheme proposes a DNA centre using liquid honey as a data-storage medium, thereby merging the natural honey-making process of bees with innovative methods of recording environmental information. Honey contains crucial ecological data about the floral ratio of the ecosystem at any given time. Collecting this data can inform future land preservation and reclamation strategies. This is particularly timely in relation to predictions that central London will be completely flooded by the year 2100 due to climate change. Over time, the digitally differentiated surfaces of the columns on the façade will create an inhabitable ecosystem for bees, whereas beneath, in the drowned world, corals will flourish symbiotically.

0.2, 0.21 **Sirikarn (Preaw) Paopongthong , Y3** 'An Agrarian Agenda, Bangkok'. A proposal for a new kind of agrarian village in suburban Bangkok, Thailand, that serves as a central hub for agricultural practices alongside an innovative residential model. Covering a large area of arable land and irrigation channels that are connected to the local canal network, a return to the traditional practice of family-based subsistence farming allows a suburban village to become self-reliant. Cultivation processes important to agrarian production, specifically paddy-field rice farming, are incorporated to devise localised earthen construction techniques.

0.5–0.6 **Konrad Pawlaczyk, Y3** 'What Do Bats Find Beautiful?, E5'. Experimenting with reversing the anthropocentric power dynamics of architecture on a site along the River Lea in Hackney Marshes, East London, the design focusses on understanding the perspectives and needs of horseshoe bats. As a result, human activity is located solely in the negative space that is left over by the bats' activities. The building's primary function is to create spaces that accommodate different activities in the daily life of bats. The constructed habitat mediates between underground tunnel spaces that serve mainly as roosts for hibernation or as overground summer 'social roosts' that function as nurseries to raise young bats.

0.7 **Luke Sturgeon, Y2** 'A Falcon's Place, NW1'. The gradual return of the peregrine falcon to major cities in Europe in recent years is both a natural occurrence and a result of artificial reintroduction. Building upon a new ecological appreciation of this endangered bird of prey, the project reveals changes taking place within London's wider ecosystems. It also considers the types of relationships that can be fostered between humans and avifauna – birds of a particular region – through a better understanding of the natural systems in our cities. The site is an ultra-narrow sliver of land behind St Pancras International in London.

0.8–0.9 **Megan Irwin, Y3** 'Chateau Camden, NW1'. The global wine industry is reshaping its agricultural activities as climate change affects weather patterns. The poleward shift of warmer temperatures is predicted to shake-up the geographic distribution of wine production; a process already underway as English winemaking expands. The project imagines an urban agricultural exploration, based on the prediction that London's climate will be like Barcelona's is today by 2050. It creates a circular economy for winemaking that revolves around three key phases: growing, making and recycling.

0.10–0.12 **Rebecca Miller, Y3** 'Theatricalities of Chalk, Surbiton'. Located in a disused Victorian-era reservoir at Seething Wells, South West London, the project mediates the slow and unseen geological timescales of the Arcadian Thames, with a specific focus on chalk and seashells imported to the site during its initial construction. The proposed landscape of hedonistic leisure – including a theatre, gallery and community centre – sits directly across from the pleasure gardens of Hampton Court Palace. These leisure activities are spatially subordinate to a chalk research facility, the purpose of which is to remind people of the threat that Britain's natural chalk faces from urban development.

0.13 **Rebecca Miller, Y3** 'Observatory of Natural Timescales, Ham'. Sited at Ham House, Richmond-upon-Thames in London, an 'ecological condenser' heightens occupants' visual and haptic perception of the natural landscape. The observatory reveals natural timescales, both above and below ground, that are often imperceptible to human understanding. The gridded building rakes in light from the surrounding environment and allows itself to be overtaken by natural weather conditions via disposable skin-like cladding elements.

0.14, 0.20 **Angharad James, Y3** 'Gospel Oak Piano and Timber Factory, NW5'. The northern hemisphere is home to ectomycorrhizal root systems: fungi that connect tree roots in what is known as the Wood Wide Web. These fungi act as major carbon sinks, yet they now face decimation due to climate change. At around 30%, the London Borough of Camden has one of the highest rates of tree-cover in Britain. The project investigates the borough's industrial past as the international centre for piano manufacturing, and proposes a new piano factory and connected forest on Hampstead Heath. As trees grow best in rich ecological forests with soundscapes of between 115–250Hz, the factory is designed to produce a new soundscape in harmony with the forest.

0.15–0.16 **Eudon Gray Desai, Y3** 'Reindustrialising Regent's Canal, E3'. The project proposes a cultural and economic regeneration of Regent's Canal in London using two naturally occurring biomaterials – bacterial cellulose and chitin – that can be sourced from the canal. Three distinct canal-side structures are situated on the stretch between Victoria Park and Limehouse Basin, and create the foundational infrastructure for the proposed biopolymer revolution. The canal-side structures include a material production factory, a water-treatment facility and a marketplace.

0.17, 0.19 **Jiayi (Silver) Wang, Y3** 'Tilbury-on-Thames, Essex'. This project asks whether tourism can regenerate riverside towns in Essex, using Tilbury as a test site. Examining existing environmental and social problems, such as vulnerability to flooding and high unemployment, the urban masterplan provides a flood-resistant townscape and a multi-level cruise terminal along the riverfront. The cruise terminal operates as a community centre and produces energy through a bank of specially designed water turbines – a dramatic architectural view that welcomes arriving boats. Parts of the structure are designed to collapse to allow for simple rebuilding after extreme storms and for maintenance.

0.18 **Jack Powell, Y2** 'Thamesmead Archipelago: Speaking with mycelium'. The project facilitates interspecies relationships by reconnecting humans with their senses. Mycelium is used as a potential collaborator in the context of climate change and rising sea levels. Utilising this underground organism to re-mediate a hazardous landfill site creates a new experiment in the wake of previous architectural interventions in the area, including the Royal Arsenal in Woolwich and the Thamesmead estate, the latter as featured in Stanley Kubrick's *A Clockwork Orange* (1971). As we enter a new age of information, finding ways to communicate with, and extract data from, other living species will provide our biosphere with tangible value.

0.2

0.3

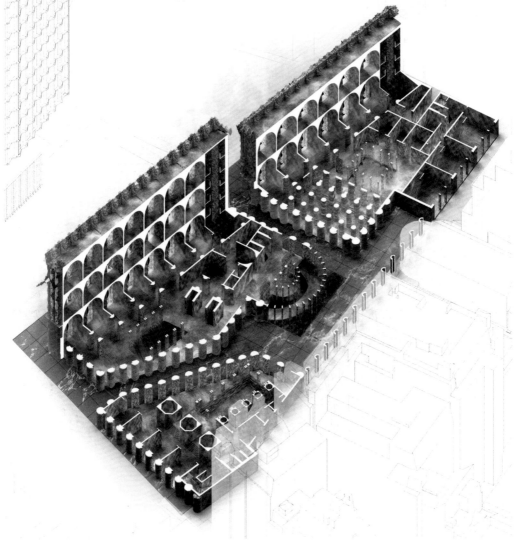

0.4

0.5

0.6

0.7

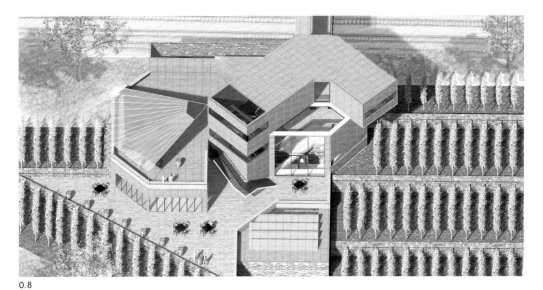

0.8

0.9

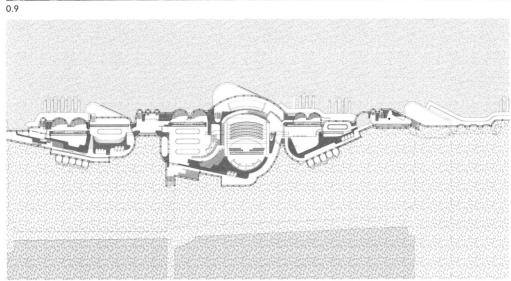

0.10

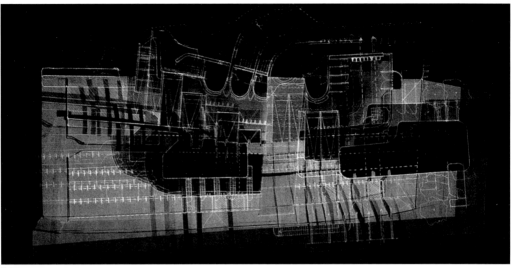

0.11

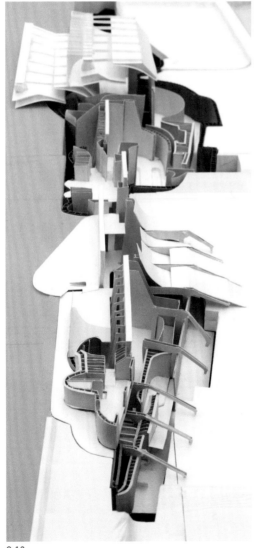

0.12

0.13

0.14

0.15

0.16

0.18

0.19

0.20

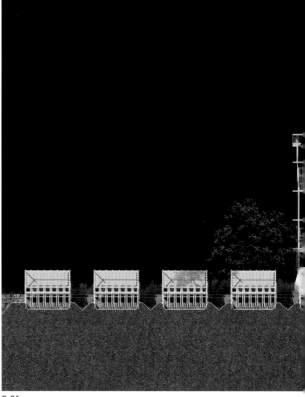

0.21

Down to Earth

UG1

Amica Dall, Margit Kraft, Toby O'Connor

Can the way we build and the way we think about building and belonging to a place change how we inhabit the Earth? Politicians and pundits continue to predict that the future will belong to the knowledge worker, yet the present remains stubbornly physical. Although many of our imaginations are increasingly committed to the virtual, we carry them around in bodies that require food, warmth, affection, shelter and a planet that sustains conditions for life.

Construction remains a deeply physical practice involving vast logistical networks made of pits, mines, furnaces, warehouses, ships, trucks and rails, all focussed on the transformation of the subterranean into the superterranean and of sludge and rocks into the city and the rest of human material culture. Even the most humble of commercial materials is touched by hundreds of hands on its journey from source to site.

This year, UG1 stayed connected to this reality, with a strong emphasis on working with our hands. Taking a firmly material approach to the questions of site, survivability and belonging, we worked experimentally with a palette of three materials – earth, timber and stone – on a set of small underused sites, selected from the Mayor of London's Small Sites x Small Builders programme.

We began by building a collective knowledge base of materials across a range of scales, from the body to the planetary, and developed skills in ways of making that are possible within a domestic environment using locally sourced materials. Students developed their own lines of design research to think about how, as architects, they can use materiality to create connections with a particular place – a sense of being at home in the world and with each other – and focussed on finding strategies, methods and treatments that are geared towards more sustainable, local and cyclic forms of building.

Individual briefs for specific sites were developed in relation to Grow, a community organisation based in London. Grow are currently creating a new urban farm in North London as an educational and cultural resource. The farm will be a place of direct embodied learning and shared endeavour.

Aiming for materially nuanced, sensitive and inventive responses to simple spatial requirements, the projects were developed to provide collective facilities within existing urban frameworks. The students engaged with established social infrastructures while creating new and transformative possibilities for the people that occupy them. The projects uniquely respond to their site but are connected by a collective aspiration to develop a deep and detailed understanding of what buildings are, where they come from, how they are made, how they feel to occupy and how they interact within their urban context.

Year 2
Dominik Do, Irene Entrecanales, Arnie Freund-Williams, Gabe Fryer-Eccles, Barney Iley-Williamson, Moe Kojima, Lim Wei Lim, Leo Osipovs, Flavia Scafella, Jerzy Szczerba, Yerkin Wilbrandt, Henry Williams

Year 3
Ahmed Al-Shamari, Megan Hague, Jacqui Lee, Poon Pairojtanachai, Wenxi Zhang

Critics: Sarah Alun-Jones, Noemí Blager, Eddie Blake, Ben Bosence, Alice Casey, Freya Cobbin, Jonathan Cook, Matthew Dalziel, Aude-Line Dulière, Alice Edgerley, Fran Edgerley, Anthony Engi Meacock, Christina Fraser, Luke Freedman, Ambrose Gillick, Anastasia Glover, Aidan Hall, Eleanor Hedley, Rainer Hehl, Gabu Heindl, Rosie Hervey, Summer Islam, Robert Kennedy, Noel Kingsbury, Louis Lupien, Quentin Martin, Ryan McStay, Ana Monrabal-Cook, Jasmine Pajdak, Roz Peebles, Amy Perkins, Kester Rattenbury, Chloe Revill, Guglielmo Rossi, Camille Sineau, Giles Smith, Steve Webb, Emily Wickham, Penny Wilson

1.1–1.2,1.22 **Lim Wei Lim, Y2** 'In the Ruins We Make'. Serving as a community-run extension of Grow, the project connects people with the natural world by finding the 'sympathy of things'. The main buildings include a makers' workshop, a furniture-upcycling centre and a farm-to-table school. In the spirit of thinking through making, the project is self-built and treats the existing urban fabric with care, employing incremental construction and reusing existing structures and locally salvaged materials. Temporary sub-structures allow for a state of 'open completion', celebrating the act of building and making.

1.3–1.4 **Megan Hague, Y3** 'Soil Remediation Centre'. The project is a pilot scheme for the research and maintenance of the soil beneath us. Carefully selected perennial flowers and grasses are cultivated to absorb pollutants like lead, arsenic and cadmium, that clean the site over time. Over a phased construction programme, the plants are harvested and combined with lime plaster to make an infill wall panel system. Anticipating future flooding, the site's ground level constitutes a wetland garden with an array of brick structures, giving access to upper levels of long-span timber construction.

1.5–1.6 **Ahmed Al-Shamari, Y3** 'Wapping School of Seafood'. Referencing Wapping's historic connection to the River Thames and the sea beyond, the project encourages direct and diverse access to nature and facilitates a range of activities for children and young people. Activities include sailing, rowing, fly fishing, the construction and maintenance of boats and fishing nets, and cooking and food production. Materials from the site are recycled and are integrated as part of a timber construction system to create an elegant, phased and flexible net-zero carbon building.

1.7–1.8 **Moe Kojima, Y2** 'Wapping Hill'. The project brings circular economy principles into everyday focus by processing Wapping's waste textiles, paper and food under a publicly accessible and farmable mountain-shaped roof. The journey from garment to ash of a Japanese Edo period (1603-1868) kimono inspires the overlay of two layers of circulation. An 'industrial route' visually celebrates the re-purposing of waste, and a 'green route' facilitates the direct experience of urban farming.

1.9–1.10 **Henry Williams, Y2** 'The Model Allotment'. A standard ten-rod allotment adjacent to the New River Path. The project is a practical tool for residents and the wider public to learn about gardening and food production. A flexible building of a barn-like typology, with a deliberate simplicity and legibility of construction, speaks in practical and imaginative terms to the agricultural history of Enfield, North London, and the potential for future adaptation and renewal.

1.11 **Yerkin Wilbrandt, Y2** 'Peace House'. The project responds to Grow's values on children's mental health and wellbeing to provide a playful and naturally built environment for yoga, meditation and mindfulness, set amongst the trunks and canopies of existing trees. The research for the project included experiments with timber, focussing on sourcing strategies, processes of production, treatments and finishes, and the testing of structural and textural possibilities.

1.12–1.13 **Poon Pairojtanachai, Y3** 'Project Camp: A centre for low-carbon life skills'. The project seeks to extend Grow's children's curriculum by providing a diverse and practical learning experience, foregrounding ecological systems and connections over time and place. To encourage collaborative and experimental forms of making and urban stewardship, the project creates a reciprocal relationship between a weekly and seasonal programme of activities. The construction of a series of buildings responds directly to specific site conditions, including layout, form, phasing, flexibility and materiality.

1.14–1.15 **Arnie Freund-Williams, Y2** 'Palmerston Forest School'. The project transforms an underused and awkward site, adjacent to the North Circular, into a set of outdoor rooms to form an accessible, self-contained and densely planted micro-forest environment for local nursery and primary school children. A series of small-scale buildings arranged in relation to the forest provides shelter from bad weather and space for tool storage, kitchens and toilets. Impact on the ground is minimised by playful stone foundations and elevated timber structures dressed in shingles above.

1.16 **Gabe Fryer-Eccles, Y2** 'Portobello Cookery School for Sustainable Urban Living'. The project proposes an urban cookery school and kitchen garden that teaches families from local schools to economically source, grow and cook nutritious food. Responding to the physical conditions of the site, the principal building is set into a slope and surrounded by a courtyard of gabion retaining walls. The material approach focusses on natural, sustainable and recyclable materials, including timber frames infilled with stone and construction rubble, internal clay render and floors of end-grain timber tiles.

1.17 **Jerzy Szczerba, Y2** 'A Warm Place for Notting Hill'. The project proposes a greenhouse-covered city farm on a disused rail embankment between Ladbroke Grove and Portobello Road, West London. Responding to the goals of the client and the needs of the local community, an immersive series of spaces encourages exploration from the street context. Different climatic zones provide direct engagement with the cultivation of fruit and vegetables found on Portobello Market's stalls and restaurants.

1.18 **Dominik Do, Y2** 'Portobello Forest Playground'. The project challenges the privatisation of outdoor green spaces along Portobello Road, West London, and proposes a green pedestrian shortcut and a loose-play forest playground. Timber, rammed earth and gabion construction methods create soft, warm and light-filled rooms, generous balconies and bridges. The proposal balances and integrates the needs for a kindergarten, cafe and bar, treetop route and forest pathway.

1.19 **Leo Osipovs, Y2** 'Farm in the City'. The project proposes a hydroponic urban farm and open kitchen, designed for agricultural education. Timber, stone and reclaimed materials are used to create large-span spaces and bridges across the three main areas of the site. The generous scale of the rooms allows space for gardening and dining. The layering and division of space is inspired by the phantasmagorical paintings of Hieronymus Bosch, such as The Garden of Earthly Delights (c.1490–1500).

1.20 **Wenxi Zhang, Y3** 'Grow Country Skills Training Camp'. The project aligns with Grow's ambition to give all young people better access to nature and proposes an urban venue for learning outdoor skills, such as camping and mountain climbing. A landscape of planted hills and terraces flow around buildings constructed using reclaimed brick, stone and timber.

1.21 **Flavia Scafella, Y2** 'A Kitchen Garden for Portobello'. The project supports an alternative approach to food and nature in an urban context. Local primary school children are provided with outdoor kitchen space, workshops and a playful terraced landscape where they can be close to nature and actively learn about how things are made. Driven by a rigorous material approach, the design explores the tactile, structural and aesthetic qualities of hyper-local materials like reclaimed brick, timber and earth.

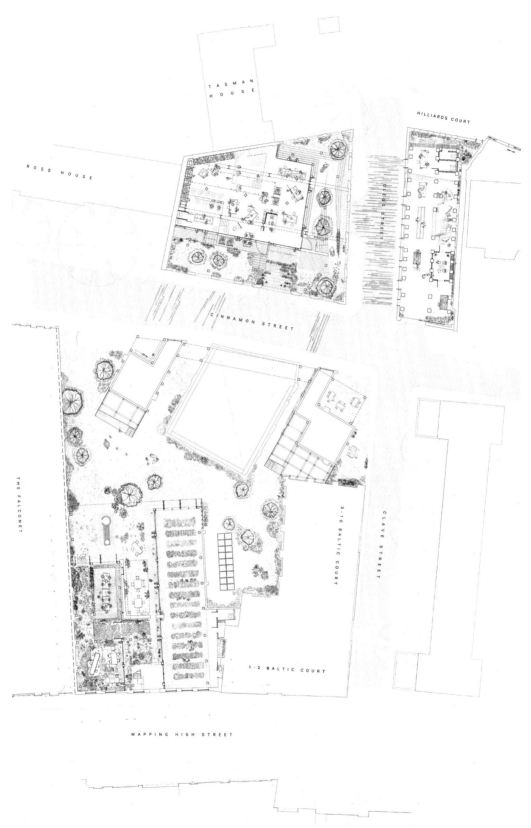

TASMAN HOUSE

HILLIARDS COURT

ROSS HOUSE

GLEGG STREET

CINNAMON STREET

THE FALCONET

3-10 BALTIC COURT

CLAVE STREET

1-2 BALTIC COURT

WAPPING HIGH STREET

1.2

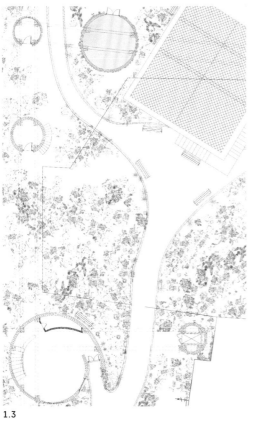

1.3

1.4

1.5

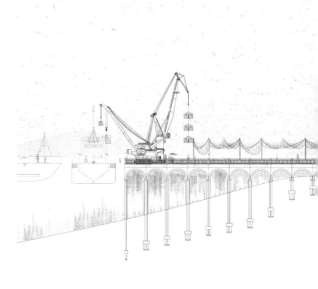

1.6

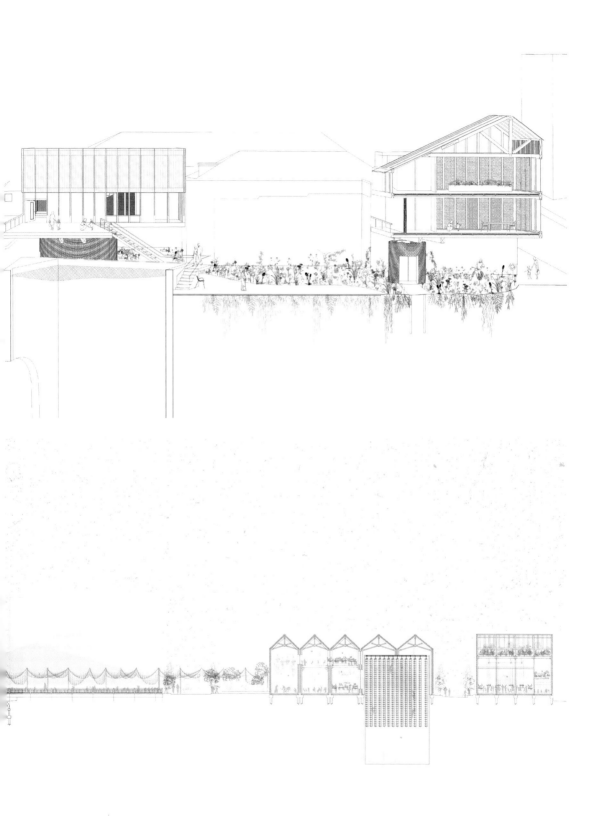

1.7

1.8

1.9

1.10

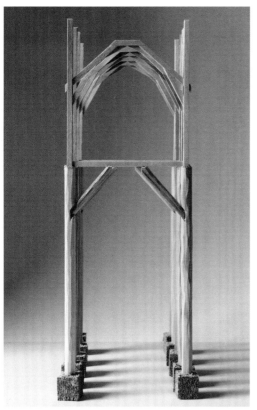

1.11

1.12

1.13

1.14

1.15

1.16

1.17

1.18

1.19

1.20

1.21

Natural State

UG2

Maria Knutsson-Hall, Barry Wark

An object of observation can be, in a number of different ways, partly natural, partly artefactual, and something that is a natural object might nevertheless not be in a natural state.[1]

The above quote by English philosopher Malcolm Budd describes how one might engage and appreciate natural objects. It alludes to the fact that even if the origin of the object is natural, if it is not in a natural state then it ceases to be appreciated as such. This year, UG2 considered the reverse: If the object in question is a human artefact and is in a natural state, can we begin to appreciate it in the same way that one appreciates the natural world?

The effects of natural phenomena, such as erosion, staining and flora propagation, perpetually alter buildings. It is, therefore, interesting to consider 'green' architecture's call to bring nature in when it is already there, we simply invest energy in design and maintenance strategies for its removal.

UG2 investigated biospatial conditions that encourage and embrace the visibility of their environment to dissolve the notion that they are separate and impervious to the natural world. The students explored projects in Rye, East Sussex, and considered how the wider environment has impacted the fortunes of human settlements, both positively and negatively. This is particularly pertinent for Rye, which is situated two miles from the sea at the confluence of three rivers, as the predicted rise in sea levels will severely affect the community, flooding entire neighbourhoods and returning it to a seaside town.

In addition to considering how to design for these scenarios, the students' proposals endeavoured to develop novel aesthetic sensibilities of what ecological architecture could be beyond its current offerings. The projects work with new biomaterials, explore architecture's role within ecology and create spaces that engage users' imaginations to consider their sense of place within the biosphere.

Year 2
Seb Bellavia, Bogdan Botis, Grace Boyten-Heyes, Kyra Johnston, Clara Popescu, Charmaine Tang, Chan Tou (Antonio) Yang

Year 3
Ho Kiu (Jeffrey) Cheung, Lavinia Fairlie, Tilly Grayson, Mankiran Kundi, Charles Liang, Harrison Maddox, Ioana-Stefania Petre

Technical tutors and consultants: Levent Ozruh, James Palmer

We would like to thank our critics: Hadin Charbel, Andreas Koerner, Deborah Lopez Lobato, Justin Nicholls, Levent Ozruh

1. Malcolm Budd (2002), *The Aesthetic Appreciation of Nature: Essays on the Aesthetics of Nature* (Oxford: Clarendon Press), p14.

2.1 Seb Bellavia, Y2 'Camber Pier'. The project develops the coastal village of Camber, East Sussex, through socio-economic and infrastructural means and acts as a coastal defence against erosion and rising sea levels. Utilising framework mesh elements and biorock to accrete material, the coastal defence becomes part of the beach itself and transforms the surrounding environment into a coexistent experiential space.

2.2 Harrison Maddox, Y3 'Myco House'. A project that explores the potential of mycelium-derived composite materials to create a modular and deployable flood defence system, with integrated housing units, for flood-prone areas in Rye, East Sussex. The project demonstrates the potential such a system has in relation to transit compatibility, interchangeability and bio-contribution.

2.3–2.4 Tilly Grayson, Y3 'Reforging Communites'. Focussing on Rye's industrial history – ironworks and Cinque Ports – is a proposal for a museum as an homage to the past. The museum functions as a community hub to combat feelings of isolation in the community. The structure is designed for deconstruction and reconstruction, and questions whether iron has a place within an ecological future.

2.5–2.6 Ioana-Stefania Petre, Y3 'The Dungeness B Recommissioning Project'. The project recommissions the existing Dungeness B Nuclear Power Station to integrate the existing nearby community and to preserve the area's authenticity. The building uses emblematic parts of the power station as a base for the proposal that includes housing, a library and art spaces.

2.7 Kyra Johnston, Y2 'Asylum Seeker Sanctuary'. A sanctuary for asylum seekers is situated around 45 minutes from the port of Dover, where most asylum seekers land after crossing the English Channel. The project explores how biophilic architecture can accommodate asylum seekers in a way that is empathetic and tranquil.

2.8 Charmaine Tang, Y2 'Out of Place'. A 'natural state' is often perceived as dirty or out of place. The project reimagines a crèche as a landscape and encourages children to explore, understand and learn from nature, not simply within the binary definitions of 'dirty' and 'clean', but in a respectful and playful way.

2.9 Clara Popescu, Y2 'Geomorphous Awareness'. The project approaches the problem of dune destabilisation in Camber Sands, East Sussex. Sitting at a key break within the dune environment, it shelters the site from prevailing winds and exploits sand deposition processes. The design allows for the integration of the environment into the building with the incorporation of nooks for plant and animal inhabitation.

2.10 Bogdan Botis, Y2 'The Preservation of Rye's Salt Marshes'. The project explores the impact of flooding and coastal erosion on the salt marshes of Rye Harbour Nature Reserve, East Sussex. It proposes a series of structures that generate new opportunities for salt marshes to develop, adapt and thrive in the ever-changing environmental conditions that they face.

2.11 Grace Boyten-Heyes, Y2 'Hydrobotanical Bathhouse'. A bathhouse that adapts to tidal flooding. Water intake is filtered using hydrobotany forming gardens that double up as social spaces. The building also monitors changing water conditions and responds to the return of Rye's old coastline using the transitioning landscape to question object permanence and anthropocentric views of buildings as defying nature.

2.12–2.13 Mankiran Kundi, Y3 'A Revitalisation of Human and Biophilic Expression'. The project brings new life to the town of Rye, East Sussex, through the creation of spaces for self-expression, specifically graffiti. Biophilic design strategies, including the gradual propagation of moss, promote occupant wellbeing.

2.14–2.16 Lavinia Fairlie, Y3 'A Transient Harbour'. The proposed harbour in Rye, East Sussex, works as a system that responds to the shifting landscape threatened by rising sea levels and daily tidal fluctuations. The harbour retains the local seafaring community's connection to the land, while improving marine biodiversity and water quality in the River Rother.

2.17–2.18 Ho Kiu (Jeffrey) Cheung, Y3 'By Land, Sea and Air: Reconfiguring fishing'. It is a global issue that current fishing methods destroy sea habitats. If these trends continue there will be little or no seafood available for sustainable harvest by 2080. Rye, East Sussex, is an inshore town with a rich history of fishing. The project explores drone fishing and biorock as sustainable approaches to reverse man-made damage.

2.19 Charles Liang, Y3 'Otter Daycare'. Otter spotting was first recorded in 1864 in a survey manual produced by the Sussex Wildlife Trust. An apex predator at the top of the food chain in its ecosystem, any river and wetland pollution results in a huge decline of otter numbers. The project proposes a kindergarten with an area for otter holts that achieves harmonious coexistence between humans and nature.

2.20–2.22 Chan Tou (Antonio) Yang, Y2 'Cohabitation Within the Fluvial Landscape'. This project addresses the disappearance of public open spaces in UK coastal towns due to rising sea levels. A theatre and public space celebrate and embrace the natural rhythms of tidal movements. Glimpses of human/non-human habitation and interaction is observed through different zones of coexistence. Control and access are traded between species by the changing of the tides.

2.2

2.3

2.4

2.5

2.6

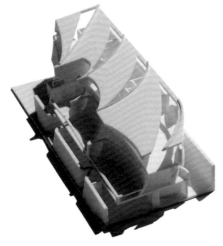

2.7

2.8

2.9

2.10

2.11

2.12

2.13

2.14

2.15

2.16

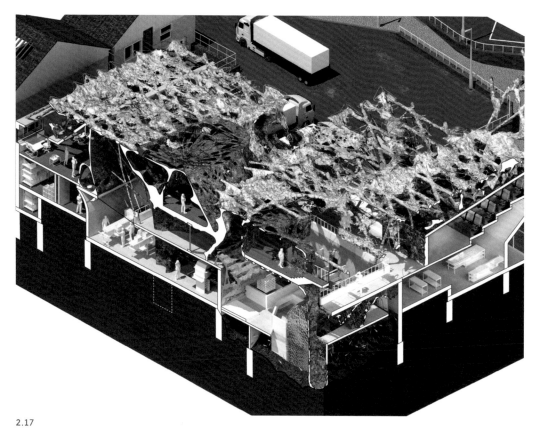

2.17

2.18

2.19

2.20

2.21

2.22

A New World of Joy

Ifigeneia Liangi, Daniel Wilkinson

This year, UG3 explored colour as a political issue for architecture, in relation to the prejudices of modernism. The term 'chromophobia' refers to a fear of corruption or contamination through colour. Throughout Western history colour has been marginalised as superficial and cosmetic, including by the founders of modernism who considered it to be deceptive, primitive and feminine, often dismissing it in relation to issues of race and gender.

As a unit, we exchanged polychromatic ideas by celebrating the cosmetic, wily and artificial as an act of defiance towards such opinions. Seeing as we could not go anywhere, we began the year somewhere we could never go: the 1925 International Exhibition of Modern Decorative and Industrial Arts in Paris, France. This citywide World's Fair was a pivotal moment for modernism, with Le Corbusier presenting his L'Esprit Nouveau pavilion there. In defending his predominant use of white for the pavilion, Le Corbusier criticised Chinese, Indian, Japanese and Persian designers, describing their use of colour as culturally inferior: 'Colour... is suited to simple races, peasants and savages.'[1]

By researching the technologies and ideologies present at the exhibition, UG3 designed architectural prototypes for 1925, the promises of which were reworked for the 21st century. The second year students did this in the Kypseli neighbourhood in Athens, Greece, while our third year students chose sites in Austria, Germany, Poland, Romania and the UK. The projects address issues of the feminine, psychedelic, sensual, animalistic and excluded, according to the personal interests that our students brought to the (online) table. This saw contemporary political issues being addressed in a way that was both critical and magical.

Year 2
Luke (Taro) Bean, Chantelle Chong, Natalia Da Silva Costa Dale, Dylan Duffy, Jack Kinsman, Luana Martins Rodrigues, Mufeng Shi, Walinnes Walanchanurak, Yeung (Julie) Yeung

Year 3
Finlay Aitken, Crina Bianca Croitoriu, Jina Gheini, Anna Knapczyk, Hanna Said

Thank you to our technical tutor Martin Reynolds

Critics: Bihter Almac, Carlos Jiménez Cenamor, Patch Dobson-Pérez, Stefana Gradinariu, Vsevolod K. Popov, Andrew Riddell, Sayan Skandarajah, Gabriel Warshafsky. Special thanks to Eleanor Crook, Tyler Ebanja, Thomas Thwaites

1. Le Corbusier (1927), *Towards a New Architecture* (London: Architectural Press), p143.

3.1 Yeung (Julie) Yeung, Y2 'The Theatricality of Crafting'. Sited in Kypseli, Athens, the project imagines a theatre transformed by turning jewellery into furniture and architecture. The theatre explores what can be considered true luxury in a community set against a background of mass modernisation and a growing refugee population. Deriving from Aristophanes' play *Assemblywomen* (392 BC), the theatre is a political arena that designates women as leaders.

3.2 Bianca Croitoriu, Y3 'The Museum of Small Jumps'. The project is in memory of Smaranda Brăescu (1897–1948), the first female parachutist in Romania and former world record holder. The design takes the visitor on a journey through Brăescu's life and death, commenting on being a woman in a male-dominated field.

3.3 Walinnes Walanchanurak, Y2 'Selene'. A moonlit theatre is established to worship the lunar deity Selene. It integrates international immigrants into Greece's local culture through acting groups that create deep-rooted bonds via a co-living space. Throughout the 28-day lunar cycle, performances are held weekly, allowing actors to practice for their roles on non-performance days. On full moon days, a special performance is given to celebrate Selene's gift of prosperity.

3.4 Anna Knapczyk, Y3 'The Marzanna Coven Hotel'. The common misconception that a 'witch' is synonymous with 'evil' stems from the notion that a knowledgeable woman is a dangerous woman. The project is a hotel inspired by the folklore surrounding its site in Łysa Góra, Poland, commonly recognised as a hotspot for Witches' Sabbath and pagan worship. It acts as a home for a coven of eight witches, as well as a hotel and place of worship for visitors practicing the old Slavic faith.

3.5 Mufeng Shi, Y2 'The Seres Museum'. A museum located in an alternative reality of Athens, in which the city's patroness Athena has been replaced by an Eastern goddess of silk. Based on the history of Greek mythology, the building translates the cultural exchange between East and West into a silk museum.

3.6 Hanna Said, Y3 'The Home Away from Home'. The project revolves around a space in Vienna, Austria, that welcomes Syrian refugees to their new homeland and encourages social and cultural exchange with the local Viennese people. This exchange takes the form of a halfway house and civic hall for the wave of refugees arriving at the city's central train terminal. The project is constructed by the migrants themselves using salvaged materials from a demolished apartment complex.

3.7 Chantelle Chong, Y2 'Under the Shade of a Bitter Orange Tree'. The design is a communal social kitchen space dedicated to the production of bitter oranges. Surrounded by an overgrowth of bitter orange trees in the multi-ethnic area of Kypseli, Athens, the programme transforms the site into a neighbourhood initiative that utilises the fruit as currency and language, bringing different communities together. The free public space welcomes migrant communities as a celebration of the bitter orange tree's similar migration from Southeast Asia to Europe.

3.8 Dylan Duffy, Y2 'Laloux's Refuge'. Laloux's Refuge is an Unorthodox Adolescent Psychiatric Centre focussed on rehabilitating its patients through methods orientated around a rewiring of posture and body trauma. The building is dedicated to the animator and director René Laloux (1929–2004), and draws inspiration for film and animation classes as a means of creative therapy.

3.9 Jina Gheini, Y3 'Dancing with the Wind'. Freedom of expression has been one of the many struggles of young Iranians. The authorities have made it especially difficult for female dancers to perform in public spaces or social gatherings. The building programme is a cabaret, inspired by the pre-revolutionary lifestyle in Iran, in which a show is performed in front of the Iranian embassy in London to tease the idea that the act of dancing is taking place close to them.

3.10 Jack Kinsman, Y2 'The Butchery of Flesh Bodies'. Set in Athens, the project draws from the lost history of ritual sacrifice that is secretly embedded in classical architectural motifs. The project reconstructs meat-bodies and defies the death of the animals sacrificed for our consumption, while uniting a neighbourhood that disbands across Greece over the summer.

3.11 Natalia Da Silva Costa Dale, Y2 'The Municipal Textile Mill'. The project explores the topic of racism by making comparisons between modern-day racism and the proto-racism of Ancient Greece, when it was believed that climate changes behaviour, and leads to discrimination and segregation. The textile mill symbolises cultural unity, where the etymology of the Greek word *histos* (weaving/cloth/material) and the Latin word *texere* (to weave) create a narrative of fluid, continuous spaces.

3.12 Luke (Taro) Bean, Y2 'An Ice Cream Theatre for the Lost Children of Kypseli'. The project is centred around the 16th-century architect Bernardo Buontalenti, acknowledging him as a mannerist designer and the inventor of gelato. The theatre reacts to the continuous migration of people into Athens, particularly from Central and Southwest Asia, and offers accommodation for unaccompanied children or those that have lost family along the way.

3.13 Finlay Aitken, Y3 'The Spore of the Ineffable'. The project is a research facility that explores the nature of psychedelia within the context of the 21st-century psychedelic renaissance. By treating the hallucinogenic psilocybin mushroom as sacred medicine and drawing upon precedents from both Eastern and Western psychedelia, the building facilitates and augments a participant's mystical experience under the watch of a trained guide. Striking a balance between the controlled and the ineffable, the fabric of the building serves to both accommodate the participant and act as a host for mycelium, which grows throughout the project's lifetime.

3.3

3.4

3.5

3.6

3.7

3.9

3.10

3.11

3.12

3.13

4.1

Convalescence

UG4

Katerina Dionysopoulou, Billy Mavropoulos

UG4 is driven by the pragmatic reality of architecture as a profession of rules, restrictions and guidelines and the deep creativity we, as practitioners, bring to our projects. Though we call on theory to reinforce our investigations, we find joy, beauty and levity in the presence and ideals of nature.

The Covid-19 pandemic has made the need for personal, collective and urban recovery more apparent than ever. In general, recovery means regaining, recuperating and returning. This year, UG4 interrogated how various definitions of recovery shape the future of London's urban landscape. We examined recovery at the scale of the individual and their immediate environment, as well as the collective and its impact on the city.

The concept of recovery became popular during the 1970s within grassroots self-help communities and the psychiatric rehabilitation profession. After the mid-1980s, recovery became the focus of extensive research and policy, with the World Health Organisation leading the global conversation. Recovery is thought of as a deeply personal and individual journey, but one that is also inherently connected to an individual's community and wider society.

Alongside place-based research, UG4 questioned the notion of recovery across histories and cultures: Can re-greening restore degraded urban landscapes and hasten recovery for individuals and communities? How might a new vision of an urban pastoral create places for convalescence and recuperation? These questions culminated in tactical site interventions, using placemaking as a tool to promote urban recovery.

We sought to invent new ways to integrate the outdoors into our spaces, neighbourhoods and cities, challenging conventional architectural approaches and exploring how green infrastructure could become part of our buildings, both laterally and vertically. We investigated increasingly redundant models of city building, such as the high street, town centre and housing estate, and tried to recover them through our use of nature. We looked at brownfield sites, rooftops, disused buildings and abandoned spaces, making them part of our proposals. By better utilising our time outdoors and creating connections with our environment, we became placemakers who break the boundaries created by socio-economic divides.

Year 2
Monika (Nina) Buranasetkul, Adnan Demachkieh, Gaeul Kim, Yan (Johnson) Lam, Ling (Stefanie) Leung, Adam Lynes, Siqi Ouyang, Zuzanna Sienczyk

Year 3
Sahba Akbar, Serim Hur, Yutong Luo, Sara Mahmud, Charis Mikkel Makmurputra, Wiam Mostefai, Jamie Stuart

Technical tutor:
Simon Pierce

Critics: Simon Beames, Kacper Chmielewski, Amy Croft, Nick Elias, Tom Greenall, Oliver Houchell, Neil Hubbard, Alex Smith

4.1, 4.20 Jamie Stuart, Y3 'Fleet Marriages in the Urban Palimpsest'. The project restores the Fleet Marriage – a 'secret' marriage ceremony held in or near Fleet prison in London during the 17th and 18th centuries – at Clerkenwell Chapel. Initially divided, the couple are brought closer to one another as they ascend around a watch repair shop, dressmaking atelier and artificial flower-making workshop. The open chapel space at the top symbolises the end of the journey to marriage. Synonymous with renewal and new beginnings, the building's programme is wedded to the subterranean themes and hidden histories that permeate the Fleet Marriage.

4.2, 4.8 Ling (Stefanie) Leung, Y2 'Everymania – Atelier & Cabaret'. Drawing from Hampstead's unique histories relating to the performing arts and washerwomen – in the early 16th century Hampstead was said to be chiefly inhabited by washerwomen – the building serves as a costume atelier for elderly women during the day and a drag cabaret by night. The co-habitation of space fosters interaction across generations as a form of urban rehabilitation in London's loneliest borough.

4.3, 4.14 Yutong Luo, Y3 'Echo of the Tide'. The stress of urban life and socialising due to a fear of missing out, increases the need for solitude and mindfulness. The project builds a space behind the sound of the tide, where introverts and people with social anxiety can hide themselves from unwanted conversation and social noise. The function, atmosphere and accessibility of the shared space changes according to the tide.

4.4–4.5 Wiam Mostefai, Y3 'In Pursuit of Awe and Wonder: The Northolt Astronomy Centre'. An initial exploration into public space and artificial lighting led to the creation of an underground network of spaces inspired by constellations, astrological myths and gas street lanterns. The centre tackles issues of obesity and low income in the area by drawing connections between healthy eating and astronomy. Inspired by Andrew Ainslie Commons' award-winning photograph of the Orion Nebula, taken from the garden shed of his Ealing home in 1883, the project provides facilities that share a core understanding of astronomy and allow visitors to practice astrophotography.

4.6, 4.16 Sahba Akbar, Y3 'Holistic Therapy'. Living in the urban environment of London, we rarely immerse ourselves fully into a therapeutic natural environment, away from the polluted atmosphere. The proposed holistic therapy centre provides an oasis of nature within central London, sited beside Regent's Canal. The space focusses on therapy through music, specifically piano, alongside aviaries for songbirds to inhabit.

4.7 Monika (Nina) Buransetkul, Y2 'Escapism'. Located in Rotherhithe, London, this project is inspired by the story of The Mayflower, which transported a group of English families in search of a new life, known today as the Pilgrims, from England to the New World in 1620. The proposed programme is a form of escapism from everyday life, where multiple types of nightclubs are designed to enable visitors to travel through a range of contrasting immersive experiences.

4.9, 4.19 Adnan Demachkieh, Y2 'CBD Spa & Wellness Centre'. Limehouse, East London, was once the focal point of a large and thriving Chinese immigrant population, composed mainly of sailors. Their desire for home-cooked meals and gossip in Cantonese led to the beginnings of a Chinatown located in Narrow Street. Applying the healing qualities of CBD, the spa and wellness centre promotes the beneficial aspects of social cohesion, relaxation and mental development.

4.10, 4.12 Charis Mikkel Makmurputra, Y3 'The Weavers Theatre'. The proposal is a learning centre that spans across a prop-making workshop and theatre. The site, located in Shoreditch, London, has a rich history in the weaving and crinoline-making industry. The building takes inspiration from the site's history, incorporating it into the functional and aesthetic elements.

4.11 Yan (Johnson) Lam, Y2 'Battersea Heritage Gardens'. The proposal celebrates Battersea's two identities – agricultural and industrial – and merges them into one space. The building is defined by both its grand undulating industrial walls at its base and the stepped landscape roof at its top. The walls create space for brewing and distilling alcohol and indoor farming, capped by a landscaped roof, and are constructed using bespoke modular units that can be combined to form multiple shapes and functions.

4.13 Zuzanna Sienczyk, Y2 'The Ice House'. The project is based on the idea of psychological and physical growth through the endurance of extreme cold temperatures. The idea was first developed by the Dutch extreme athlete Wim Hoff, also known as The Iceman, who puts himself in the most extreme conditions in order to study the effects of cold temperatures on the body and mind. The Ice House is situated in Battlebridge Basin, London, as a tribute to its fascinating history. During the 19th century, Swiss entrepreneur Carlo Gatti established an ice-importing business next to the site.

4.15 Sara Mahmud, Y3 'The Ornate Urban Experience'. The project creates unique and harmonious experiences that challenge conventional approaches to recovery through its exploration of architectural pattern, ornamentation and sensory experience. As we recover from the Covid-19 pandemic, the need for a space for human and architectural urban recovery has become evident. A study conducted by Imperial College London revealed how the combination of natural fragrances, scent, memory and emotion can improve wellbeing and reduce stress levels.

4.17–4.18 Adam Lynes, Y2 'The Floating Tea Expedition'. During the lifetime of the English naturalist and botanist Joseph Banks (1743–1820), Soho Square, where he lived, was described as a tropical paradise. Today, it is neglected and overwhelmed by the urban context. The building reflects Banks' interest in economic botany and his enthusiasm for tea through the onsite cultivation and production of Earl Grey. 'The Floating Tea Expedition' is a community craft centre comprised of an orangery, tearoom and model-boat workshops. The building cultivates recovery by connecting people to the outdoors, forging community and promoting intergenerational relationships.

4.21 Serim Hur, Y3 'Masked Ambiguity: A transparent safe haven'. The project explores the ideas of disguise and ambiguity inspired by masquerading and masks. A variation of transparency throughout the building is achieved using unique timber structures inspired by the movements of the human body, fencing and nets. The timber structure wraps around the entire building like a shell, creating a beacon in a centre of urban green space.

4.2

4.3

4.4

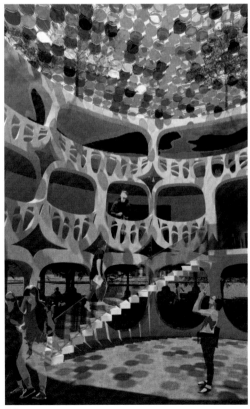

4.5

4.6

4.7

4.8

4.9

4.10

4.11

4.12

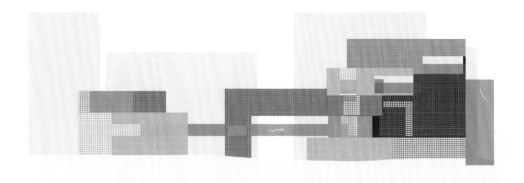

4.13

4.14

4.15

4.16

4.17

4.18

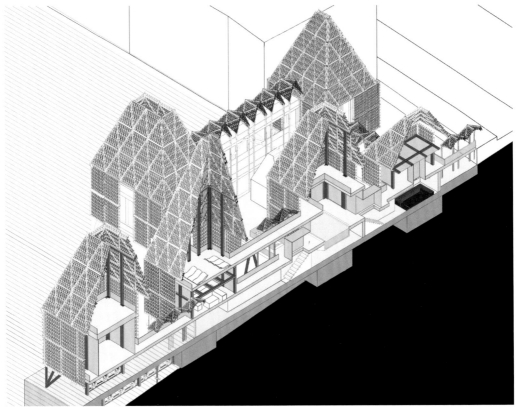

4.19

4.20

4.21

5.

Goodbye Anthropocene, Hello Symbiocene

UG5

Julia Backhaus, Ben Hayes

As the Earth's climate changes, so must our architecture. The architectural profession is deeply invested in the logic of economic growth and, as a consequence, the built environment accounts for almost 47% of greenhouse gas emissions in the UK. Are architects unavoidably complicit?

Last year we challenged what it means to live and design in the Anthropocene. This year we focussed on how we, as future architects, can break this destructive cycle and shift our creative efforts towards a new epoch: the Symbiocene. We explored how the concept of symbiotic alliances can be applied to the practice of architecture and in this our research focussed on ecology's driving principle of adaptation. A powerful and central idea of the past century, symbiotic alliances transform the study of natural and social sciences, guide the engineering principles of computing and continue to offer a mechanism to mediate between the natural, synthetic and digital.

Guided by research and instinct, we speculated about buildings that behave like generous neighbours in like-minded communities, accommodating the cohabitation of natural and manmade organisms, moderating the microclimate, cleaning the air, offering tomorrow's food and much more. We explored how tools of care, storytelling, play and activism might guide us towards a generative, less destructive and alternative future.

Driven by geographical curiosity, we became eco visionaries and took each other on virtual journeys across the globe to find sites that became the testbed of our explorations. Confined to our bedrooms and kitchen tables, our research took us across different time zones, from London to Tokyo. We cared for construction workers on building sites, rediscovered vernacular bamboo-weaving techniques, explored architectures of activism, cleaned up toxic ground conditions and studied circular economies and productive demolition processes.

Together, we imagined a multi-sensory world where we can hear, smell, taste and feel our environments. In the spirit of collaborative survival, we engaged in multi-species thinking, explored entangled existences and studied how dependencies and exploitation could be translated into a beneficial and intimate co-existence.

Year 2
Benson Chan, Park Jin Chan, Keane Chua, Esme Dowle, Oska Smith, Adam Stoddart

Year 3
Sophia Brummendorf Malsch, Jasmine Lam, Rebecca Radu, Xin Ze Seah, Lion Tautz, Jeffrey Wen, Xiaotan (Alexander) Yang

Thank you to our consultants: Damian Eley, Anja Kempe and Jack Newton

Thank you to our critics: Pedro Font-Alba, Murray Fraser, Elie Gamburg, Kaowen Ho, Donn Holohan, Bruce Irwin, Ana Monrabal-Cook, Luke Pearson, Theo Games Petrohilos, Stuart Piercy, Ben Stringer, Michiko Sumi, Mika Zacharias

A special thank you to our guest speakers: Ernest Ching, Donn Holohan, Jono Howard, Kit Lee-Smith, Jack Newton, Ewa Roztocka, Gwilym Still, Superposition, Martin Tang, Sharil Tengku, Ron Tse

5.1, 5.12 Xin Ze Seah, Y3 'Remembering Hanami'. The Hanami viewing festival in Japan celebrates life and the coming of spring. Friends and family gather under cherry blossom trees to enjoy the fleeting occasion of their flowering. This project memorialises and preserves the ephemeral nature of cherry blossoms. The building programme is a public memory archive that furthers the community's memory of Hanami and seeks to expand the demographic of its visitors to include dementia patients.

5.2, 5.10 Xiaotan (Alexander) Yang, Y3 'Reconstructing Unseen Industrial Narratives (R.U.I.N)'. The project proposes a set of reconfigurations to a derelict Capital Steel complex in Beijing, China, specifically the residential quarters and bunker warehouse. In response to the global trend towards a circular economy, the programme celebrates every existing corner of the site and considers them not as redundant wasteland but as a bank of recyclable materials.

5.3 Oska Smith, Y2 'The Industrial Allotment'. How can we derive new life from something once thought redundant? The project attempts to find a life that is both uniquely forward thinking for a Symbiocene future, but is also in symbiosis with the industrial past of Teesside in the North East of England. An allotment is manipulated and explored through its connotations of collective growing and its constant state of flux. Characteristics of industrial architecture explore where ambition for a future driven architecture is seen as a shared collective intention.

5.4–5.5 Jeffrey Wen, Y3 'Permanently Temporary'. The project is a construction school and mock-up park set in London's Royal Victoria Dock, surrounded by multiple redevelopments. The architecture comprises specific areas for working and relaxation, seeking to facilitate both the workers' physical and mental health while encouraging the enhancement of new and improved skills. The playful interaction of fabrics and colours inspires both the workers and the public.

5.6–5.7 Rebecca Radu, Y3 'The Last Pristine Biome Laboratory'. The island of Surtsey, Iceland, serves as an unexplored territory with great scientific value due to recently formed ecosystems and discoveries in the inception of life. The laboratory hangs on the island's cliff-side and serves as a habitat for six researchers to live for the duration of their research. The proposal creates a temporary modular architecture that can be removed from the island at the end of its lifetime.

5.8 Benson Chan, Y2 'The Great Andaman Fishery'. The project is inspired by the Sentinelese tribe and the delicate equilibrium through which they maintain their habitat. It takes fishing, a fundamental practice for the tribe that combines religion, craftsmanship and culture, and turns it into a space for community. The building is a paradigm shift for the Andamanese, returning to this tradition through the repeated learning and practising of a sustainable culture and serving as a beacon of a new Symbiocene.

5.9 Adam Stoddart, Y2 '(Ex)traction: A new productive landscape'. Situated in the scars of a disused quarry, the project critically explores the future of our landscape within the Symbiocene. Taking a speculative approach, the project interrogates the importance of an architecture that is intrinsically linked to its environment and how this can lead to the re-mediation of a forgotten land. The proposal for a community research facility acts as a mediator between the forgotten landscape and its surrounding context.

5.11 Esme Dowle, Y2 'Nomad'. A proposal for a travelling surveyor of large-scale construction migrating to industrial projects, the most current being one of the excavation sites of HS2 located in the Colne Valley. 'Nomad' is an allegorical project that occupies space for as long as possible, scavenging materials for its own

fabrication. When the building leaves, a rammed chalk wall remains as a monument to its existence. A protective barrier prevents dust, sound and light pollution from penetrating the local woodland.

5.13 Keane Chua, Y2 'Power-Down Pasir Panjang'. Rapid expansion and the transformation of Singapore's landmass and economy has placed Pasir Panjang's coastline in great risk. Today, Pasir Panjang remains the only natural rocky shore habitat on mainland Singapore. The project responds to recent developments on the site with a counterproposal that can 'power-down' the district by raising awareness of this dwindling habitat.

5.14–5.16 Jasmine Lam, Y3 'Igniting Hornsby Quarry'. The project proposes a bakery and storytelling centre for the Guringai people, the traditional landowners of the site in bushfire-prone Hornsby in Sydney, Australia. Set against a backdrop of native grass fields cultivated using traditional fire regiments, this project investigates how people and architecture can engage with fire through traditional aboriginal practices. While the project focusses on the impact of fire on the landscape, the building proposal focusses on fire in a domestic setting as a tool to bring community together.

5.17 Lion Tautz, Y3 'Design for the People: Rethinking the city'. The automobile has shaped urban thinking for the better part of a century. As we transition away from cars towards more sustainable and active means of travel, a host of redundant typologies will be left behind. Using a soon-to-be-abandoned gas station in Bremen, Germany, as a case study, the project imagines a hopeful future in which the remnants of the car age are re-purposed and utilised to form close-knit communities in our cities. The project also proposes to install a semi-permanent framework into private garages, revitalising our streets and laying the groundwork for more people-friendly cities.

5.18 Park Jin Chan, Y2 'Grande Reverence'. The project is inspired by Jennifer Homans' book *Apollo's Angels: A History of Ballet* (2010), which argues that contemporary artforms are replacing, or have already replaced, classical forms of ballet. The death of ballet becomes a real possibility as repertoire fades into distant memory. Situated on a performance stage in Richmond Park, London, the architecture adapts and responds to the seasons and the surrounding landscape, and is in constant motion: shifting, changing and calibrating for the next performance.

5.2

5.4

5.5

5.6

5.7

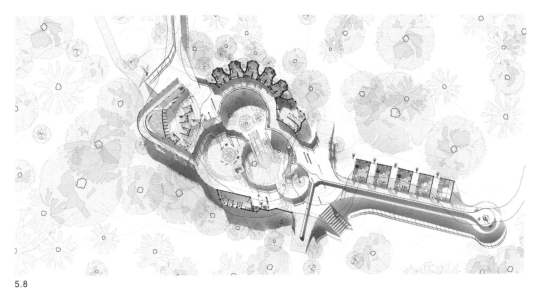

5.8

5.9

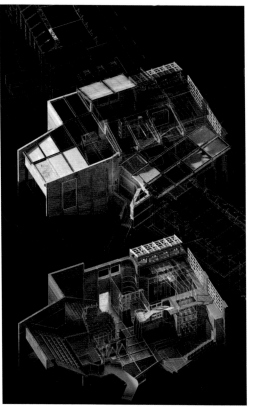

5.10

5.11

5.12

5.13

95

5.14

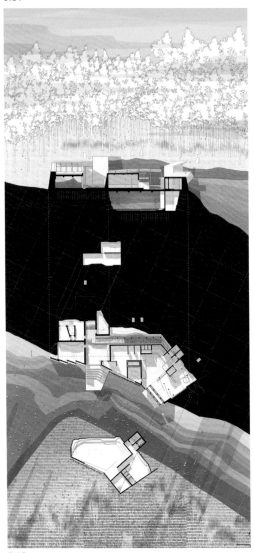

5.15

5.16

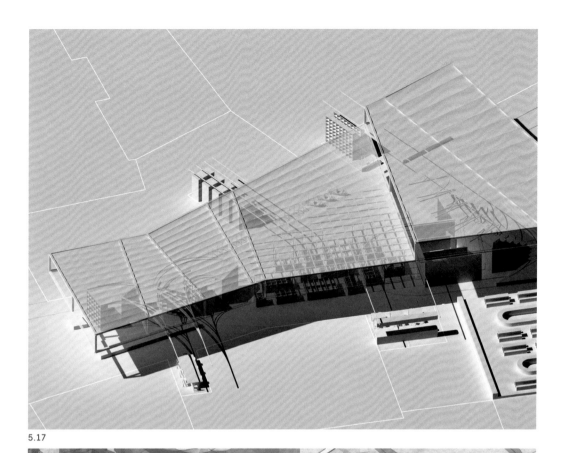

5.17

5.18

A New Brave World

Pascal Bronner, Thomas Hillier

As we technologically advance at a blistering pace, we leave in our wake a devastating and ever-growing trail of destruction that scars our landscapes and destroys our fragile ecologies. From enormous rubbish gyres in the Atlantic Ocean to mountains of radioactive mining waste in Florida, and Amazon's imposing global fulfilment centres, nowhere is left untouched by human impact.

While achieving this wonderful life of comfort and luxury, our ability to create such monstrous objects is only outdone by our skill in covering up these collective sins. We sweep them under Earth's carpet, leaving large parts of our planet virtually uninhabitable. But what if there is a second life for these scars? What if they can be reconfigured for a new world? Could they become new sites? Could their histories and obsolete technologies help develop a new architectural language?

These continue to be unprecedented times, where lockdowns and travel restrictions affect us all; however, this should not stop discovery. For UG7's field trip, the world was the student's oyster. They could travel far and wide, to the ends of the Earth and back, just not in person but, rather, in mind and spirit. While on this virtual field trip, they constructed and assembled a new world around them, creating semi-fictional diaries that regaled us of their travels to sublime and alien landscapes of human ruin.

While their field trip was used as a launchpad to develop a unique mode of thought and new forms of representation, their second project was as much about methods as it was the result. The students explored how the agency of drawing can be used to communicate ideas and tell stories. We asked the students to envisage and create a new architecture of joy, built from a world of ruin. The stories, sites and outcomes from the field trip became the prologue to the main building project. Architectures were propelled into a new realm that fed on the technological advances (or mistakes) of the past and were extrapolated into a brave new building typology for the future. As always, the work aimed to embody the unit's agenda of craft, experimentation, wonder and delight, with drawings becoming real places in an effort to explore and construct architectures entirely within the confines of the student's workplace.

Year 2
Nana Boffah, Oi Lam (Tiffany) Chin, Christian Coackley, Daniel Collier, Glory Kuk, George Neyroud, Joe Russell, Jiahui Zhang

Year 3
John Clayson, Alvin Lam, Michela Morreale, Yasmin North, Sevgi Yaman, Kelvin Zhang

Thank you to our technical tutor Martin Reynolds and computing tutor Sean Allen

Critics: Simon Beames, Amy Croft, Katerina Dionysopoulou, Nick Elias, Tom Greenall, Oliver Houchell, Neil Hubbard, Billy Mavropoulos, Alex Smith

7.1 John Clayson, Y3 'A(lice) I(n) www.onderland'. This project charts the tale of Alice, the White Rabbit and the adventures of the Queen of Hearts in www.onderland. Using Lewis Carroll's *Alice's Adventures in Wonderland* (1865) as a basis, the architecture explores how the relationship between the physical and the virtual can manifest, building on the idea that humans and machines are beginning to inhabit the world in a similar way. The building is a privatised data bank in which material stored on servers can be organised and experienced, and symbolically protected through VR by the bank's wealthy clients, in a virtual landscape known as www.onderland.

7.2 George Neyroud, Y2 'Shadow Chorography'. Betrayed by the state, feeling neglected and lost, sculptor Hennie Smit absconds from Johannesburg. He stumbles across Laanglate, a former goldmine left abandoned and in ruin. Inspired by his surroundings, Hennie begins to inscribe into this scarred landscape a new language of notation. In a barren terrain of dust and decay, each building fragment becomes a new landmark for Hennie to decipher and reconfigure. He follows the lines he has carved into the surface, placing clay-coated skeletons formed from the ground beneath his feet to provide a dark, shadowed refuge from the relentless sun beating down on him.

7.3–7.5 Oi Lam (Tiffany) Chin, Y2 'The Column of Farnsworth'. Located on the site of Mies Van der Rohe's Farnsworth House (1951), 'The Column of Farnsworth' is an archive of (re)collection that stores objects, smells, sounds and tastes to evoke long lost memories for those who visit. The engrained narratives built into the historic columns, alongside modernism's rejection of ornament, are intentionally aligned to provoke and create a new tectonic in the form of a 250-metre-tall column comprised of 25 columns. Each one is delicately carved to create a series of surreal and immersive internal spaces.

7.6 Joe Russell, Y2 'The Great Recognition'. The project explores the negative long-term effects of the Covid-19 pandemic on public mental health and proposes a need for a mental health revolution. Inspired by the Great Exhibition of 1851 – a celebration of industry emblematic of the economic and technological advancements of the 19th century – the project celebrates openness and kindness around issues of mental health to help combat a mental health crisis in the 21st century.

7.7 Daniel Collier, Y2 'The Aral Cathedral'. The project takes place in the year 4021, 1,500 years after the fall of the last great Aral Giant, a lost civilisation that designed their architecture to move and retreat with the rapidly rising sea levels surrounding the Aral Sea. After the unearthing of new and largely intact archaeological remains of a fallen Giant, a new group of sectarian religious scientists have attempted to revive the worship of the Aral people by reanimating the newly discovered relic, in order to reconnect us with its functionality and true meaning.

7.8 Glory Kuk, Y2 'The Whale Monastery'. Nestled within L'Esperance in the South Pacific, and cast from the whale bones scattered across the site, 'The Whale Monastery' lies at the heart of this graveyard landscape within the island's central volcanic crater. A building created for silence, the denizens of this place walk silently and softly across the sand-covered ground to heighten the sound of the surrounding ocean. Sound tunnels weave through the island and into the building, capturing the sombre songs of the whales that swim nearby.

7.9 Jiahui Zhang, Y2 'The Craft Chronicles of Shaxi'. Located in Southwest China, on the Ancient Tea Horse Road, sits the village of Shaxi, famed for its rich tradition in ceramic-crafting techniques, seen by many as a symbol of escapism from the surrounding cities.

At the centre of a circular cornfield on the edge of the village lies 'The Craft Chronicles of Shaxi', a new building that takes visitors through time, reinterpreting and reinvigorating these crafts for a new generation.

7.10 Yasmin North, Y3 'A Shrine to a Priori'. To represent the idea of a greater transience this non-denominational shrine to faith captures the sublime – power and greatness beyond measure and calculation. It is through a philosophical enquiry into the sublime and the beautiful that their parameters are understood and explored. Concepts of the obscure, the uncanny, the power of nature, suddenness and light are used to overwhelm the occupant's emotions and provoke the greatness of the divine.

7.11 Nana Boffah, Y2 'At the New Road'. Vancouver Island is situated on the West Coast of British Columbia. Like most of British Columbia, Vancouver Island was once covered by rainforest. Over the past 50 years 96% of these rainforests have been heavily logged. This project contributes to the transition from old-growth to second-growth logging by providing a reforestation facility where trees are cultivated to reforest clear-cut areas. This helps to preserve the ancient forests and satisfy environmental groups, while providing enough trees for controlled logging in the future.

7.12 Sevgi Yaman, Y3 'Cappadocia's Overground City'. Located above the UNESCO World Heritage site in Cappadocia lies the 'Overground City', a new floating world dedicated to the environmental protection of the natural wonders below. The project provides a cloud-like protective blanket that increases the area tourists can visit and protects the unique icons of the underground city formations and fairy chimneys that lie beneath.

7.13 Kelvin Zhang, Y3 '2021_A Nemo Odyssey'. Located at Point Nemo in the South Pacific Ocean, the Nemo Space Archive – a floating island four times the size of the UK – sits in the most remote location on Earth. Also known as the Oceanic Pole of Inaccessibility, the building is more than 3,000km away from the nearest coastline. The project responds to the environmental impact of the modern day space race by proposing an architecture that retrieves, recycles and archives the excessive amounts of space debris left in the Earth's orbit over the last 60 years.

7.14–7.16 Alvin Lam, Y3 'The Quiet Corner'. A film set inspired by *The Truman Show* (1998) that explores the poetry of longing for home through architecture. Sited in Hong Kong's Mong Kok district, which translates as 'busy corner', a single street is enveloped with a cage-like structure and is converted into a series of film sets. In a touching yet delusional frenzy, the architect (the protagonist) places themselves within the film in the hope of finding comfort in the virtual world they have created.

7.17 Christian Coackley, Y2 'Second Chance'. The project speculates on the revival of the revolutionary ideals embodied by the late John F. Kennedy (1917–63), 35th president of the United States. JFK is associated with the space race, technological power, the Cold War, unification and integration, idealism, romance, prospect, false hope, failure and his death, leaving his legacy in mystic and allegorical ruin. The ruins of a failed lunar colony base serve as the foundations for a newly constructed Earth Embassy on the Moon. An outpost at an urban scale, where the nations of Earth can send diplomats and scientists to engage in a united effort towards undoing the scars of the anthropogenic. It serves as a reminder to this generation and the next that Earth does not belong to man: man belongs to Earth.

7.2

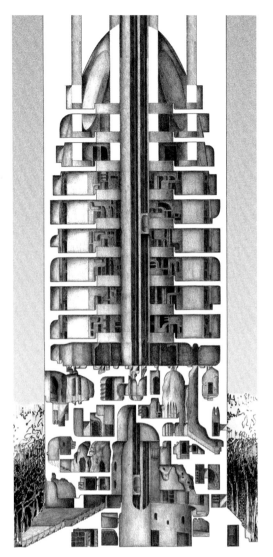

7.3

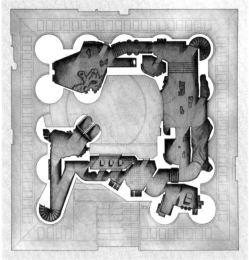

7.4

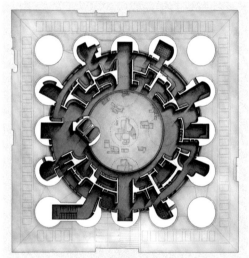

7.5

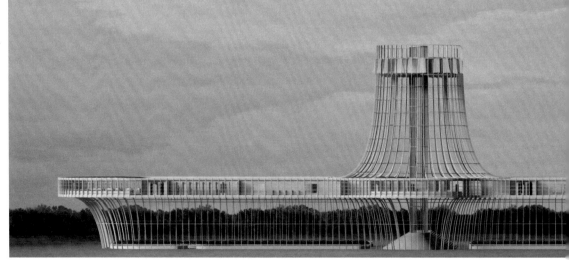

7.6

7.7

7.8

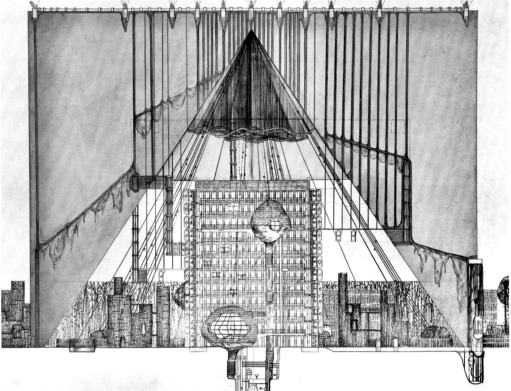

7.9

7.10

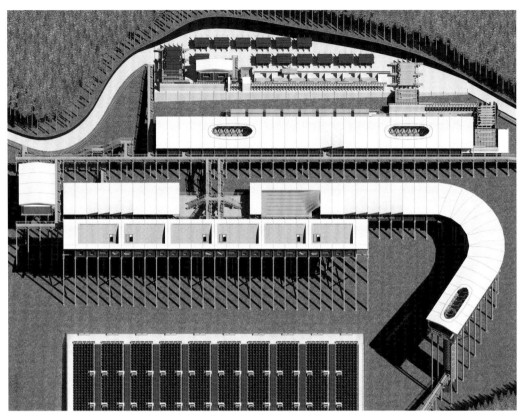

7.11

7.12

7.14

7.15

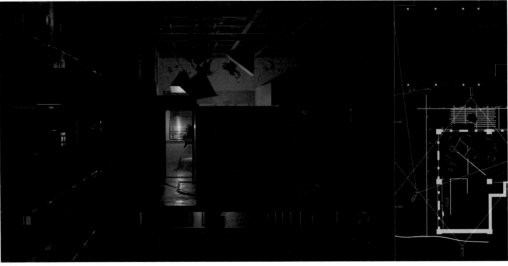

7.16

7.17

8.1

At Truth's Edge

Charlotte Reynolds, Greg Storrar

This year UG8 investigated the agency of architecture in today's culture of misinformation and the roles that architects play in the defence of fundamental truths. By reorienting ourselves in ambiguous states, we explored conspiratorial narratives and critical doubt. Daring to meddle in the murky world of paranoia and mistrust, we sought to address the critical need for new architectures that confront the post-truth age.

In our first project we unravelled the social, spatial and architectural mechanisms behind the false narratives of conspiracy theories by developing tools to disarm conspiratorial plots. We employed investigative systems and forensic techniques to learn the ways of the conspirator, to demystify the magic in the mundane and distinguish 'conspiracy' from 'conspiracy theory'.

In the building project that followed, we developed designs for cultural buildings dealing with complex spatial, structural and climatic conditions. We asked, How could architecture be reimagined or refigured when it becomes the refuge from, or target of, mistrust? We learnt from the creative stagings and precision props of others: Jeff Wall's photographic reconstructions, NASA's neutral buoyancy simulation labs, Marguerite Humeau's pseudo-scientific installations, Miriam Bäckström's parallel-reality stage sets, Thomas Demand's political facsimiles and Forensic Architecture's evidentiary systems that reconstruct physical and virtual worlds to fight socio-political injustice. We treated each forensic (re)staging as a critical tool rather than simply an architectural end-product, each becoming a model for questioning and (dis)organising ideas. We embraced first principles – starting with a basic assumption that cannot be deduced any further or refuted – see-sawing between intuition and precision, (mis)using digital technologies to advance physical learning and prototyping over and over again.

Interested in material, structural and spatial experimentation at a range of scales, UG8 champions innovative architectural strategies that boldly address the environmental challenges of our time. Despite the challenges of lockdown and remote working, the unit's well-established practice of prototyping and hands-on thinking was maintained through close collaboration with our technical and digital tutors. Together we explored the potential of new technologies and age-old crafts. Through these working methods we were able to move fluidly between the analogue and digital, technical and psychological, and remote and physical to develop a well-judged selective sharpness in these times when the truth often appears blurred.

Anna Dixon, Max Hubbard, Yuto Ikeda, Michalis Philiastidis, Rafiq Sawyerr, Libby Sturgeon, Ying (Sunny) Sun, Kate Taylor, Peixuan (Olivia) Xu

Year 3
Ivy Aris, Ling Fung (Grace) Chan, Chelsea Dacoco, Andrei Dinu, Alice Guglielmi, Tom Keeling, Parin Nawachartkosit

Thank you to Tom Budd and Steve Johnson

Critics: Valentina Billios, Theo Brader-Tan, Tom Budd, Barbara-Ann Campbell-Lange, Nat Chard, James Della Valle, Sarah Frith, Stephen Gage, Freddie Hong, Steve Johnson, Johanna Just, Stefan Lengen, Emma-Kate Matthews, Jack Newton, Cira Oller Tovar, Luke Olsen, Thomas Pearce, Danielle Purkiss, Matthew Simpson, Oliver Wilton

8.1, 8.6, 8.24 Ling Fung (Grace) Chan, Y3 'Bedding In At the Edge of Origin. A new museum for Shekou'. A study in stone, seven ways. This city museum tells the story of Shekou in Shenzhen, China, through the life cycle of its bedrock granite. The project looks to new models of museology, understanding that visitors better relate to exhibited artefacts through an experience of the work in its context.

8.2, 8.3 Ivy Aris, Y3 'Where's North from Here?'. The processes of papermaking, printing and archiving are brought together in this new home for Westbourne's society of self-publishers. Led by the collaborative principles of the zine and constructed entirely from paper, the building brings together documenters and disseminators and challenges architecture's relationship with the Fourth Estate: press and news media.

8.4, 8.5, 8.11 Chelsea Dacoco, Y3 'Can You See Me Now?'. The Westminster Guild of Filmmakers investigates the authenticity of what is seen. Drawing on research into the mechanics of the human eye and filmic production, the building looks to recreate ways of seeing, both mimicking and provoking the industry it serves.

8.7, 8.21, 8.23 Andrei Dinu, Y3 'The Westminster Faith Exchange'. A new headquarters for the multi-faith congregation of the Westminster Faith Exchange, a council that promotes inter-religious community engagement in London. The building challenges the way we interpret contemporary spaces of worship, acknowledging the distinctions between beliefs while identifying places of common ground.

8.8, 8.9 Peixuan (Olivia) Xu, Y2 'Beyond the Visible'. A cinema and media art centre for visual and acoustic experimentation, welcoming filmmakers, artists and the public. An ode to superstitious beliefs, the building explores how cinematic techniques can offer experiences of the phenomenological and supernatural.

8.10, 8.27–30 Parin Nawachartkosit, Y3 'And the Truth Will Set You Free'. A radio station and open-education media centre for the congregation and broadcast of the voices of the community. Located on the site of the former Royal Doulton clay-pipework manufacturing plant, the building takes cues from the site's industrial past, translating casting processes into spaces for the production and dissemination of radio.

8.12 Alice Guglielmi, Y3 'Thames Habitat Frameworks'. Nestled on the Victoria Embankment in London, between river, bridge, railway and street, this environmental-monitoring station looks to reframe our relationship with the city. Responding to the circadian rhythm of the site, the building shifts with the tide and the movement of the sun to promote habitat growth.

8.13 Kate Taylor, Y2 'Tempering the Mundaneum'. A repository for the lost narratives of musical history, this public-facing archive resists the reclusive nature of the City of Westminster in London and offers new insights into the handling of musical artefacts.

8.14 Rafiq Sawyerr, Y2 'Amplifying a Stateless Truth'. Victims of geopolitical conflict are offered food, temporary accommodation and workspace in the city, as part of this new embassy for the stateless.

8.15 Anna Dixon, Y2 'The Lost Living Museum'. Public collection displays and an archival research centre form this new home for the disputed artefacts of London's alternative histories and the beginnings of a new cultural quarter in the City of Westminster.

8.16-17 Tom Keeling, Y3 'Urban Prosthesis'. An aquatic filtration facility and leisure centre looks to revive London's interconnected cultural, fluid and infrastructural networks. Taking cues from biological processes and metaphors, the project embraces the potentials of a metabolic architecture; a new landscape for photoreactive ecologies and buoyant human bodies.

8.18-19 Max Hubbard, Y2 'Red Sauce and Refuge'. A café complex at the centre of London's legal district offers a last bastion to the demise of the 'greasy spoon' and the community that it fostered.

8.20 Michalis Philiastidis, Y2 'Observations in Residence'. A thinktank for the research of residential living in London's Westminster. Projecting forward the history of housing typologies, the adaptable building reconfigures to accommodate residencies in speculative models of urban living.

8.22 Yuto Ikeda, Y2 'Institute for Prototypical Housing'. In this showroom and laboratory for future homes, radical approaches to new construction methods are fabricated, tested and promoted. Facing off against the Houses of Parliament, the building is a new landmark for London's changing built environment.

8.25 Ying (Sunny) Sun, Y2 'Shifting Therapies'. A facility for art and dance therapeutics negotiates the space between bank and river in Westminster, London. Responding to exacerbated post-Covid-19 physical and mental health problems in the city, the building creates a new safe space for the local community.

8.26 Libby Sturgeon, Y2 'Disrupted Choreographies'. A riverside community arts centre, wedged between two iconic London bridges, serves as testament to the reclamation of public river space and the future pedestrianisation of the city.

8.2

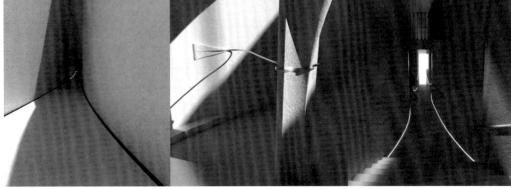

8.3

8.4

8.5

8.6

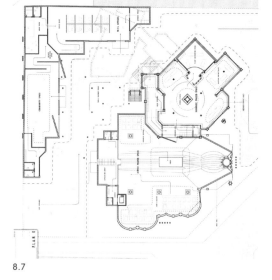

8.7

8.8

8.9

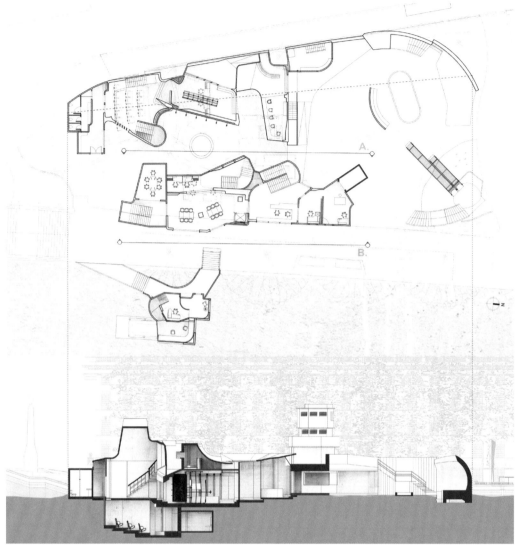

8.10

8.11

8.12

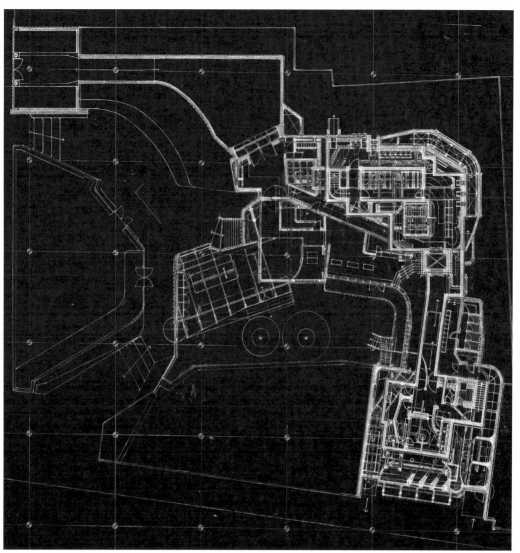

8.13

8.14

8.15

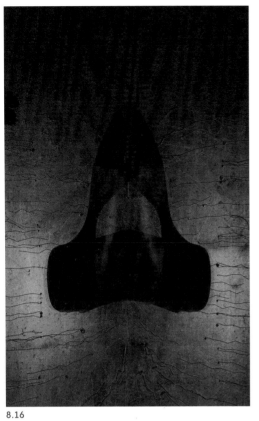

8.16

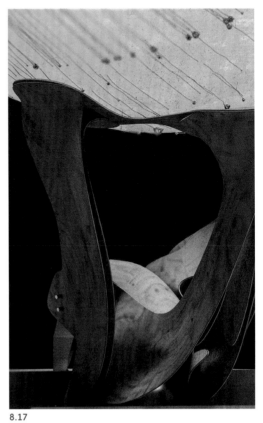

8.17

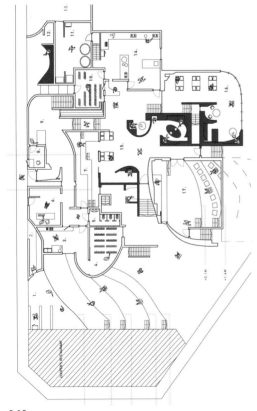

8.18

8.19

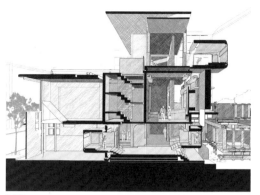

8.20

8.21

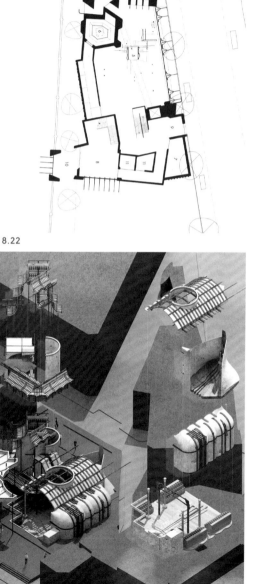

8.22

8.23

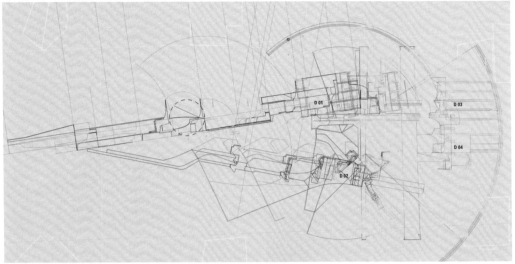

8.24

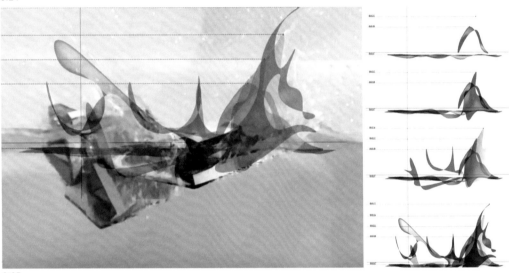

8.25

8.26

8.27

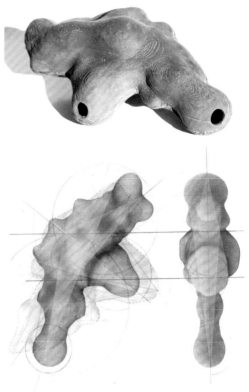

8.28

8.29

8.30

121

9.1

Tales from the Boundaries UG9

Chee-Kit Lai, Douglas Miller

Recording borders – the drawing of maps – has always had social and political ramifications. Used in warcraft to establish primacy over a territory, as an indicator of ownership over a place, it is a source of data on which an invader relies. As systems of cartography modernised, competition to develop maps created cartographic espionage, involving copyright traps secretly embedded in drawings. Now, Google, as a cartographic superpower, bleeds into every aspect of data collection, technology and tracking, yet glitches of imperial secrecy and political ambition persist.

This year, UG9 looked at borders across shifting scales and locales, beginning by interrogating the complex apparatus that surrounds and maintains them. With students scattered across the globe, themes of control, subversion and the political mechanisms that surround borderlines in multiple contexts began the year's explorations. Inspired by illustrations, comics and films, we set out to draw new maps and create narratives, discovered and invented, which tell a story of boundaries by subverting and reimagining them.

Our first investigations touched on the political and the personal. In London, a battle for control over land rights in Walthamstow Wetlands was augmented with architectural structures that proposed to manipulate ownership data over many years by blurring digital and physical datums. Meanwhile, in Bangkok, Thailand, a forensic recording of childhood memories was designed as an interactive architectural game, to pick apart the logic behind the subjective maps we draw in our minds on a daily basis that often live with us forever.

Our main projects for the year were located in lands of contentious ownership, sites of material mediation and locales balanced between climatic conditions. Students were given total autonomy to find a site relevant to their research interests, including places in the US, Iceland and China.

Alongside our ongoing investigations, a select series of talks and workshops led by artists, architects and designers encouraged students to merge disciplines and techniques beyond conventional architectural drawing and gave insight into the world of graphic novels, game design, installation, model making, virtual and augmented realities. We drew upon these representational methods in our drawings and models throughout the year.

Year 2
Daniel Langstaff, Oliver Li, Sean Louis, Eleanor Middleton, Shannon Townsend, Nathan Verrier

Year 3
Xintong Chen, Tia Duong, Marie Faivre, Ben Foulkes, Guiming He, Harris Mawardi, Nandinzul Munkhbayar, Kirsty Selwood, Ewan Sleath, Prim Vudhichamnong, Yunzi Wang

Thank you to our technical tutors and consultants: Tom Budd, John Cruwys, Tae Woo Hong, Jessica In, Greg Kythreotis, Evan Levelle, Gareth Damian Martin, Anna Mill, Sophie Percival, Owen Pomery, George Proud, Ellie Sampson, Arinjoy Sen, Don Shillingburg, Kate Strudwick, The Bakerloos

Critics: Laura Allen, Bamidele Awoyemi, Tom Budd, Blanche Cameron, Nat Chard, Krina Christopoulou, Oli Colman, John Cruwys, Sam Davies, Tamsin Hanke, Penelope Haralambidou, Colin Herperger, Jonathan Hill, Jessica In, Will Jeffries, Madeleine Kessler, Asif Khan, Constance Lau, Stefan Lengen, Syafiq Mohammed, Ana Monrabal-Cook, Luke Pearson, Kevin Pollard, George Proud, Guang Yu Ren, Ellie Sampson, Bob Sheil, Donald Shillingburg, Ben Spong, Manijeh Verghese, Stamatis Zografos

9.1–9.6 **Ben Foulkes, Y3** 'Seeding Swanscombe Marshes'. On the isolated windswept peninsula of Swanscombe Marshes in north Kent is a regenerative and resilient courthouse. The slow and steady construction of the court subverts current proposals for the development of a London resort theme park. Acting under the guise of an ecological mandate, the court stands as a figurehead for our companionship with the landscape.

9.7 **Eleanor Middleton, Y2** 'The Debatable Forest'. Set against the backdrop of current politics, the project focusses on two villages – Nookfoot and Alberig – with opposing views on Scottish independence, located either side of the Anglo-Scottish border. The architecture facilitates debate between the two communities and offers a space for reconciliation.

9.8 **Daniel Langstaff, Y2** 'Hveragerði Water Cremation Centre'. The project addresses mass deforestation in Iceland and the lack of infrastructure to deal with the country's death-cycle. Through micro-reforestation of the land and the provision of a carefully choreographed public cremation centre, a place for memorialising loved ones is created.

9.9 **Guiming He, Y3** 'Generations Under One Roof'. Sited in the mountainous region of rural Luoyang, China, a multi-generational house is proposed for four generations of the He family. The architecture is autobiographical, constructed using fictional narratives based on the author's personal experiences. The spaces explore the relationships between different family groups and utilise traditional Chinese courtyard culture.

9.10 **Nandinzul Munkhbayar, Y3** 'In Season'. In Ulaanbaatar, Mongolia, a community library is proposed on the border between the informal *ger* districts and modern centre. The community library looks to find robust and adaptable solutions to extreme weather conditions. Mobile built elements can be reconfigured by users throughout the year to encourage community engagement while maintaining optimal levels of comfort for occupants throughout the seasons.

9.11 **Kirsty Selwood, Y3** 'The Multiple Garden Houses'. A proposal for a mixed-tenure social-housing scheme, located in Welwyn Garden City, Hertfordshire. The proposal offers an alternative scheme for the site; currently a large high-rise development is under construction, which is widely considered to go against the values of the town.

9.12 **Shannon Townsend, Y2** 'A Shifting Landscape: The future of Cuckmere Haven'. Cuckmere Haven, East Sussex, has entered a stage of managed retreat, promising to reclaim the wetlands but, in doing so, disrupting life for locals. This project proposes architectural responses to aid the transition by representing the stages of grief that the residents will experience at the loss of their homes. The scheme unfolds into a sequence spanning 100 years, during which time four individual structures are built, aligning with key transformative moments of the landscape and resulting in ruination.

9.13, 9.16 **Ewan Sleath, Y3** 'Risen from Rubble'. On the border of the River Lea, where the channel splits in two, a wetland emerges from the cracks of a cloistered depot. Splitting apart the site reveals modest materials, which are reassembled into structures that take part in the terraforming process, with the old site gradually crumbling to create and maintain an ecologically complex and sustainable wetland.

9.14 **Harris Mawardi, Y3** 'Castle Lane Homeless Shelter'. The City of Westminster in London reports the highest cases of homelessness in the city. The project, sited in an unoccupied terraced building in Castle Lane – once home to local workers – proposes temporary accommodation for homeless adult men in the borough

through retrofit and careful augmentation of the existing building. The project explores themes of individuality, privacy and forms of rehabilitation for the most vulnerable.

9.15 **Yunzi Wang, Y3** 'Yangmeizhu Moving Market'. The design investigates the use of mechanics to create a transformable theatre and market in the Yangmeizhu *hutong* (street) in Beijing. The proposal is both symbiotic and modular. It responds to the needs of the programme and negotiates with the existing historic neighbourhood, which is under constant threat of demolition.

9.17 **Nathan Verrier, Y2** 'Lee Boatel'. The 'boatel' is a canal-side short-term residence designed for members of the local boating community. By carving a new channel into the neighbouring park, the project unites the secluded boating community with park users through a network of open space. The design recognises the established presence of canal residents and opens a dialogue with those that inhabit the land.

9.18–9.19 **Prim Vudhichamnong, Y3** 'Through Risk and Comfort: Education within bridging realities'. A day care and educational facility, centred around play spaces for children aged between 0 and 5 years, in Bangkok, Thailand. Each space is designed to maximise a child's physical and mental development through a mixture of risk, stimulation, play and comfort in real-world and digital reality augmentations.

9.20–9.22 **Marie Faivre, Y3** 'Carbon Landscape Laboratories'. A proposal for a carbon sequestration landscape and research laboratory situated on the peninsula of the former docklands and London City Airport runway. Built using materials from the runway, the laboratory embodies as much carbon as possible in its design. The greater the embodied carbon in the structure, the more carbon is removed from the atmosphere. A research woodland adjacent to the laboratory allows mature trees to create a constantly deepening carbon sink.

9.23–9.24 **Tia Duong, Y3** 'The Little Hanoi in London'. The project recreates the atmosphere of Hanoi, Vietnam, in a small hotel in Beckton, East London, through the manipulation of environmental conditions and their effects on the building fabric. As the seasons change throughout the year, the building remains atmospherically entangled, shifting with the Hanoian climate, and responding to its local context.

9.25–9.27 **Xintong Chen, Y3** 'The Unauthorised Camp'. A proposal for an assembly of protesters on the site of the Former Embassy of Iran in Washington, D.C. The project seeks to desegregate the city by positing a landscape of power through guerrilla tactics and constructed protest structures, which provide long-term infrastructure to support these unauthorised communities.

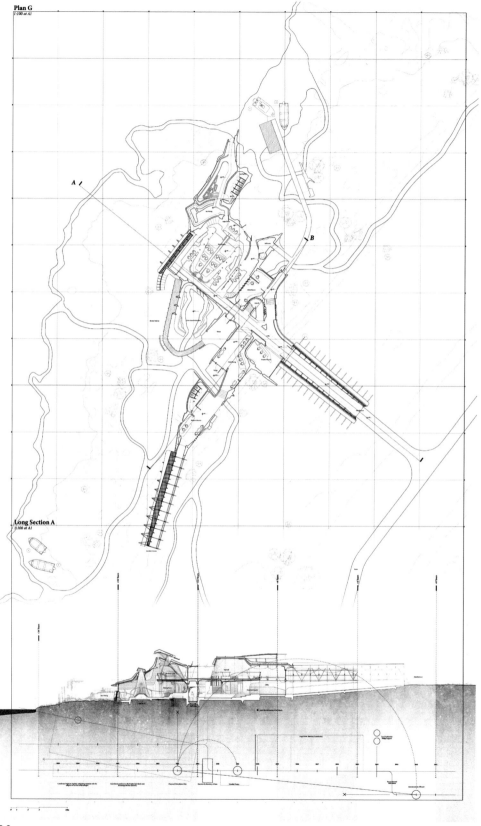

Plan G
1:100 at A1

A

B

Long Section A
1:100 at A1

9.2

9.3

9.4

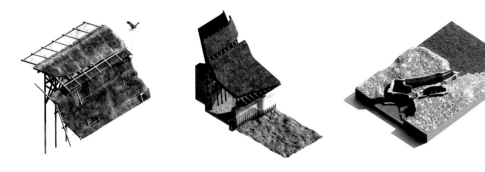

9.5

9.6

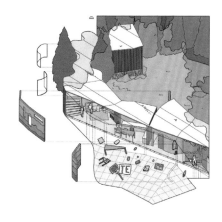
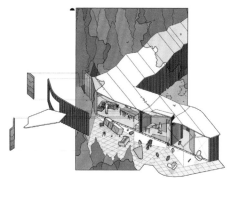

9.7

9.8

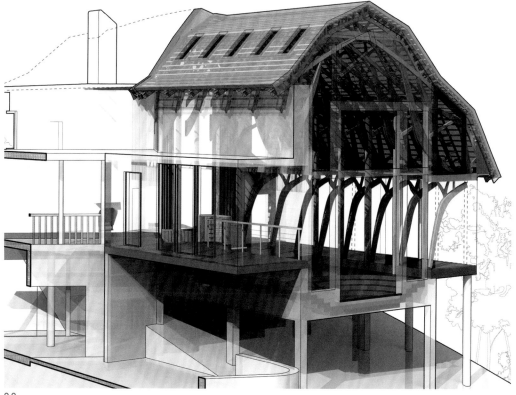

9.9

9.10

9.11

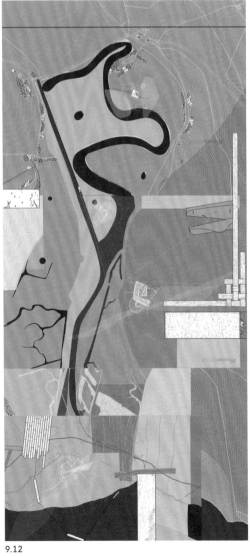

9.12

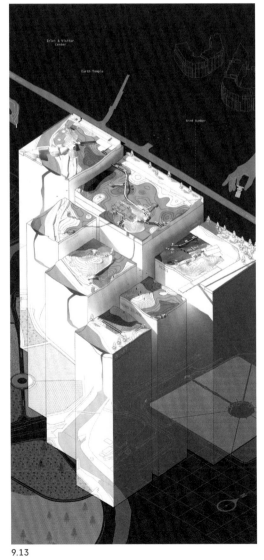

9.13

9.14

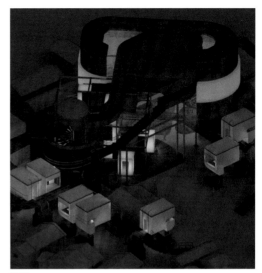

9.15

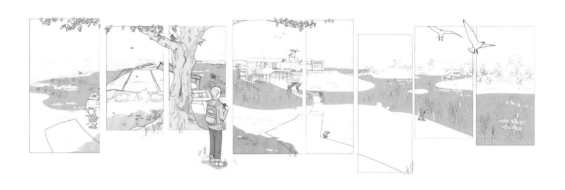

9.16

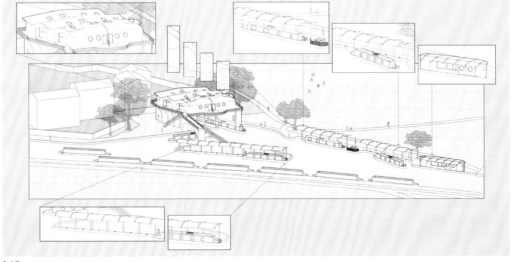

9.17

9.18

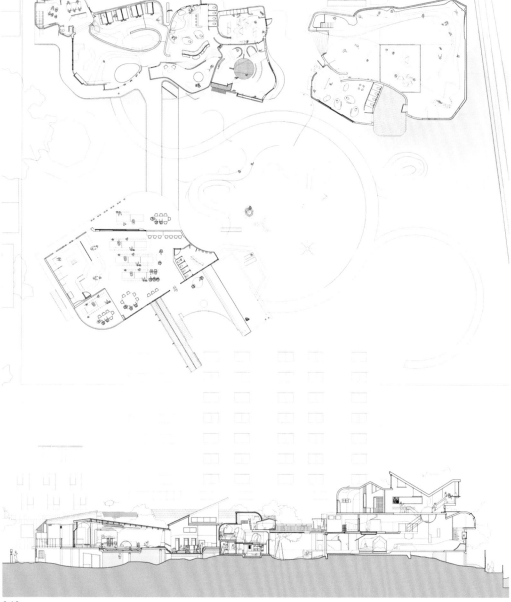

9.19

9.20

9.21

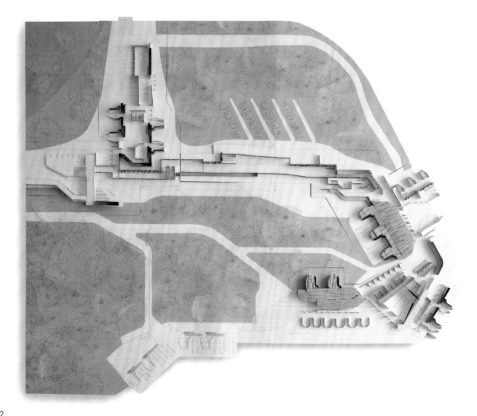

9.22

9.23

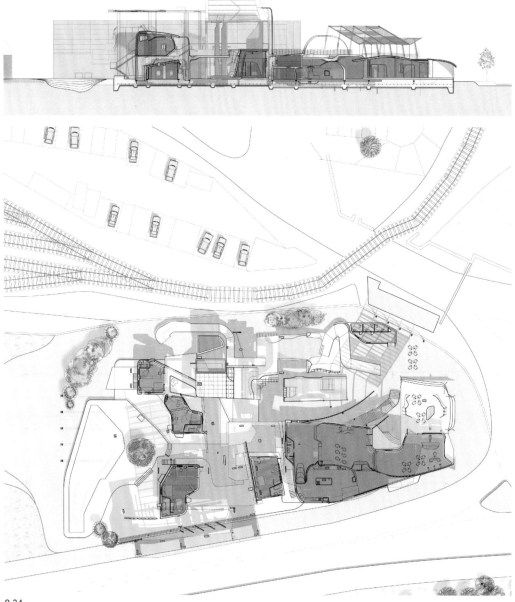

9.24

Lectures in the
People's Assembly

9.25

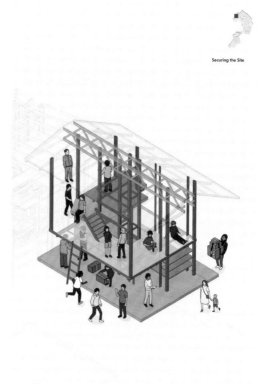

Securing the Site

9.26

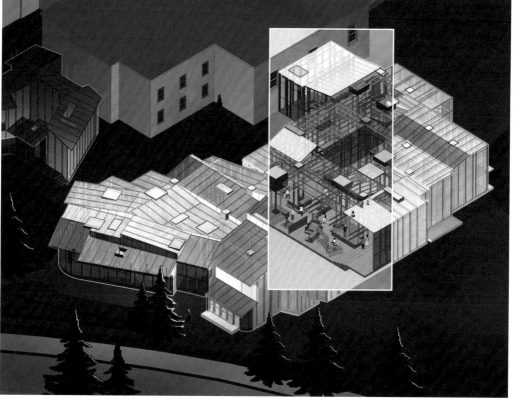

9.27

10.1

Polyrhythms

Freya Cobbin, Pedro Gil-Quintero

UG10 acknowledges the Global North/South paradigm. In doing so, we aim to expand the curriculum by raising awareness of Latin American culture, using its traditions as a lens through which to design. Within our unit's agenda we explored both contemporary and historical relationships between the UK and Latin America and engaged in radical ideas across design activism, entrepreneurialism, resilient futures and transculturation. Our work highlights the differing phenomena and cohabitations between these diverse contexts, exploring what has been borrowed, drawn upon and taken from both sides of the Atlantic.

For our inaugural year, we selected Venezuela as our region of focus due to its rich and diverse history, people, land, nature, art, architecture, music and food. In the first term, we generated a series of postcards in response to The Bartlett's 'Build a better future' manifesto,[1] and set up a socio-environmental framework for the year. This short exercise led to the production of small-scale propositions, following in-depth research into Venezuela's various social, political, historical, economic and/or environmental cultures.

In terms two and three, we built on the manifesto and socio-environmental framework, in order to develop proposals in and around a London-based site: Grafton Way in Fitzrovia. This locality has a long-term connection with Venezuela, dating back to the 19th century, when key political figures, including Francisco de Miranda and Simón Bolívar, lived there in order to secure fiscal and military support for the country's (and much of South America's) independence from Spain. More recently, establishment buildings and institutions have opened, including the Venezuelan Consulate and cultural arts centre Bolivar Hall, continuing the country's presence and influence in Fitzrovia.

Our projects demonstrate a diverse range of themes, addressing issues including water scarcity, future food production, female and under-represented community empowerment, consumerism, mental health and wellbeing.

In place of a field trip, we organised a virtual series of talks and presentations, fashioned as a miniature cultural festival, presented by various Venezuelan guest contributors including designers, architects, academics and artists.

Year 2
Blenard Ademaj, Nasser Al-Khereiji, Emma Bush, Eunice Cheung, Aaron Green, Lolly Griffiths, Eleanor Hollis, Jovan Jankovic, Kah Miin Loh, Esma Onur, Zahra Parhizi

Year 3
Noor Alsalemi, Conor Hacon, Dongheon (Julian) Lee, Asya Peker, Michael Rossiter, Fergal Voorsanger-Brill

We are very grateful to all our guest contributors and workshop tutors: Liam Bedwell, Maelys Garreau, Alex Mizui, Levent Ozruh, Neba Sere

Critics: Barbara-Ann Campbell-Lange, Edward Dension, Rosie Gibbs-Stevenson, Jaime Gili, Mina Gospavić, Stefan Gzyl, Carlos Jiménez Cenamor, Christo Meyer, David Ogunmuyiwa, Rebeca Ramos, Layton Reid, Max Rengifo, Josymar Rodríguez, Neba Sere, Bob Sheil, Jessica Tang

Venezuelan contributors: Rodolfo Agrella, Rodrigo Armas, Cruz-Diez Art Foundation, Jaime Gili, Stefan Gzyl, Alejandro Haiek, Julio Kowalenko, Ana Lasala, Isabel Lasala, Tomás Mendez, Rebeca Ramos, Max Rengifo, Josymar Rodríguez, Ignacio Urbina Polo

1. The Bartlett (2021), 'Build a better future', *The Bartlett* (accessed 6 June 2021), ucl.ac.uk/bartlett/about-us/our-values/build-better-future

10.1, 10.8 Asya Peker, Y3 'La Casa del Agua'. The project explores the relationship between rainwater and the built environment. Following research into the eco-cosmological belief systems of the Ye'kuana – a rainforest tribe who live in the Caura River and Orinoco River regions of Venezuela – the project asks how an architecture can facilitate an understanding of the natural world and re-situate humans within a larger ecosystem. Set in the year 2070, on Grafton Way in Fitzrovia, the location of the Venezuelan Consulate in London and once home to the revolutionary Francisco de Miranda, the building and public exhibition space conserves, harnesses and celebrates rainwater.

10.2–10.3 Fergal Voorsanger-Brill, Y3 'Polyrhythms'. A musical festival in Leytonstone, East London, that celebrates the unacknowledged, yet culturally important, music of Venezuela. The festival is a platform that encourages collaboration between musicians from Venezuela and the UK. The project visualises the intrinsic and overlooked influences that underpin our music and lives.

10.4–10.5 Aaron Green, Y2 'Learning Above London/ Aprender encima de Londres'. The project investigates areas above the London streetscape as viable spaces for use. It proposes a London satellite for the Central University of Venezuela's international relations department. Akin to informal developments in Venezuela, the project's activities are split to form small architectures that fit into the spaces between roofs and leave little lasting impact on the existing structures.

10.6–10.7 Zahra Parhizi, Y2 'Escuela De Danza Venezolana'. A Venezuelan performing arts and dance school in the garden of Fitzroy Square, London. The layering and curvature of the architecture is inspired by joropo dresses, traditional Venezuelan clothing worn for national dances. The project is designed to theatrically communicate dance and allow the building to become an interpreter between the dancers, the audience and the architecture.

10.9–10.10 Michael Rossiter, Y3 'Centre for the Venezuelan Diaspora'. 5% of the world's displaced people are Venezuelan, and many have found themselves in London in search of a community. The project proposes a new civic hub for London's Venezuelan community in an appropriated Georgian terrace in Fitzrovia. The centre's agenda is to maintain and celebrate Venezuelan culture, to empower Venezuelans in London and connect them to NGOs at home.

10.11–10.13 Dongheon (Julian) Lee, Y3 'Psychological Hidden Oasis'. The project encapsulates the experience of finding sudden peace and quietness in the middle of a busy city. It provides a hidden space where people can achieve mental relaxation and personal welfare through various types of meditation exercises.

10.14–10.15 Eunice Cheung, Y2 'Arepa School of Culinary Arts'. Political turmoil in Venezuela has led to many of its citizens seeking refuge in foreign countries. As a result, Venezuelans have found it difficult to source yellow cornflour in their new homes. Yellow cornflour is an essential ingredient in arepas; a round cornmeal cake typically stuffed with meat and cheese and a cornerstone of a Venezuelan diet. Sited in Fitzrovia, London, the culinary school provides space to prepare arepas and facilitates the dissemination of this culinary craft to a new generation. By 2040, the UK will be warm enough for the building to be surrounded by a cornfield, turning the landscape into a visual spectacle.

10.16–10.17 Conor Hacon, Y3 'Sweet Chestnut Coppice'. We may consider artefacts to be object-tools that we use to navigate the world, and metaphors might be described as abstract-tools for the same ends. This project investigates how our object-tools shape our encounters with the world.

10.18–10.19 Lolly Griffiths, Y2 'Latin American Student Centre'. The project explores how architecture can be used as a tool to narrow the attainment gap at UCL and provides practical space, resources, community and a platform for educational equity. The proposal revolves around a rectangular module, where each unit is available for appropriation and students are encouraged to use it as a framework for adaptation. Equitable structures for higher education counteract educational spaces that manifest and perpetuate racial and structural inequalities. The building is part of the institution's pledge to invest equitably in the future of its students.

10.20–10.21 Nasser Al-Khereiji, Y2 'RE_TELIER'. Located on Oxford Street, London, the building challenges high-street fast-fashion culture to foster a meaningful relationship between garment and wearer. Adopting the atelier model of traditional fashion houses, and taking inspiration from transgenerational mochila bags – hand-woven using local materials by the Wayuu tribe of Venezuela – the project injects a sense of intimacy, missing from disposable fashion, between humans and garments.

10.22 Jovan Jankovic, Y2 'Beisbol Barrio'. The project is a rooftop baseball club, inspired by research into urbanism and sports in Caracas, Venezuela, where architectural interventions are made within the unplanned *barrios* (neighbourhoods) that lack amenity spaces, such as sports enclosures and public squares. The proposed 'club de beisbol', a ubiquitous typology in Venezuela, is situated on a rooftop on Grafton Way, Fitzrovia.

10.23–10.24 Blenard Ademaj, Y2 'The Cult of Healing'. The project creates a place that celebrates the Venezuelan cultural practice of rituals that use smoke to connect to spirits and heal. A space for therapy by day and aromatherapy by night, the programme promotes healing through nature and burning as a method to restore, celebrate and unite. Through everyday use, the building comes alive with smoke, steam and mechanisms that create a relaxed and reflective atmosphere.

10.2

10.3

10.4

10.5

10.6

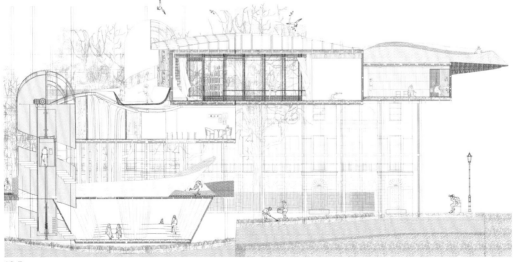

10.7

10.8

10.9

10.10

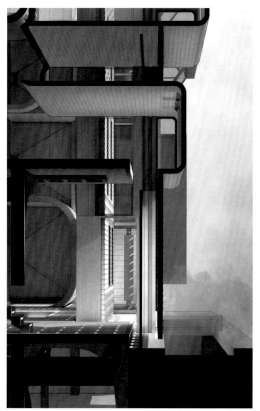

10.11

10.12

10.13

10.14

10.15

10.16

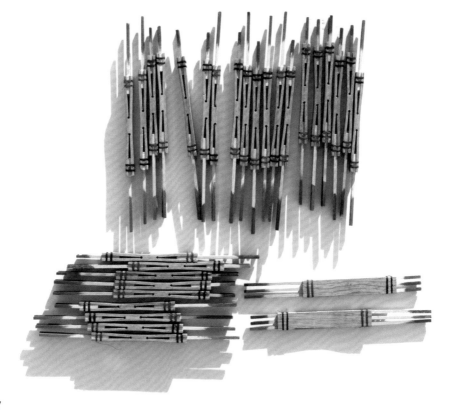

10.17

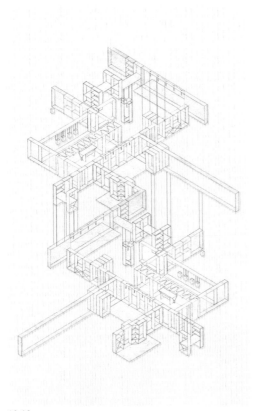

10.18

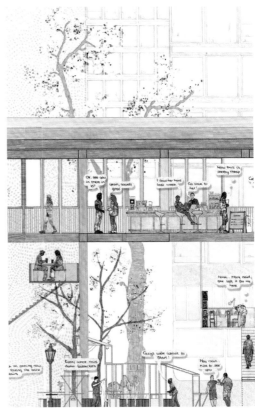

10.19

10.20

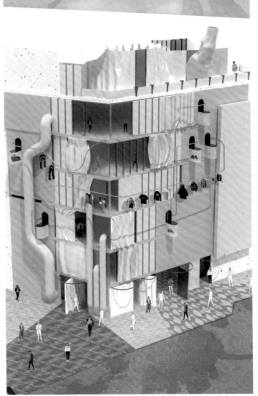

10.21

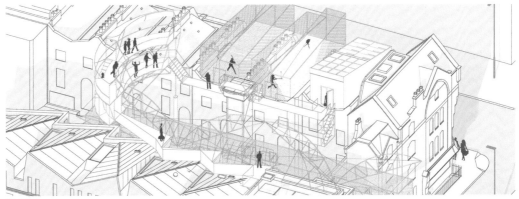

10.22

10.23

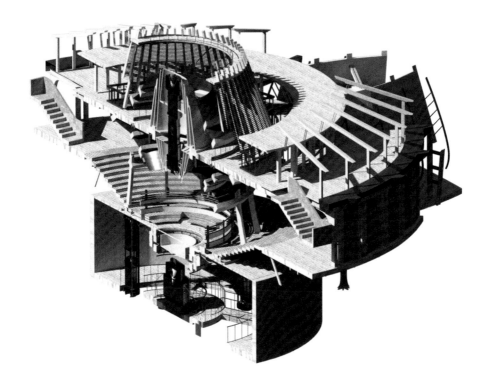

10.24

THE FRESH WATER LAGOON IS UTILISED AS A SOURCE OF HYDROPONIC FARMING, ENABLING THE BRAVE FRONTIERS TO GROW, HARVEST AND PROCESS THE VERY MATERIALS NEEDED FOR THE SELF BUILD.

ATTEMPTING TO AVOID UNSUSTAINABLE AND ECOLOGICALLY DEVASTATING CONSTRUCTION METHODS, A STRAIN OF CANNABIS - HEMP SATIVA - BRINGS NEW HOPE TO A LARGELY DAMAGING INDUSTRY ...

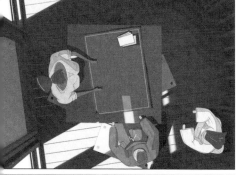

01

02

04

12.1

NO I THINK WE'RE OKAY. I'M SO EXCITED TO SEE EVERYTHING LIT UP ...

DO YOU GUYS NEED ANY HELP PREPARING FOR THE STREET LIGHTS PARTY?

EVERYONE OUTSIDE IS SO EXCITED !!

05

Citadel:
The body of bodies

Johan Hybschmann, Matthew Springett

As we slowly recalibrate to new patterns of existence, as a result of the Covid-19 pandemic, we must (re)consider the boundaries of where we live, work and play. With the human constructs of community and shared belonging being challenged, UG12 considered the building typology of the citadel. We reflected on places of autonomous refuge, protection and defense to explore future citadel typologies. Through detailed research and enquiry, we explored more traditional citadels and defined communities that have chosen to self-isolate. We asked, What might a modern interpretation of a citadel look like?

This year, we embraced the uncertainty and change that we are all facing. Our brief did not only reflect on the turmoil of the past year but also looked forward to a better place. Our working methodology encouraged new processes and established an original and elevated rhythm of research, design and production.

The students were free to select the sites for their projects through independent local research and immersed us within their chosen area of exploration. With the lack of a physical field trip, the unit virtually travelled across the globe to engage in personal and localised investigations.

Precedents of existing citadels were researched at a range of scales and ages, using constructs and propositions to explore our notion of what they could be now and in the future. The unit explored themes of personal and community boundaries; what it means to be inside or outside of a citadel and how this is mediated through thresholds and permeability. The role of protection and security was discovered as both a real and constructed reality for the proposed inhabitants and community, and a cause for reflection on what it means to be in a state of isolation.

The scale and complexity of the intended artifice was developed through a focus on what is and is not essential to distill in finding the quintessence of each citadel. Above all, we designed, understood and demonstrated the anatomy of the places created – the citadel as a body of bodies. As always, we did not know where this would take us but that was the excitement of this year's work.

Year 2
Vanessa Chew, Samuel Field, Kai McKim, Jacob Meyers, Ayaa Muhdar, Joanna Van Son, Elise Wehowski, Joy You

Year 3
Latisha Chan, Victoria Chan, Silvan-Mihai Cimpoesu, Maria Garrido Regalado, Will Hodges, Betty Liang Peng, Carmen-Theodora Noretu, Katherine Ralston, Reem Taha Hajj Ahmad

Technical tutor and consultant: Kevin Gray

Thank you to our critics: Laura Allen, Margaret Bursa, Barbara-Ann Campbell-Lange, Rhys Cannon, Michael Carlin, Brian Cohen, Peter Culley, Kevin Gray, Ashley Hinchcliffe, Danny Kahn, Fiona MacDonald, Brian O'Reilly, Jonathan Pile, Eva Ravnborg, Sara Shafiei, Bob Sheil, Mark Smout

12.1, 12.15 Will Hodges, Y3 '[RE] Stabilised Grounds'. The masterplan responds to the unfolding climate crisis to sustain the traditional coastal typology, integrating key moments of architectural resistance with biotic and abiotically resolved systems. A pioneering urban community is embedded within the natural ecology, and sets a precedence for an architecture constructed of complex interactions between anthropogenic processes and biophysical systems.

12.2, 12.24 Samuel Field, Y2 '1.5 Canary Wharf'. Situated on an urban slipway connecting the River Thames and Millwall Dock in the Isle of Dogs, East London, the project creates a new urban typology for social housing, using Canary Wharf as a study for material reuse. Housing and studio spaces are connected by communal streets and elevated walkways have a dual function of boat yard and prefabrication facility.

12.3, 12.22 Betty Liang Peng, Y3 'The Fifth Wave: Renaissance of the Docklands'. The project proposes a new public district and extra-care home in the Isle of Dogs, East London, marking the beginning of its fifth development wave. The development negotiates the boundaries between private and public territories, reclaiming the commons through the management of private and social interests. The project enhances the everyday quality of life of the local community and alleviates feelings of loneliness among the elderly population by encouraging and facilitating intergenerational interactions and cohabitation.

12.4, 12.20, 12.26 Latisha Chan , Y3 'The Embassy for the 'Betwixts''. A proposal for an embassy that supports people with dual Hong Kong and UK heritage who fear that they will lose their cultural attachments when they travel back to Hong Kong. The 'Betwixts' are the people stuck between Hong Kong and the UK. The embassy provides a space for them to meet people of similar backgrounds and receive cultural support, in order to restore a sense of belonging.

12.5 Joy You , Y2 'Community & Care: Highgate Senior Home'. Situated in the residential neighbourhood of Highgate, London, the proposal combines public community spaces and private co-living units to form an urban citadel. The project utilises a courtyard typology, with central gardens providing space for people to look, socialise and play.

12.6 Elise Wehowski, Y2 'Domplatz – Citadel of Communication'. A proposal for a mediation centre that promotes communication between opposing parties. Rather than fuelling confrontation, the building design supports the process of reconciliation. To achieve this, routes and spaces form the structure of the building as well as the process of mediation itself.

12.7 Joanna van Son, Y2 'Citadel of Ruins'. An archaeological research centre, gallery and residential programme on the uncovered ruins of Gobëkli Tepe, Sanliürfa, Turkey. By interrogating the archaeological transitions of the site, the project creates a lens of remembering and forgetting for a spatialised history.

12.8, 12.23 Carmen-Theodora Noretu, Y3 'Fragments of Change'. The project proposes a new type of social infrastructure for the new financial district in Bucharest, Romania, that responds to overlapping social communities. It applies a flexible and adaptable approach to construction through an engagement with human-operated mechanisms. The building is a living being that embraces visitors behind its (movable) walls, producing a change in the neighbourhood through its adaptable social spaces.

12.9, 12.12 Kai McKim, Y2 'Rasmussen's Carcass'. Floating within a fjord in Greenland, the project extends the period that ice can be used as transport infrastructure each year by embedding and anchoring it to the shore. Providing apparatus to support subsistence hunting practices and sustainable food production, the project alleviates the community's dependence on expensive imports. Further, with increased ice melt during summer and winter periods, the building's skeletal frames emphasise the impact of climate change in places on the West's periphery.

12.10 Victoria Chan, Y3 'Bridging Life and Death'. A proposal for student housing units for a university in rural Hong Kong, joined to a crematorium and cemetery that adopts green and sea burial methods. The proposal encourages sustainable funerary rituals and develops a new housing typology that normalises living in proximity to the dead. It expands the possibilities of residential land use in Hong Kong and reduces the burden of the city's housing crisis.

12.11, 12.21 Jacob Meyers, Y2 'Fort Canning Arts Centre'. A proposal for an art centre located in Fort Canning Park, Singapore. The building embodies a 'trojan horse' response to the city-state's chronic shortage of space for creative production. Studio, workshop and performance space are carved out from an inhabited wall of public circulation infrastructure; viewing points and public amenities enhance access to the adjacent underused urban park.

12.13 Vanessa Chew, Y2 'Open Citadel'. A series of temporary structures celebrate and host cultural and agricultural activities. The project reflects on the effects of gentrification in Hong Kong and explores how architecture can preserve cultural sites, such as the rural village of Nim Shue Wan. The 'Open Citadel' does not protect the site using walls but instead adapts it to the topography and surrounding structures.

12.14, 12.19 Reem Taha Hajj Ahmad , Y3 'Down to Earth'. A landscape that weaves together foster-care housing with a secondary school. It encourages a communal lifestyle and promotes a flexible learning environment that helps to connect and settle foster children into their new community.

12.16 Ayaa Muhdar, Y2 'Mental Wellbeing Respite Centre'. A safety refuge situated within the vicinity of Ealing Hospital, West London. The project explores the qualities of therapeutic architecture and the ways a biophilic and salutogenic design approach can promote mental wellbeing. It generates a restorative environment for young people and provides overnight facilities for those in an immediate crisis. A public walkway over the building connects the refuge to the surrounding area and encourages reintegration.

12.17 Katherine Ralston, Y3 'I Respite Where You Dance'. A respite centre for homeless women and children in Islington, North London; the borough with the largest wealth divide. Its design maintains anonymity for the centre's users and makes daily and essential tasks safe and easy to perform. It is a citadel for the homeless where community can thrive, preventing dehumanisation by offering an opportunity to re-enter society.

12.18, 12.25 Silvan-Mihai Cimpoesu, Y3 'New Justice District of Lasi'. The project places the judiciary of Romania under public surveillance to undermine and counter corruption in the legal system. Through a design that rebalances power, the building places the Lasi community 'above' the judiciary system and creates an opportunity for its citizens to survey them.

12.2

12.3

12.4

12.5

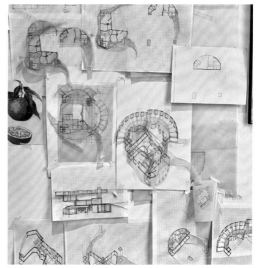

12.6

12.7

12.8

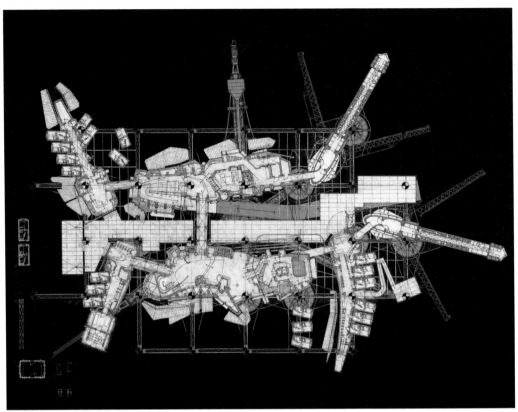

12.9

12.10

12.11

12.12

12.13

12.14

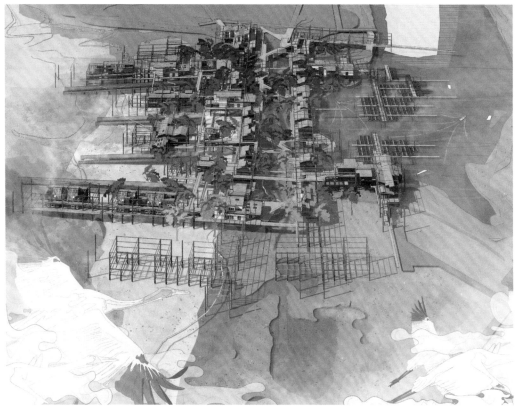

12.15

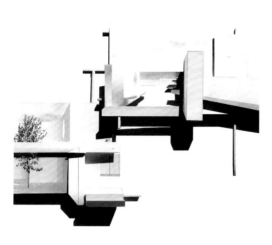

12.16

12.17

12.18

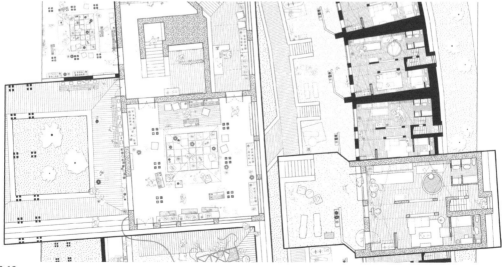

12.19

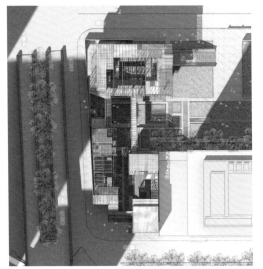

12.20

12.21

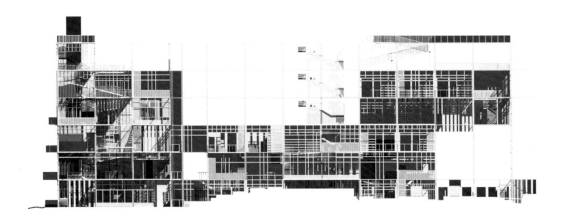

12.22

12.23

12.24

12.25

12.26

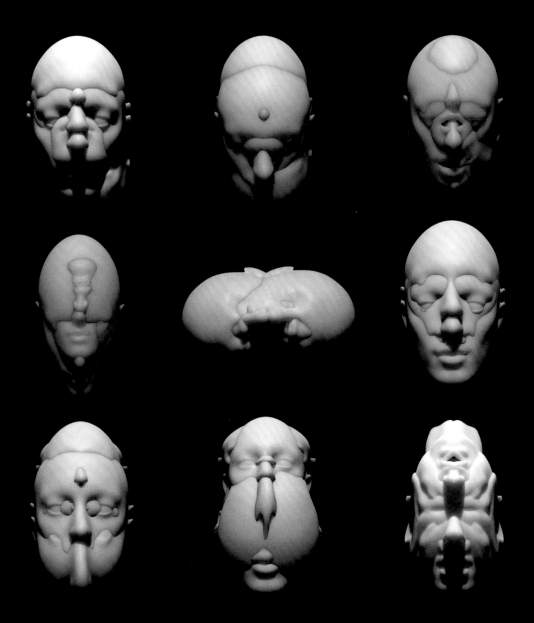

13.1

Something Missing (and Almost Alive)

UG13

Tamsin Hanke, Colin Herperger

This year, students looked at the nature of limitation and the cultural importance of occasional impossibility. Sometimes limitations manifest themselves as a tiny absence borne from an impossible script in the rendering engine. Sometimes it is an entire masterpiece that fails in the last round of fundraising. We are interested in the instances when limitation has been met with nonchalance, where the absence has been so completely considered that the yet-made project has become fully alive.

Students investigated unmade projects that have become, through persistence, no less whole than those that have been built, acted or shot. These works often contribute more actively to a genre as they attempt to realise a feat that is technologically, culturally or ethically ahead of their time. They must work harder to convince and answer questions of validity and possibility.

Nimbly and with persistence, students sought to construct a journey to achieve an invented vision. The development of the projects included the invention and construction of the site as a digital environment. This may be borrowed from reality or a found or invented narrative, and is ultimately communicated with exacting precision and utter belief in its existence. Students worked to consider a continuously growing range of cultural influences beyond architecture to find and build upon opportunities for insight.

In UG13, we help students to find a way of working and line of enquiry that drives them as individuals, which can be sustained beyond the limitations of the graded project. We encourage students to find agency through clear and confident decision making, and to explore and communicate complex ideas of architecture and design through simple programmes.

Year 2
Cosimo De Barry, Leonard Ide, Natthasha (Ying) Jintarasamee, Veronika Khasapova, Krit Pichedvanichok, Josef Slater, Zhelin (Simon) Sun, Yen Ting, Fangyi (Erica) Zhou

Year 3
Grace Baker, Selin Bengi, David Byrne, Zijie Cai, Alfie Gee, Ruoxi Jia, Mariia Shapovalova, Martins Starks

Technical tutors and consultants: Sam Davies, Patch Dobson-Pérez, Egmontas Geras, Syafiq Jubri, Sonia Magdziarz, Kevin Pollard

Critics: Nat Chard, Sam Davies, Freddie Hong, Madhav Kidao, Freddie Leyden, Kevin Pollard, Javier Ruiz Rodriguez, Simon Withers. A special thanks to Mark West

159

13.1 Alfie Gee, Y3 'My Partner, A Ghost'. An architecture that refuses a passive and static life, preferring instead the world of dolls and ghosts: bodies looking for life and lives in search of bodies. These studies explore the limits of sympathy and revulsion and their blurring into an architecture of punishment.

13.2 David Byrne, Y3 'Entrance to the Referenced Heterotopia'. Analysis of Mark Fisher's work on cultural hauntology – a concept that considers how the present is affected by the metaphorical 'ghosts' of lost futures – leads to an exploration of referencing and plagiarism in popular culture. Through investigations of designers and their modes of referencing, the design produces a bewildering experience in which one can dissect and explore the references and precedents held within.

13.3 Josef Slater, Y2 'In Praise of the Berceuse'. Drawing initial inspiration from capsule hotel typologies, this project proposes a hotel that acts as a lullaby, while emphasising and manipulating the relationship between users and workers. Sited in Camden, the project considers how a capsule hotel might function in a London setting and comments on the obscuration and actualities of labour within society.

13.4–13.5 Leonard Ide, Y2 'Relocating Smithfield Market Tenants' Association'. The proposal allows for the Smithfield Market Tenants' Association – the trade union representing the market's working body – to compromise on forced emigration, due to the expansion of the city's financial centre, and relocate to a new site. The building takes on a defensive stance, acting as an anchor for Smithfield's legacy.

13.6–13.9 Martins Starks, Y3 'Playce'. An inner London kindergarten provides children growing up in small flats in Haggerston a chance to roam freely and explore their urban surroundings. Through the application of parametric simulation techniques, a new mode of kinetic architecture is proposed, allowing the corridors of a school to transform into an immersive game world.

13.10–13.13 Mariia Shapovalova, Y3 'Blurring Performance'. The project is a performance space and gastronomy centre located at Trinity Buoy Wharf, the confluence of the River Thames and River Lea. The building negotiates the interaction between the performance and gastronomy space, questions the depth of space and architectural boundaries, and modifies how an audience transitions into a performance and a performer relates to the stage.

13.14 Alfie Gee, Y3 'My Partner, A Ghost'. A ballet school haunted by ghosts sits on the water's edge at Trinity Buoy Wharf, London. Both host and occupant, the school dances in partnership with its students, provoked by their inhabitation and provoking in return. Applying animation as the main design process, both literally and conceptually, the school proposes a cohabitant architecture. A stage is an empty floor but the dancer's posture can transform its resonance. This ballet school is an architecture for animists, not automata.

13.15–13.17 David Byrne, Y3 'Queering Vauxhall/ Disrupting Normativity'. Through the production of heterotopias, interior spaces allow for the experimentation and production of novel Queer identities, away from the homo and transnormative modes of identity produced through exterior surveillance.

13.18–13.20 Zijie Cai, Y3 'Dream at Trinity Buoy Wharf'. The film industry has developed various techniques and devices to describe the dream in visual terms since cinema's invention. The hotel provides an architectural departure from the reality of urban life into the dream space of its interior. The project defines dream as the distortion of reality and challenges the physical constraints of architecture to propose a personal dream through digital media.

13.21–13.22 Ruoxi Jia, Y3 'Soft Immersion: Hotel in the aesthetic'. Drawing from the aesthetic movement in Britain (1860–1900), a hotel complex is proposed to investigate an artist's formal softening approaches. The hotel intends to cure urban melancholy with recreation, bathing and landscape fusions onsite.

13.23 Grace Baker, Y3 'Decommissioning Fear Towards a Post-Nuclear Future'. Capitalism has normalised destructive forces. The global effects of climate change now outweigh the catastrophic risks associated with nuclear power. The proposal analyses the fears of past disasters and weaves a narrative of suggestions for a more harmonised and sustainable world, as a way to cultivate acceptance of future green technologies.

13.24 Cosimo De Barry, Y2 'Nourishing the Culinary Underbelly'. A restaurant in St James's, London takes on a labyrinthine form of subterranean kitchens and bars. The intimate site allows for the underground world of chefs to flourish in the heart of central London, while appealing to a clientele seeking exclusivity and hedonism.

13.25 Krit Pichedvanichok, Y2 'Broadway Terminal'. Responding to the world's gradual transition to electric vehicles, the project takes as its focus the longer time period required to refuel an electric car. The typical five-minute pit stop for petrol cars is reimagined and re-purposed to become a multi-purpose hub for car enthusiasts and passing drivers to utilise and unwind.

13.26–13.27 Selin Bengi, Y3 'Architecture as Landscape'. The building design envisions a new Farringdon Station in London, embodying a sense of adventure and the unexpected contrasted with the inherent order found in nature. Many repeating and interwoven habitats within the building reveal themselves along circulation paths and create a sense of dynamism. The new station turns the daily commute into a calming and inspiring experience as one moves from the alluvial forms of the ground floor to a dwarfing canyon, and into the nooks of the cavernous library that reach the vast valley of the Crossrail terminal, 30 metres below ground.

13.28 Natthasha (Ying) Jintarasamee Y2 'The Next Phase of Trinity Buoy Wharf: A performative stage of its own'. A project that uses performance as a tool and understands it as a form rather than something that *is* a performance. It features a designer's flagship store that focusses on the experience of the building's users, and the building itself, to recreate performance.

13.29 Yen Ting, Y2 'On the Rocks and Under the Sea'. A hotel that explores the coastal character of the Broomway, a public right of way over the foreshore at Maplin Sands, off the coast of Essex. The architecture ties together notions of tide, changing sea levels, danger and accessibility. Parts of the building are allowed to flood and the presence and proximity of the sea is felt throughout.

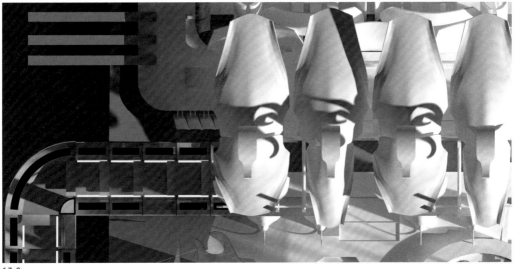

13.2

13.3

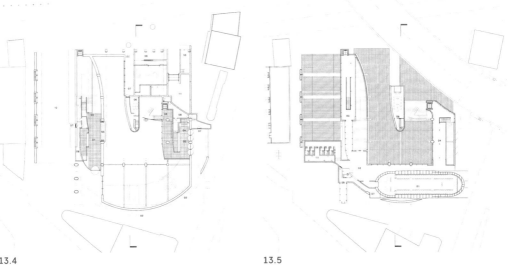

13.4   13.5

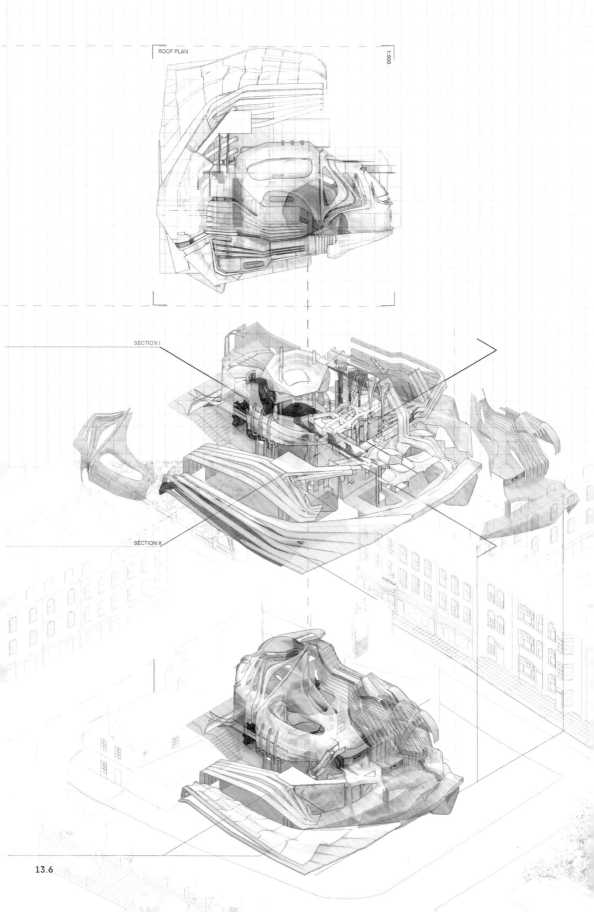

ROOF PLAN   1:500

SECTION I

SECTION II

13.6

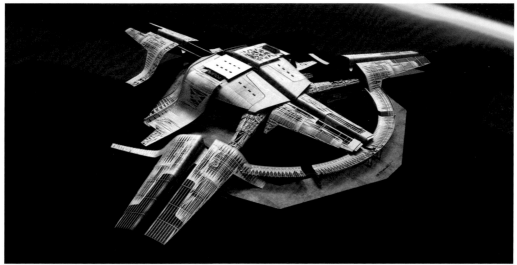

13.7

13.8

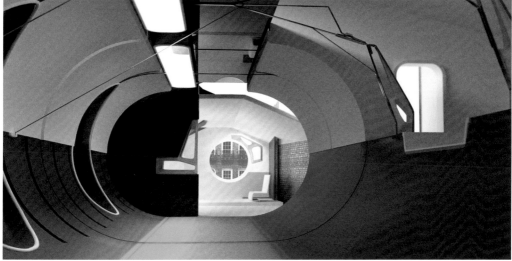

13.9

13.10

13.11

13.12

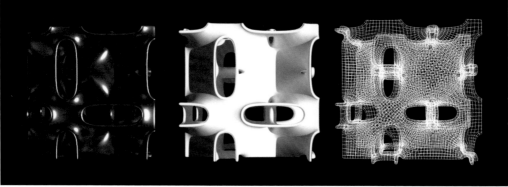

13.13

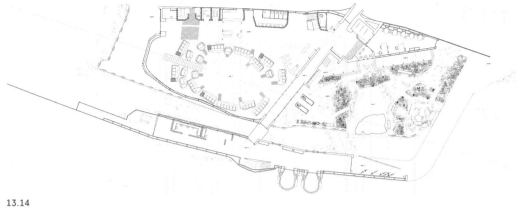

13.14

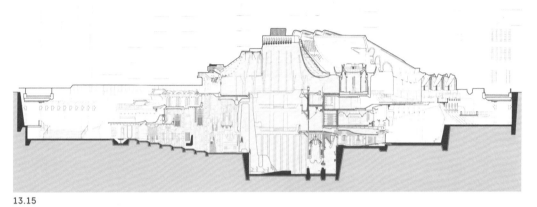

13.15

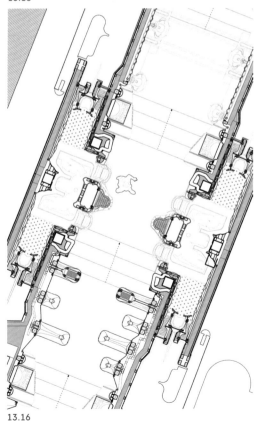

13.16

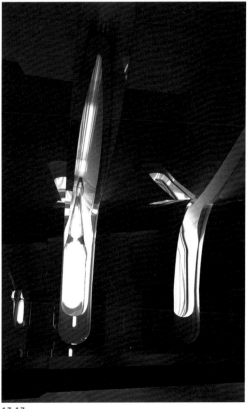

13.17

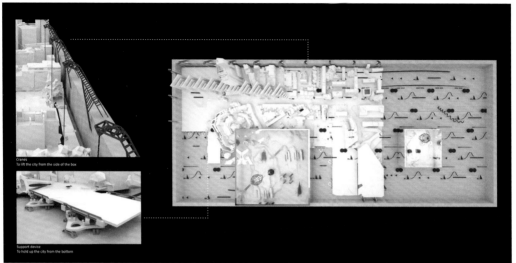

Cranes
To lift the city from the side of the box

Support device
To hold up the city from the bottom

13.18

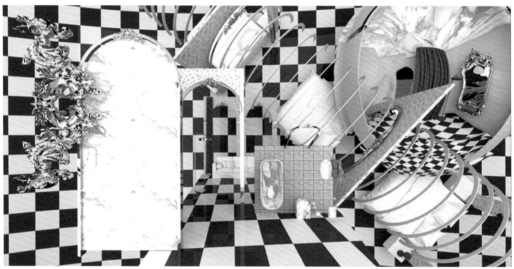

13.19

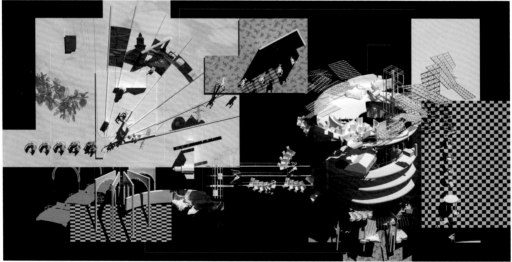

13.20

13.21

13.22

13.23

13.24

13.25

13.26

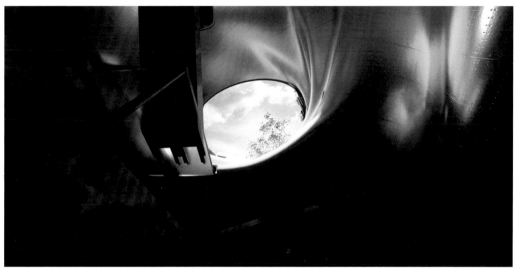

13.27

13.28

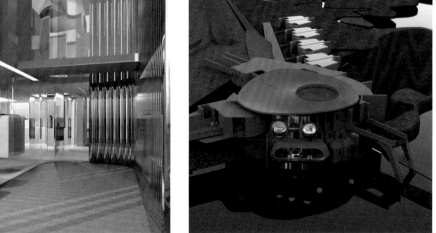

13.29

Remember to Forget

David Di Duca, Tetsuro Nagata

Last year, UG14 studied how societies remember through architecture and rituals. This year, we looked at how we forget or, more specifically, the tension between collective memory and social amnesia.

Modern society is built on the prevalence of change, making forgetting a key characteristic of contemporary life. The political economy encourages us to live our lives at a progressively greater speed, accessing and producing immeasurable quantities of data. We are urged to feed into a consumerist culture, which is increasingly industrialised and globalised. In tandem, the world today has been designed as a topography of forgetting. The size and extent of our cities make them immemorable to the human brain, while the speed at which we repeatedly construct and destruct our built environment has eroded the foundations on which we build and share our memories.

2020 brought a halt to these proceedings. Despite the collective efforts of governments, the non-stop processes of 21st-century capitalism have been stagnated by Covid-19, presenting us all with a moment to withdraw and reflect. Unsurprisingly, this has provided an opening for the restoration of our communities, as well as for political expression and an unprecedented level of introspection. Statues have been toppled and new ones erected and cancel culture has left controversial public figures and companies isolated. Collectively we are asking ourselves whether the things we are told to remember are what we should remember. This leads to a fork in the road: After the pandemic, do we return to the way we were or change our practices? What do we really want to remember and forget as a society? If we rip down our statues, should we also demolish our buildings that no longer fit our new histories? And how does this tally with our need for sustainable development?

UG14 always considers architecture in four dimensions: buildings only exist when they are experienced and this can only occur through the axis of time. We believe in a design process with a focus on how people perceive, interact with and remember space – the connection between body, imagination and memory. To complement these studies in temporal architecture, we participated in a series of online workshops, run by film and theatre professionals, exploring ideas and techniques in immersive storytelling to arouse an emotional response.

Year 2
Praew Anivat, Thomas Bloomfield, Marten Hall, Eugene Kulakova, Natnicha (Amy) Ng, Chisom Odoemene, Alexander (Sasha) Pozen, Orm Sivapiromrat

Year 3
Ben Dewhurst, Brendan Du, Yushen (Harry) Jia, Anatasiia Stoliarova, Sharon Tam, Tianpei Wang, Oscar Wood, Leyun (Kitty) Zhu

Technical tutors and consultants: George Adamopoulos, Danielle Purkiss

Thanks to our workshop leaders: Loukis Menelaou, Henrik Pihlveus, Daniel Sonabend, Josef Stöger, Punchdrunk Enrichment

Critics: Stephen Gage, Stefana Gradinariu, Kevin Kelly, Eleanor Lakin, Benjamin Lucraft, Benjamin Mehigan

14.1, 14.3–14.4 Yushen (Harry) Jia, Y3 'Urban Resurrection'. The project explores our relationship to death and memorial through an alternative approach to body decomposition: the transformation of human flesh into fertiliser. The resulting soil is subsequently cast into a façade, which dissolves over ten years. As the façade weathers into a communal landscape, the commemoration transitions from the specific individual tribute to an ambiguous terrain of mass remembrance.

14.2 Marten Hall, Y2 'Requiem for a Futurist'. The project offers an alternative history for The Hill Garden and Pergola in Hampstead, London, envisioning a series of three occupants over the 50 years since its original abandonment. The invented narratives result in a proposition for a building in the present day that serves as a tapestry of imagined uses and moments; each able to be re-read and re-told through the physical proposal.

14.5 Anastasiia Stoliarova, Y3 'Donskoy Cemetery'. Sited in the old Donskoy Cemetery, Moscow, the project brings back erased memories of the past and connects them with new rituals of the future. A new crematorium and columbarium delicately thread between the old graves. The building uses concrete in forms that are usually found in steel, functioning as a form of visual play on the precast constructions commonly found in neighbouring Soviet-era buildings.

14.6 Orm Sivapiromrat, Y2 'Rice Capsule'. There is a saying in Thailand that 'rice is the backbone of our country'. The building programme is a rice museum and restaurant, designed as a place where people of different communities can come together regardless of their background. The site – originally the British Embassy in central Bangkok – is a heritage home nestled amongst skyscrapers and luxury shopping malls.

14.7 Praew Anivat, Y2 'Reimagining Kemthong Nursery'. Kemthong nursery in Thailand was abandoned eight years ago, however, the land is designated by the government for educational purposes only. Thailand's education system is known for its conservativeness, with teachers having full control over their pupil's activities. The reimagined nursery envisions an alternative school environment that embraces the risk of frequent flooding.

14.8 Brendan Du, Y2 'London Wall Workshop Museum'. In the City of London, the urban fabric has been constructed around remnants of the London Wall. Some of these fragments lie preserved but forgotten. The project investigates how providing functionality to the London Wall can facilitate community engagement and lead to a future of better maintenance and protection. The building is a conservation centre and gallery.

14.9 Alexander (Sasha) Pozen, Y2 'Contingency Centre'. The project is located in South East Spain, in an area where challenges of sustainability and changing social values are threatening communities. A community centre uses data to find trends and predict the evolving needs of the local community. It reappropriates four holiday homes, formerly left uncompleted following the global financial crisis of 2008.

14.10 Natnicha (Amy) Ng, Y2 'The Gateway to Bangkok'. Sited at the old Customs House in Bangkok – a significant example of architecture in Thai history – the project explores Thailand's cultural heritage through the management of indigenous plants. Throughout the design of the building, the story of Nang Phom Hom (The Fragrant-Haired Lady) is told and acts as an allegory for the delicacy and beauty of Thai handmade crafts.

14.11 Eugene Kulakova, Y2 'Eating Order'. Medical treatment for eating disorders can involve behavioural and cognitive therapy. The project provides a facility for an emerging method of treatment: rehearsed eating in varying levels of privacy. The architecture creates a range of spaces with varying levels of privacy and enclosure. The design employs experimental calcite materials that challenge preconceived aesthetic expectations for treatment spaces.

14.12 Tianpei Wang, Y3 'The Crystal Palace Gin Farm'. Inspired by the design of the Wardian case – an early type of terrarium – the gin distillery represents and explores global food cultures. Gin derives flavour from botanical ingredients; some of these are native only to specific regions. The appearance, smell and taste of the plants cultivated, and the subsequent gins produced by the distillery, become representative of their geological origin and regional culture.

14.13–14.14 Ben Dewhurst, Y3 'Lichen are Queer Things'. Restoring the abandoned Abney Park Chapel in Stoke Newington, London, the project is a proposal for a Queer bathhouse, comprised of lichen, mud, algae and fungi to create a natural space that challenges notions of Queer bodies as unnatural. Lichen, as an example of biological symbiosis, offers ways of thinking about sexuality beyond a heteronormative framework. Blurring the boundaries between buildings, bodies and organisms, the project challenges preconceptions about architectural categorisation.

14.15–14.17 Sharon Tam, Y3 'Silo D'. A derelict grain silo in the post-industrial district of Silvertown, Newham, is turned into a brewery and is host of an annual festival. The brewery acts as a community hub that helps to counter some of the negative effects of gentrification, e.g. the displacement of long-term residents through rising rents, and celebrates the area's industrial heritage, which is in danger of being forgotten.

14.2

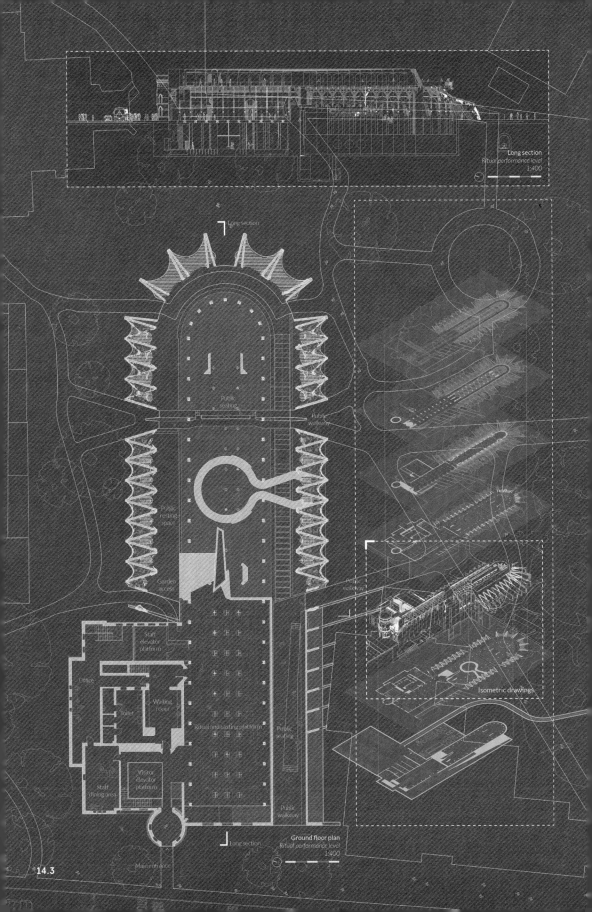

Long section
Ritual performance level
1:400

Long section

Public
seating

Public
walkway

Public
resting
space

Garden
access

Public
walkway

Staff
elevator
platform

Office

Waiting
room

Toilet

Ritual and casting platform

Public
seating

Staff
dining area

Visitor
elevator
platform

Public
walkway

Long section

Isometric drawings

Ground floor plan
Ritual performance level
1:400

Main entrance

14.3

14.4

14.5

14.6

14.7

14.8

14.9

14.10

14.11

14.12

14.13

14.14

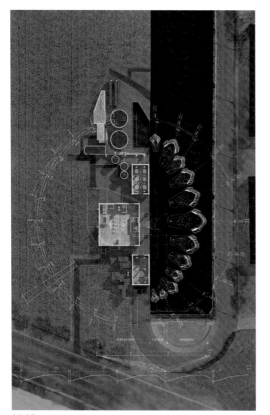

14.15

14.16

14.17

21.1

Uncertainty

Abigail Ashton, Tom Holberton, Jasmin Sohi

The mathematician Giovanni Cassini was a pioneer of accurately drawing the universe. In 1679 he produced the first scientific map of the Moon and concealed a tiny figure of a woman in the Bay of Rainbows. No one knows why he hid this fictional maiden within a scientific drawing. Perhaps it was a playful admission of the limits of truth? Despite painstakingly measuring the shadows and smudges of the lunar surface, the drawing still concealed an unknown and uncertain world.

We are living in uncertain times; the Covid-19 pandemic and political instability have shaken our collective sense of the world as relatively predictable. We crave social categories and identities as anchors that make our interactions predictable, surrounding us with shades of certainty. It is easy to live in the echo chamber that is the internet, where algorithms feed false certainty. News and truth are manipulated to group people using confirmation bias, offering the comfort of social categories and a digital environment that reinforces, rather than engaging with, the unfamiliar or ambiguous.

Science offers a different perspective, where the measurement of uncertainty is a vital tool for critical thinking. Quantifying what we do not know is as important as what we do. Artificial Intelligence allows machines to gradually make their dreams converge with reality and creates a succinct internal model of a fluctuating world; each iteration creating a new fiction where uncertainties are tested against real data.

Buildings offer the constants of shelter, structure and environment, but architecture often plays and manipulates uncertainties. Every drawing, model and building carries ambiguities through tolerances and translation.

This year UG21 was interested in designs that are not determinate or fixed but are instead uncertain. The unit looked towards the beautiful and eerie landscape of Dungeness on the coast of Kent. Frequently called 'the UK's only desert' – an alternative truth – and 'the fifth continent', Dungeness is home to one third of all plant species found in the UK. 30,000 tonnes of shingle are manually relocated there every year to protect the land from the certainties of longshore drift. Strange buildings and military installations and infrastructure have all been created to confront and watch for the unknown coming over the horizon: smuggling, swamps and atomic fission.

Year 2
Yu Kan (Colin) Cheng, Junyoung Myung, Nicolas Pauwels, Eoin Shaw, Xavier Simpson, Benjamin Woodier, Ron Zaum

Year 3
Rory Browne, Zixi Chen, Ioana Drogeanu, Beatrice Frant, Lucas Lam, Gregorian Tanto, Zhi Qian (Jacqueline) Yu

Technical tutors and consultants: Julian Besems, Alex Campbell, Maya Chandler, James Potter, Bethan Ring, Jasmin Sohi

Critics: Paddi Benson, Julian Besems, Roberto Bottazzi, Calum MacDonald, Luca Dellatorre, Naomi Gibson, Andrew Porter, Kat Scott, Sayan Skandarajah, Priscilla Wong

21.1, 21.11 **Rory Browne, Y3** 'Orchestrating Geochronology'. Geochronology determines the age and history of Earth's rocks. The project is orchestrated to quantify durations of time in order to construct a geochronology museum and research facility. An artificial geology, based upon the formation of the landscape through computation of site tidal data, is constructed. It forms a stratigraphy that encodes time to create an architectural geological landscape.

21.2, 21.15–21.16 **Zixi Chen, Y3** 'Mise-en-Dungeness'. Promoting filmmaking as a way of preserving and growing local culture, the project explores how mise-en-scène (spatial staging), using layers, frames and views, can be applied as a process to create architectural experiences. The inhabitation and distortion of this architecture creates aspects of the intangible and blurred around each constructed moment.

21.3–21.5 **Beatrice Frant, Y3** 'Scattered Potential'. A seed-bank tower in the Dungeness Power Plant complex, paralleling the decommissioning of the reactor. The building is actively involved in the re-population of flora through a choreographed seed release, controlled by the deterioration of paper over time, that reduces remaining radiation levels as the neighbouring area is demolished and emptied.

21.6–21.7 **Zhi Qian (Jacqueline) Yu, Y3** 'The Playscape Garden'. The project is conceived as an urban landscape with undulating interacting planes, mountainous structures, excavations, punctures and a 'sifting roof', where visitors can explore and discover the unlimited possibilities of the body and physical perceptions. The enclosed programme and mixture of spaces for adults and children to learn, play and interact with each other creates a fun and engaging environment for the community.

21.8 **Nicholas Pauwels, Y2** 'Laminar Horizon'. Located in Kent, on the coast of South East England, the structure induces an internal landscape that manipulates prevailing winds and is divided between negative, positive and neutrally charged climates. This establishes an infrastructure through which to conduct research on the relationship between meteorological activity, psychological wellbeing, cognitive ability and physical performance.

21.9 **Eoin Shaw, Y2** 'A Garden for Lost Queer Icons'. Sitting as a picturesque landscape garden behind the Dungeness nuclear power station is a scattering of pylons, towers and platforms dressed in bright green fabrics and blue inflatables. This is an infrastructure to support a mixed-reality landscape, using AI and choreographed digital architecture, and is dedicated to lost Queer icons such as the filmmaker Derek Jarman.

21.10, 21.22–21.23 **Gregorian Tanto, Y3** 'Reinventing Dungeness's Photographic Icon: A photography gallery complex masterplan'. A masterplan for a photography gallery complex, situated within the boundaries of Romney, Hythe & Dymchurch Railway in Dungeness. The project reinvents Dungeness' iconic photographic identity and is built on a parametrically designed landscape that exaggerates the subtle fluctuating terrain of the coastline. It is an intervention that conceals and reveals, choreographing circulation and regulating significant view framing. Each gallery shows a distinct photographic genre and the design approach is tailored to evoke spatial atmospheric qualities in response to the work exhibited.

21.12–21.13 **Ioana Drogeanu, Y3** 'Building a Bathhouse at Scale 1:1'. The project is concerned with the scale at which people think, design and interact with architecture. It researches the ways in which designing a building at scale 1:1, using VR in conjunction with body-augmented tools, can create a new architecture.

21.14 **Lucas Lam, Y3** 'Dungeness RNLI Museum'. The building's form is sculpted by the wind, making it fluid-like and creating extreme curvature in the building's façade. A timber structure is chosen due to its malleability that narrates the site's history with the RNLI Lifeboat. The steam-bending forming method was chosen as it provides strong structural integrity and less material waste.

21.17 **Yu Kan (Colin) Cheng, Y2** 'Acoustics – Music & Noise'. The building project promotes the magic of sound by exploring the certainty of a controlled environment versus the uncertainty of nature. The project focusses on the possible coexistence between carefully controlled acoustics and natural white noise. The contrast between the two extreme elements creates a programme for a recording studio. The building is embedded within a hill and its spaces are split into insulated acoustic and open natural environments.

21.18 **Xavier Simpson, Y2** 'Pumping for Lug: A fanatic's fantasy'. A clubhouse for bait-hunting fanatics, full of contrast and textural nuances. It is a space where local fishermen can reconnect and share knowledge. Questioning the need for an entirely enclosed envelope, it reinforces the notion of a boundless Dungeness. Placing filigree structures amongst heavier cast concrete forms helps render these clear boundaries into uncertain ones.

21.19 **Junyoung Myung, Y2** 'Dungeness Obsidian'. Obsidian is a dark-coloured igneous rock, which renders the overall look of the building and creates a connection with the landscape of Dungeness. Children interact with diverse geological environments through educational activities. A colour spectrum is distributed according to height level and the climbable connectors act as triggers for children to explore and engage with the environment along a guided route.

21.20 **Ron Zaum, Y2** 'Dungeness – The Musical'. A sampling process for colour and form, developed as an architectural tool, inspired by the song 'Think Pink' by Funny Face (1957) used in Derek Jarman's film *The Garden* (1990). Pre-evolved colours are turned into characters on a stage using theatrical placement.

21.21 **Benjamin Woodier, Y2** 'Imperial College Biotechnology Facility'. A biotechnology centre based on a design philosophy that uses steel frames to contain concrete structures, as well as glass and modular aggregations, influenced by the binary output of a neural network that analyses rice-seed data and genetic information. Mesh-like screens are created that only allow certain amounts of light through.

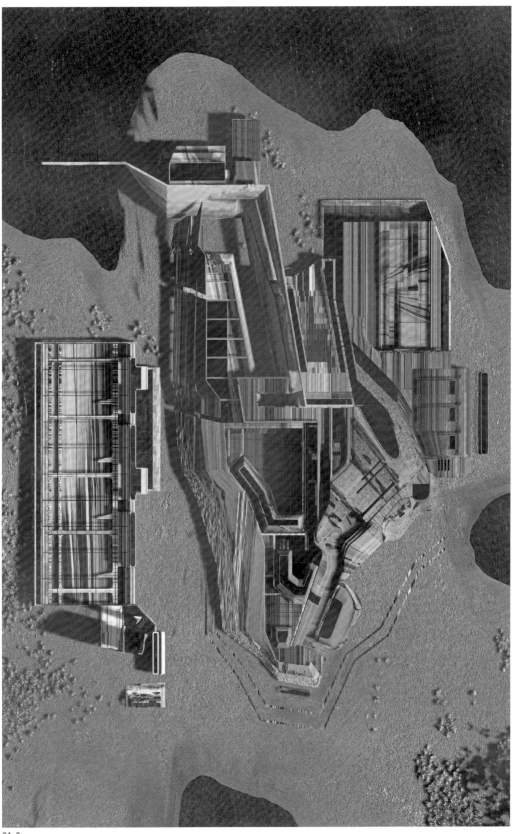

21.2

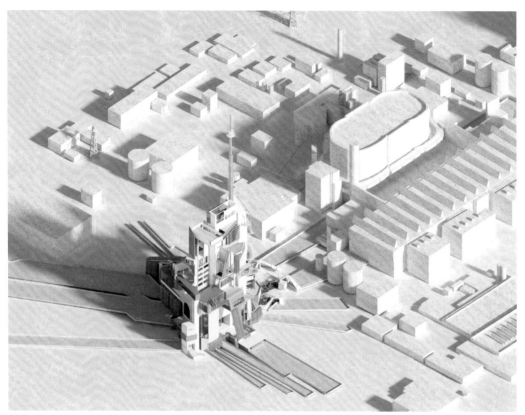

21.3

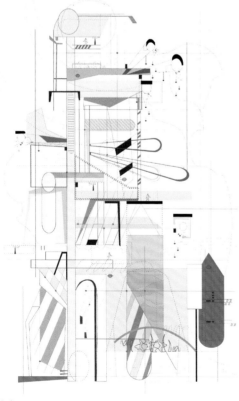

21.4

21.5

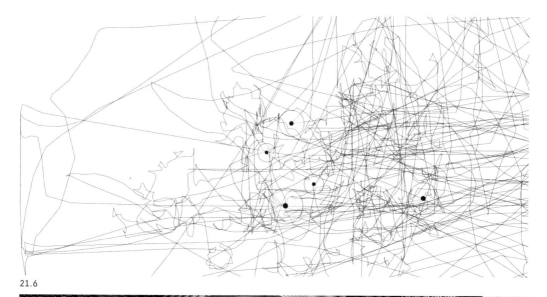

21.6

21.7.

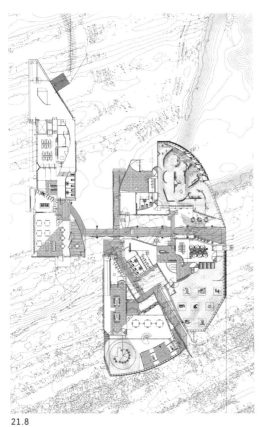

21.8

21.9

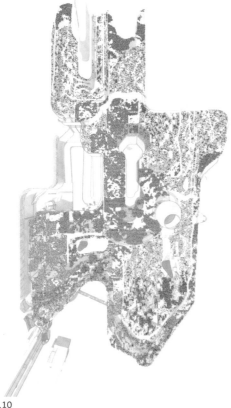

21.10

21.11

21.12

21.13

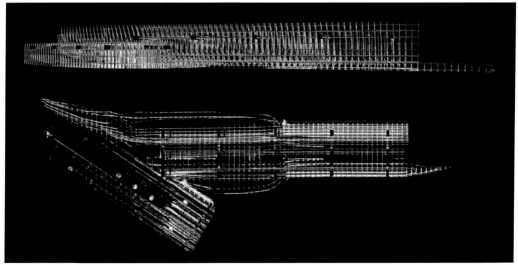

21.14

21.15

21.16

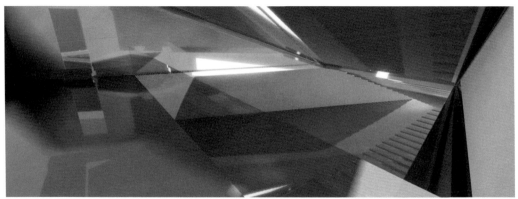

21.17

21.18

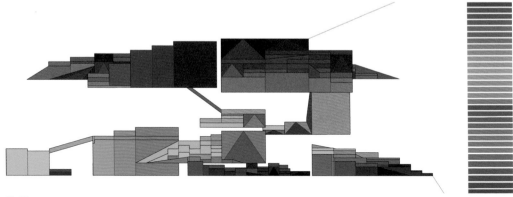

21.19

21.20

21.21

21.22

21.23

Architectural & Interdisciplinary Studies BSc weaving
workshop with Áine Byrne, for Store Projects.

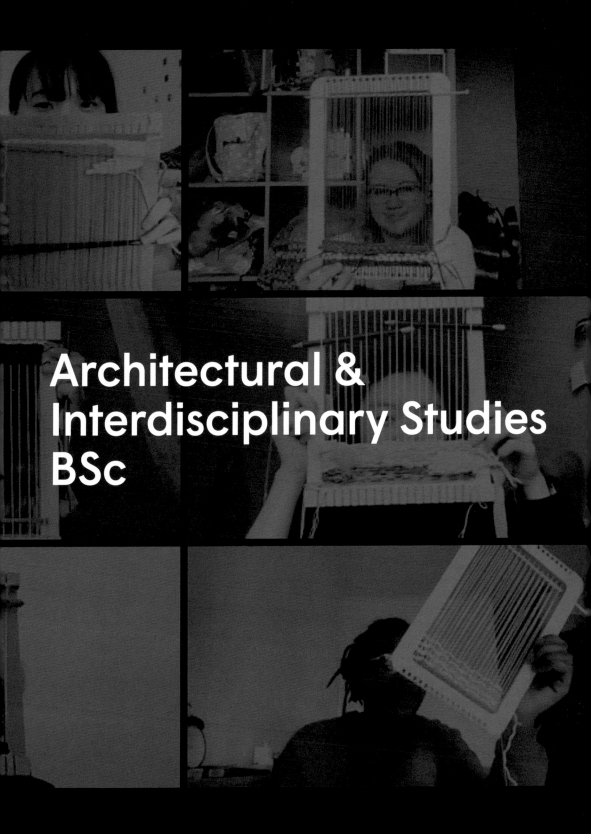

Architectural & Interdisciplinary Studies BSc

Architectural & Interdisciplinary Studies BSc

Programme Director: Elizabeth Dow

Architectural & Interdisciplinary Studies BSc is a degree that is not only unique within UCL but also in the UK, as it allows students to select their own modules and tailor their studies to their wider interests. By bringing together architectural research with design and creative practice, and complimenting these subjects with modules from across UCL, our students are able to demonstrate that architectural culture is not centred singularly around the accredited profession. They are able to recognise and benefit from the fact that there are many other people working in related fields – film, media, public engagement, policy, conservation, curation, design and creative practice – who shape debates and ideas around architecture in significant and important ways and are actively participating in these conversations through their studies and beyond.

The greatest strength of the programme is its interdisciplinary nature. We encourage our students to navigate their studies in a focussed manner, while choosing from a diverse range of modules from across UCL alongside their architectural studies. They develop a range of skills and build a unique knowledge-set tailored to their interests, empowering them to go on to apply themselves to careers such as journalism, art, design policy, activism and environmental and urban studies.

There are two specially tailored modules for Architectural & Interdisciplinary Studies students: Design & Creative Practice and Architectural Research. Images from the resulting design projects and an excerpt of work produced on this year's 'Architectural Research III' essay-based module can be found on the following pages.

Architectural Research Tutors
Edwina Attlee, Ruth Bernatek, Brent Carnell, Stelios Giamarelos, Sophie Read, David Roberts, Maria Venegas Raba

Design & Creative Practice Tutors
Kirsty Badenoch, Kevin Green, Thomas Kendall, Freddy Tuppen, Gabriel Warshafsky, Henrietta Williams, Michelle Young

Computing for Design & Creative Practice Staff
Blanche Cameron, Bill Hodgson, Artemis Papachristou

Programme Administrators
Beth Barnett-Sanders, Pani Fanai-Danesh

Special thanks to our fantastic critics, workshop and seminar leaders: Siufan Adey, Aisyah Ajib, Camilla Allen, Thomas Aquilina, Eleanor Beaumont, Douglas Bevans, Alfonso Borragan, Jos Boys, Jane Brodie, Barbara-Ann Campbell-Lange, Ben Campkin, Zoe Childerley, Sabrina Chou, Charlie Clemoes, Anna Drakes, Oliver Evans, Dmitri Galitzine, Niamh Grace, James Green, Stephen Henderson, Naomi House, Tim Iveson, Tom Jeffreys, Marcy Kahan, Tom Keeley, Aisling O'Carroll, Yeoryia Manolopoulou, Laura Mark, Claire McAndrew, Russell Moul, James O'Leary, Brenda Parker, Frederik Petersen, Jonathan Prior, Michael Rand, Aeli Roberts, Merijn Royaards, Tania Sengupta, Sayan Skandarajah, Amy Smith, Julia Tcharfas, Nathaniel Télémaque, Colin Thom, Eva Tisnikar, Gabriel Warshafsky, Tom Wilkinson, Lili Zarzycki

Architectural Research III

Module Coordinator: Brent Carnell

Architectural Research III is a final-year module within which students explore and develop an interdisciplinary architectural subject of their own choosing, undertaking rigorous primary research and writing an 8,000-word essay. Concurrent to individual research projects, students also work collaboratively on the production of a group output for dissemination in June. This year, as a response to the restrictions imposed by the Covid-19 pandemic, this component took the form of a blog: a common digital space, accessible from anywhere in the world. This blog enabled students scattered across different time zones to share and comment on each other's work and offered a more democratic and inclusive way of disseminating it. The blog has now become an online archive and a unifying platform for highlighting connections between diverse projects, loosely organised into thematic categories: 'At Home', 'In School', 'Through the Landscape', 'Across the Landscape', 'Across The City' and 'Into Cyberspace'. It can be accessed at: archresearch3.com/

Over the year, students hone their research methods whilst distilling the fruits of their own unique interdisciplinary education, gained at The Bartlett and other departments across UCL, to develop a unique understanding of the multifarious ways in which architecture interrelates with society and the world. This year's projects are truly interdisciplinary, tackling real-life case studies and contemporary debates in architecture and beyond. They offer an impressive range of investigations into the built environment, which demonstrate the strengths of the module and the diversity of the programme. The teaching team are profoundly impressed with the rigour, commitment and development of each study; a significant feat given the unique challenges of this academic year.

Module Tutors
Stelios Giamarelos, Sophie Read, David Roberts

Students
Rasim Aroglu, Lok (Recina) Chau, Yuge (Julie) Chen, Anna Chippendale, Yoon-A Chung, Gurmukh Dhanjal, Tyler Ebanja, Sandra Engardt, Camille Eymieu, Tsz (Bernard) Ho, Lily (Ren) Ketzer, Joseph Kingsley, Nelli Mazina, Mungeh Ndzi, Erika Notarianni, Chinwe (Siobhan) Obi, Morgan James George Pollard, Herb Ronson, Eloi Simon, Chetz (Chloe) Tan, Rosy Todd, Helen Visscher, Emma Yee

The Complexities of Invisible Boundaries within a British-Chinese
Takeaway Home
Emma Yee

By recounting my own experience of growing up in a Chinese
takeaway and analysing that of others, I argue that the private and
public spheres in a takeaway complicate British-Chinese children's
already complex bi-cultural identities. It is not the British-Chinese
identity itself that is complicated for an immigrant child, but the
process of its acquisition, the feeling of belonging and the burden
of forging a complex cultural identity derived from their native land
and their immigrant home.

Growing up in a Chinese takeaway made me realise that home
is a complex notion. In my experience, family dwelling involves the
customary juxtaposition of private and public spaces, with an added
layer of cultural complexity. For the Chinese immigrant family, the
takeaway is both a home and a business. Under some circumstances,
the spheres of the (private) upstairs home and the (public) downstairs
business overlap. The two cultures that co-exist in the same space
provide a unique spatial quality that affects the self-identification
of young British Chinese children. Generally, homes and businesses
are disconnected. But when they are intertwined, complex invisible
boundaries between these private and public spheres shape the
cultural identity of the British-born Chinese.

The takeaway home presents layers of complexity that have an
exponential effect on the identities of their young British-Chinese
residents, resulting from the tensions between private and public
spaces and British and Chinese cultures. In addition, the blurred
boundaries between these two cultures within the same sphere
reinforce and complicate the processes of self-identification for
these young takeaway children; sometimes, we felt more Chinese
than British and vice versa. Because of this blurring of boundaries
in my takeaway home, I am neither more British nor more Chinese,
and certainly not one or the other. I am British-Chinese, a unique
identity that blends and blurs the two.

Design & Creative Practice 1, 2 & 3

Design & Creative Practice is a 15-, 30- and 45-credit module that is taught across Years 1, 2 and 3 of Architectural & Interdisciplinary Studies BSc, and is taken by Bartlett students, affiliate students and those from other departments. Inspired by Performa's 2020 online exhibition, *Bodybuilding*, Year 1 explored the intersection between architecture and performance. Students pushed beyond the idea that performance is solely a form of output and expression, and asked, How can performance serve as a method to design and explore, as a means of engaging with society, and how can it challenge architecture and the built environment? Each student created a series of brief initial works that responded to a set of key references through re-enaction, adaptation and reappropriation. Students then developed their projects propelled by three workshops: 'Mapping the Performance', 'Performing to Camera' and 'Sharing the Performance'. The resultant and wide-ranging proposals are thoughtful, mature and humourful responses to themes such as identity and culture, gender and immunity and contemporary issues such as community engagement, social media activism and the idea of cult and influence.

Year 2 explored two distinct themes: the act of walking and the concept of utopia. Throughout human history, some of the greatest writers, politicians, philosophers, artists and architects have embraced walking as an apparatus for deep thinking, storytelling and radical environmental engagement. Similarly, the concept of utopia has provided a frame for engaging with our future, using stories and invention to forecast new worlds. We invited students to leave the safety of their desks and explore the relational ecology between their body and the environment through these themes. We started the year with a self-guided walk across our various isolated landscapes and soon took twists and turns through the worlds of film, photography and sound to investigate topics as diverse as disease engineering, DNA weaving, blood cults and more. Individually and as a collective we traversed, meandered and marched towards our own paradise.

Year 3 is driven by an interest in interdisciplinary practice that looks outside of the institution and promotes public-facing, socially engaged group and individual projects. We experiment with strategies for creative practice that are sustainable within a wide cultural context, while collectively exploring a theme relating to architecture and the built environment. This year we explored the figure of 'The Outsider' and investigated ways in which times of global turmoil drive people to develop new models of kinship and communal living. We started the year with an exploration of alternative ways of living through a programme of workshops, talks and film screenings. The subsequent student-led projects analyse existing models of community and propose radical alternatives for the future.

Year 1
Connor Cartwright-Larkin, Eric Castellarnau Feitoza, Adam Dalton, Katharina De Mel, Mahika Gautam, Stela Kostomaj, Yuyang (Sunny) Li, Qiqi Liu, Christa Lockyer, Katherine McClintock, Merle Nunneley, Muinot (Angel) Quadry, Ionela Mihaela Suciu, Javas Tan, Yifan Wang, Xiaoyan (Ivanka) Zhao

Year 2
Yasminah Alhaddad, Saumark Bhaumick, Isobel Binnie, Anya Blanchfield, Margaret Chao, Zahra Chatha, Louison Deutsch-Filippi, Maia Dubois, Ikaay Ebi, Omotara Edu, Daniela Gil Nieves, Richard Hardy, Patrick Howard, Fatjona Kabashi, Shiori Kanazawa, Jiying (Emily) Luo, Clara Lyckeus, Franka Matthes, Daniel McCarthy, Laurence Milton-Jefferies, Elina Nuutinen Vera Tudela, Siobhan Rothery, Alexandra Savova, Leyao (Vesper) Wang

Year 3
Evelyn Cavagnari, Lok (Recina) Chau, Yuge (Julie) Chen, Anna Chippendale, Indigo Clarkson, Tyler Ebanja, Martin Eichler, Sandra Engardt, Camille Eymieu, Yingqi (Jessic) Gao, Stefan Gosiewski, Francesca Green, Tsz (Bernard) Ho, Mungeh Ndzi, Morgan Pollard, Rosy Todd, Carla Veltman, Helen Visscher, Motong (Mog) Yang, Emma Yee

DCP1.1 Mahika Gautam, Y1 'Discovering the Displaced, Replacing the Stolen'. This project explores the performative nature of the food-giving ritual in Indian culture. Through this lens, the giving, taking, making and packing aspects of the ritual are explored. In unpicking what each of these acts represents, unspoken acts of communication between people sharing food are uncovered. The subject of food, specifically ingredients and their origins, is used to understand immigration and colonisation. The UK's national dish is chicken tikka masala, which celebrates the multicultural population. The project highlights the falsehood of this narrative by discussing hostile childhood experiences of eating curry and the difficulty of sharing family recipes, to rediscover and reclaim white-washed Indian histories in the UK. A series of acts of resistance and decolonisation were performed, revealing the inextricable link between invaders and the invaded, as a result of colonisation. The performances highlight the significance of marginalised bodies in public space and how they can be used as a historical counter-monument.

DCP1.2 Ionela Mihaela Suciu, Y1 'NOTHING ABOUT THE ROYAL WEDDING'. This project explores the boundaries of performance and authenticity. Intentions of the creator are scrutinised indirectly, using self-incriminating clues inserted into the performances.

DCP1.3 Merle Nunnely, Y1 'What Do We Do with Public Spaces?'. This project focusses on public spaces, in particular those in Greenwich, London, and pockets within these that are underused and unloved. It asks, How can we make them into successful community spaces? Is it the responsibility of local residents to create this change or should it be done by the council or a developer? If we assume the latter, how do we ensure that community voices are still heard in the planning process? These questions are addressed through filmmaking. Change is inevitable and sometimes unpopular. It can be stopped through community activism but can also be viewed positively.

DCP1.4 Muinot (Angel) Quadry, Y1 'A Conversation: Around gender and space'. It is only through the sharing of ideas that people can try to understand the opinions of others. This project is a critique of both societal and familial pressures and how the effects of oppressive systems, like racism and patriarchy, are enforced. It focusses on issues around gender and the intersectionality of being a woman of colour in the UK and across the world. A conversation-based practice was developed to recognise the power of dialogue in gaining and understanding new perspectives. It explores how these pressures manifest, how they are managed and how different cultures encourage behaviour. By viewing ideologies as cultural products, language and traditional practices can be used to interrogate them. Is behaviour the consequence of the context of the spaces we inhabit? How do we begin a discourse to challenge these spaces and ideas? The project attempts to provoke further thinking into the power of conversation. Although the focus was critiquing the ideology of gender, the most vital aspect of the work was conversation itself.

DCP1.5 Stela Kostomaj, Y1 'Voyeurism Through Sleep'. Sleep is a performance explained by its moment-to-moment preparation. This is usually a private performance, done only for the actor or perhaps a partner or family member. It is constrained and methodical, every movement is purposeful, be it to unwind, walk to get some water or brush your teeth. As everyone enjoys sleeping, it only seems logical that the next step is for sleep to become a political movement. This project asks, How can sleep become a public performance? The surveillance of sleep, using technology or other people, has various issues and complications.

First, how can people be convinced to join this new existence? Second, how can the people that have joined the movement to sleep more exist? Third, how can huge numbers of people be controlled to make sure they are following the rules of this new world? The answer to these questions come from small individual actions, e.g. sleep garments to wear around the house that gradually influence more people to join in.

DCP1.6 Eric Castellarnau Feitoza, Y1 'The Body and Immunity'. The project responds to Gaetano Pesce's *Habitat for Two People* (1972). It explores the idea that we protect ourselves from our surrounding environment. Specifically, it re-envisions the rubber shoes worn by visitors entering Pesce's subterranean habitat. The project discusses notions of a second skin, immunity, opposition between the organic and inorganic, and body enhancements (or hindrances). This analysis of the relationship between body, enhancements and surroundings culminates in a movement-based performance.

DCP2.1 Alexandra Savova, Y2 '43.1370° N, 24.7142° ETHE STARTING POINT OF DECAY'. This project unpicks the vernacular of decay that fragments an object's surface. Small-scale material experiments are intruded upon by notions of how one can capture and translate the essence of time. The project is a series of archaeological and photographic uncoverings and recoverings of two sites: a seductively rotting Bulgarian house and a decaying garden in London. The final act is the suspension of a latex skin, full of the trappings of decay, onto a female figure.

DCP2.2 Jiying (Emily) Luo, Fatjona Kabashi, Y2 'A Tale of Two Cities'. The project is an urban sound project focussed on two cities: London and Beijing. These urban environments were explored by recording and drawing sound. With the reproduced soundscape, audiences were able to travel to Beijing and London. The parallels and differences in sounds between the two cities were captured in a collective drawing experiment. The guidebook created contains an invitation to join the journey and explore and draw more soundscapes around the world. The final outcome is a neverending list of sounds and an exponential drawing project that explores multiple cities.

DCP2.3 Richard Hardy , Y2 'The Nature Of Decay'. This project seeks to investigate and challenge our understanding of the nature of decay. Using film and photography as a medium, it looks to present the process of decay as a utopia, a place of life and a world within worlds, rather than something negative or dystopic.

DCP2.4 Anya Blanchfield, Y2 'Arboreal Connection'. It is easy to take trees for granted as they have been planted on almost every street in our cities and our green spaces. Forests are defined as having 20% canopy cover in a specified area. London has a canopy cover of over 21%, making it the biggest urban forest in Europe. Flora, fauna and humans are connected through webs that we are often unaware of. Indigenous beliefs about how the natural world is living and connected have been around for hundreds of years, but there has never been any Western science to back them up. In the 1980s, scientists such as Sarah Simbard began to research how trees are connected to each other. We know trees form communities using mycorrhizal networks that allow them to share nutrients and communicate in their own unique way. Can a visual representation be created?

DCP2.5 Margaret Chao, Y2 'ECHO'. Centred around memory, this project creates a personal utopia where a user can relive their favourite memories in a virtual space. The initial focus was how to capture the essence of a memory in a reconstructed form, exploring the topics of space, emotion, identity and perception.

ECHO focusses on the fluidity and instability of our visual perception and memory in relation to physical presence, and how spatial relationships can be disrupted and are open to interpretation. It takes the form of an augmented reality app, which allows users to utilise 3D layers to share, build and recreate their memories.

DCP2.6 Siobhan Rothery, Y2 'The Suburban Myth'. A photographic exploration into the future of Maidenhead's suburbs, as the Age of Peak Oil comes to a close. It depicts affection for a place alongside a growing discomfort at what the suburban way of life means on an ecological scale. It takes the viewpoint of the monomythic hero returning home to see the landscape around them, as it truly is, for the first time. The photographic documentation depicts a landscape of an imagined and changing suburb, leading the viewer into a place shaped by storytelling. The final film is both a reflection on suburbs and an invitation for the suburbanite to change their relationship with the landscape.

DCP2.7 Ikaay Ebi, Y2 'Ego'. The project is sited in The Hill Garden and Pergola, a scenic terrace garden located on Hampstead Heath, regarded as the hidden jewel of North London. To be Black and British is to be cautious and sceptical: Who was this built for? Who was it built by? How much did this extravagant display of wealth cost? And, most importantly, who did it cost? These are all questions that occupy the Black mind, triggered by Edwardian architecture and opulence of a bygone era. The project attempts to get white British people to think critically about the spaces they occupy and the legacy they uphold. The UK has a deeply entrenched denial of its imperialist past and racist present. Denial, however, equals complicity. The project attempts to disrupt that denial by presenting the sordid reality behind even the most utopic space. It is aimed at members of the African diaspora as a gift, validating the feeling of being unwelcome, which is often hard to articulate. Ego attempts to articulate and validate those feelings, and interrupt the narrative that tells Black British people that they should not feel a certain way. Myths of a post-racial society are common, and it makes racism that much harder to comprehend.

DCP2.8 Clara Lyckeus, Daniel McCarthy, Y2 'Matter Out Of Place'. The investigation was guided by a fascination with intimate and domestic objects found in the London streetscape. Such objects hold human traces that can generate feelings of disgust. In this process, the project explores the temporality of matter. The desire for the removal of dirt is not merely due to its ability to subtract from the aesthetic qualities of the space it inhabits but also its agency to contaminate and accumulate. Such agency is generally lacking in what is commonly perceived as 'beautiful'.

DCP3.1 Sandra Engardt, Y3 'Rhythmic Walking'. This project creates a walking experience that makes the walker engage more actively with the environment. It is a response to the new conditions of Covid-19, as our daily routine increasingly includes a limited set of spaces, which through frequent use and repetition, become progressively more mundane.

DCP3.2 Emma Yee, Y3 'ReLearn/ReMake'. A group project that seeks to find a new form of communication in community building, through a collection of remakes of home necessities such as tables, lamps and chairs, using discarded objects found on the streets. People from around the world are invited to participate using a kit mail-out.

DCP3.3 Yingqi (Jessie) Gao, Y3 'Time Composition'. This project composes a spatial somatic time with bodily measurements of the universe. Time is inherently connected to light. Night is the time for restoration and finding deeper connection with oneself and the universe.

In order to resist the inescapable mass information of modern society, time composers believe that we need to abandon the standardised and abstracted unity of time and space and reconnect with our bodies, and their time and position in relation to the universe.

DCP3.4 Tyler Ebanja, Y3 'Degrees of Exchange'. This project asks, Where does architecture fit into culture? In the ways in which art and music can directly represent and reveal the essence of a particular cultural group, architecture does not, at this current moment, do the same thing. But what makes architecture interesting is that it can facilitate culture and align itself with it.

DCP3.5 Rosy Todd, Y3 'Re-Understanding Loss: Dementia'. Reflecting on cultural assumptions about dementia in the UK, this project seeks to challenge stigmas that characterise those living with dementia as lacking in agency and 'lost' in both time and space. The outcome is a film, *Reorientation*, that looks at connections between wayfinding, care and dementia. Made in collaboration with individuals living with dementia, their carers and healthcare workers, the film considers the dichotomy between ecological and cognitive approaches to wayfinding.

DCP1.1

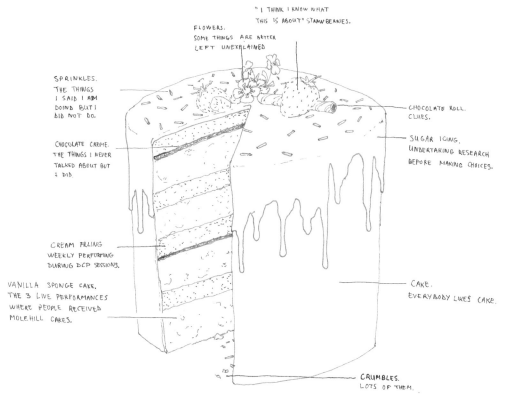

DCP1.2

DCP1.3

DCP1.4

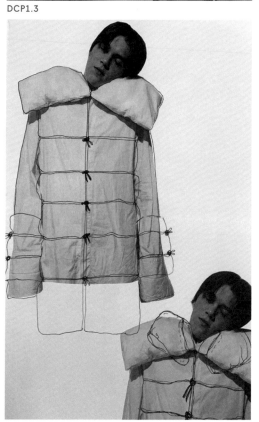

DCP1.5

DCP1.6

DCP2.1

DCP2.2

DCP2.3

DCP2.4

DCP2.5

DCP2.6

DCP2.7

DCP2.8

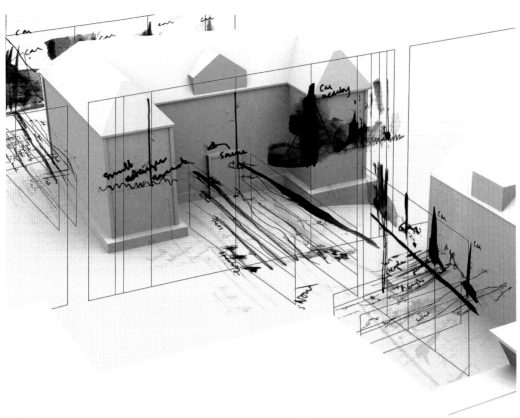

DCP3.1

DCP3.2

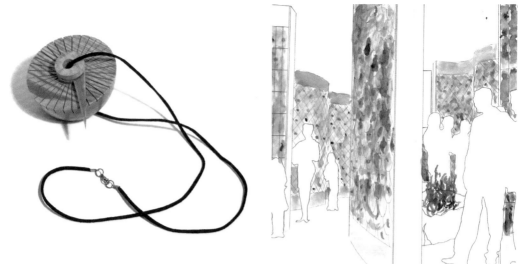

DCP3.3

DCP3.4

DCP3.5

Engineering & Architectural Design MEng group work in progress. Stills from short film by Clara Obeid.

Engineering &
Architectural Design
MEng

Year 1
Aretha Ahunanya, Lavanan Ainkaran, Sara Akhmetova, Inaya Akhtar, Shamsa Al Mehairi, Aaishah Ali, Lola Artiles San Juan, Saad Basharat, Arnav Bhatia, Leonie Bredenbals, Gabe Brown, Arthur Camara, Tiger Campbell-Yates, Po-Han Chang, Marie-Sophie Chen, Jiajia Chen, Flora Cheung, Myriam Chourfi, Ackley Da Silva, Aidan Davies, Reda Dbouk, Ako De Siran De Cabanac, Zelie Devulder, Adam Ekin, Orlando George-Ibitoye, Isaac Greaves, Luisa Groetsch, Beliz Gurmen, Michael Hammond, Sarah Haydon, Jucheng Hu, Alex Iordache, Danny Jiang, Bartosz Kurylek, Amaliyah Legowo, Erine Lellu, Aleksandra Lemieszka, Qiqi Li, Xufeng Li, Juliette Loubens, Shakthi Manoharan, Elisa Martini, Alessandra McCutcheon, Natasha Merricks, Marjoleine Mooijman, Sara Motwani, Joel Muhangi, Ananya Narendra Nath, Ina Natseva, Claudia Navarro Canovas, Ariadne Ntoriza, Clara Obeid, Nicolas Ortega Poblete, Teni Otulana, Daveriel Purugganan, Malena Royo Rodic, Amane Ryomura, Jun Sakamoto, Irin Satheinsoontorn, Yumeng Shi, Constantina Shiacola, Martha Stevens, Eleonora Trotta, David Vicent Tornador, Maria Vogeler Balcazar, Gabriel Vollin, Yi Wong, Celia Wu, Borbala Zebko, Wenting Zhao

Year 2
Tara Abdol Hossein Zadeh, Jamila Aboueita, Kimia Alexis, Azman Azhari Rizal, Bianca Bodo, Cheuk Cham, Paraskevi Chatira, Yu (Phoebe) Chen, Tatyana Cheung, Regina Dufu Muller-Uri, Danielius Grabliauskas, Masaki Hattori, Phoebe Hensley, Liana Hoque, Eddie Jones, Andreina Kostka, Joshua Labarraque, Kexin Li, Jingchi (Jason) Li, Haiyun (Isabella) Long, Ekaterina Lopatina, Cynthia (Marjorie) Luque Escalante, Bihi Mohamed, Max Ostroverhy, Daniel Perski, Sanara Piensuparp, Bevan Pun, Logan Scott, Sara Sesma Costales, Aya Souleimani, James Standing, Thomas Steip, Sheung (Emily) Tse, Ciying Wang, Emily Wang, Isaac Wang, Yueyao Wang, Hanaa Yakoub

Year 3
Tamanna Abul Kashem, Yuval Ben-Giat, Wenhui (Alex) Cao, Yuzhe (Eason) Chen, Yi (Alex) Chen, Ruiyi (Renae) Du, Andreea Dumitrescu, Victoria Ewert, James Grimmond, Panagiota Grivea, Sarah Hassan M Alsomly, Jessica Ho, Iman Jemitola, Young Choel Moses Jeon, Hans Kei Kaeppeler, Leo Kauntz Moderini, Pedro (Antonio) Merino Ramon, Julie Motouzka, Victor Noorani, Iuliana-Andra Padurariu, Sarina Patel, Franca Pilchner, Jakub Plewik, Mateo Rossi Rolando, Kimberley Rubio Ugalde, Ralf Saade, Samuel Seymour-Blackburn, Nikie Siabishahrivar, Allegra Simpson, Johanna Stenhols, Harry Sumner, Emma Temm, Yile (Aloe) Wu, Zhuofan (Marco) Wu

Year 4
Cecilia Cappellini, Zhe (Gigi) Chen, Federico Chiavegati, Kasikit Dumnoenchanvanit, Michael Fordham, Simran Khurana, Michal Kierat, Clement Lefebure, Cheuk (Peter) Liu, Yuhan Liu, Sheung (Marcus) Lo, Olivia Narenthiran, Fatema Panju, Praefah Praditbatuga, Jahnina Queddeng, Toekinah Sabeni-Lefeuvre, Yan (Ellie) To, Tin (Jason) Tse, Rabia Turemis, Lan Wang, Kaia Wells, Sheryl Wylie, Yibin (Ben) Xu, Hetian (Jessie) Zhang, Yunxian Zhu

Engineering & Architectural Design MEng

Programme Director: Luke Olsen

Engineering & Architectural Design MEng is a pioneering and progressive programme, uniting the three major disciplines of architecture, civil engineering and building service engineering. Spanning professional, pedagogical and cultural boundaries, the programme is hosted by The Bartlett School of Architecture and is designed and developed with the UCL Institute for Environmental Design and Engineering and the UCL Department of Civil, Environmental and Geomatic Engineering. The programme synthesises structural and environmental engineering, maths and physics with architectural design, history, theory and practice, to test innovation in progressive laboratories.

Our Year 1 students operate within one of five studios. This year they explored the theme of 'The Circus Comes to Town!', and worked with digital processes to test 1:1 experimental pavilions deployed as virtual and augmented reality. Year 2 work within three studios to develop original buildings as spaces of environmental and structural mutability. This year's theme was 'Surface to Air: Environment in flux', with students exploring the landscape of Dungeness in Kent.

Year 3 and 4 operate within a vertical studio system, with students from both years testing ideas from multiple perspectives influenced by their studios' unique vision. The theme of this year's Studio 1 was 'Re-generation', looking at the adaptive reuse of buildings and structures such as Margate Lido; Studio 2 travelled along the Jubilee River, the River Thames and the UK's 'tornado alley', which passes through Eton, Berkshire, to connect ecologies of environment, education and politics; Studio 3 focussed on developing hybridised and symbiotic architectural and engineering interventions on specific toxic ecologies, disrupted by past and contemporary collective consumerist cultures; and Studio 4 found alternative futures for London's industrial heritage, in particular Greenwich Power Station, to explore collective memory and the politics of identity and sustainable design in the face of a changing climate.

Our pioneering Year 4 students – the first students to join the programme – graduate this year. These students possess the ability to bridge and enhance the increasingly disparate disciplines of engineering and architecture, and propose creative solutions for a net-zero carbon future, ecologically responsible schemes, energy efficiency, culturally sensitive practices and resilient and technically innovative buildings. They possess the confidence to know how to construct propositions that not only demonstrate what might be possible to affect meaningful change but are also inspiring, resilient and lovable places to inhabit.

Staff
Yasmin Didem Aktas, Hector Altamirano, Jonas Andresen, Sabin Andron, Salam Al-Saegh, Simon Beames, Bedir Bekar, Sarah Bell, Santosh Bhattarai, Peter Blundy, Andrea Botti, Esfandiar Burman, Bim Burton, Dan Carter, Simon Chambers, Hadin Charbel, Tara Clinton, Matthew Coop, Daniel Ovalle Costal, Pippa Cowles, Ben Croxford, Dina D'Ayala, Satyajit Das, Klaas de Rycke, Simon Dickens, Luke Draper, Shyamala Duraisingam, Tim Dwyer, Dave Edwards, Sam Esses, Fabio Freddi, Mark Garcia, Laura Gaskell, Agnieszka Glowacka, Daniel Shinzu Godoy, Virginia Gori, Timo Haedrich, Laura Hannigan, Jack Hardy, Matthew Heywood, Mark Hines, Delwar Hossain, Oliver Houchell, Anderson Inge, Aurore Julien, Ivan Korolija, Vasiliki Kourgiozou, Tony Le, Christopher Leung, Deborah Lopez Lobato, Liora Malki-Epshtein, Valentina Marincioni, Emma-Kate Matthews, Josep Miàs Gifre, Shaun Murray, Dejan Mumovic, Sahar Navabakhsh, Luke Olsen, James Purkiss, Caroline Rabourdin, Michael Ramwell, Olivia Riddle, Yair Schwartz, Andrew Scoones, Bob Sheil, Sandra Smith, James Solly, Michael Stacey, Sam Stamp, Tom Svilans, Farhang Tahmasebi, Jerry Tate, José Torero Cullen, Melis Van Den Burg, Amelia Vilaplana De Miguel, Michael Wagner, Andrew Walker, Alice Whewell, Isabel Why, Graeme Williamson, Michael Woodrow, Yi Zhang, Marek Ziebart, Stamatis Zografos

EAD.1 Praefah Praditbatuga, Y4 'Hydro Playfield'. A project that looks far into the future, measuring invisible climatic changes and using hydropower to maintain operations. 'Hydro Playfield', named after the pinball machine that inspired the trajectory of its water courses, operates under cycles of seconds and decades. The fluxive canopy maps the non-visible motion of wind in seconds as the canopy measure oscillates atop its mast. Over decades the layers of sedimentary rock erode, deposit and compose the built 'topography'. Water carves the landscape, powers turbines and stores heat, and is to be enjoyed.

EAD.2 Allegra Simpson, Y3 'Multidisciplinary Theatre in Eton'. The multidisciplinary theatre building encourages the integration of physically segregated departments within Eton College, with the flexible theatre space and main hall hosting interdisciplinary activities for both the Eton boys and the public. The original and adjacent Eton College buildings and Chapel, constructed in 1440, appear to have extensively followed the proportions of the golden rectangle from the scale of the buildings to their windows. These divine proportions are adopted in the proposed structure, with the timber grid-shell roof pattern being constructed from golden spirals, like those found in a sunflower, to determine the position and scale of the spaces within the building.

EAD.3 Adam Ekin, Alex Iordache, Amaliyah Legowo, Erine Lellu, Juliette Loubens, Y1 'Singing Forest, Whittington Hospital Forecourt'. Singing Forest is an example of engineering and architecture that can influence one's psyche, e.g. hypnotic instruments and immersive interactive soundscapes of healing frequencies. It explores how elements of both visual and audio perception can be used to hack one's awareness of time and space. Inspired by psychology and circus hypnosis acts, particular focus was given to creating a space that would allow the occupants to become submerged by a state of deep relaxation and catharsis. The project was developed for the Whittington Hospital Forecourt and was designed as an interactive hypnotic space of light and sound that promotes psychological health and wellbeing.

EAD.4 Regina Dufu Muller-Uri, Y2 'Infusion Gardens, Dungeness'. The meta-brief for Year 2 was sited in a decommissioned quarry in the uniquely strange landscape of Dungeness. Infusion Gardens speculates on the environmental parameters affecting virtual interventions on the Dungeness headland, which is exposed to extreme weather conditions throughout the year. The project takes the form of a therapeutic retreat and is comprised of a series of bespoke cultivation and treatment spaces, with garden rooms for rosemary, ylang ylang, lavender and jasmine arranged around an immersive sauna along the quarry's edge. The image depicts the view across the quarry and the roof's form.

EAD.5 Clement Lefebure, Y4 'Margate Coastal Foraging Centre'. A proposal for the regeneration of the Cliftonville Lido as a multi-programme building dedicated to the promotion of coastal foraging and, by extension, low-impact living and environmental stewardship. Inspired by Margate's rich history with the sea, the building – straddling the shoreline and nestled in the chalk cliffs of the Thanet coast – becomes a threshold space between land and water, night and day, summer and winter. Coastal foraging is a low-impact approach to procuring food. The practice depends on the responsible behaviour of foragers, recognising their potential at destabilising an ecosystem, and calls on them to only gather what they need for personal consumption. The concept of environmental stewardship is particularly relevant in the context of the climate emergency and planetary ecosystem imbalance.

EAD.6 Fatema Panju, Y4 'Transforming Margate Lido'. An accessible and inviting community centre in the historic Margate Lido complex. The project tackles issues of racism and discrimination in Margate by bringing education and conversation to the fore, whilst supporting the community's artistic pursuits through open galleries inspired by Ancient Roman *stoa* (covered walkways). The project is governed through four stages of involvement, which ensure that the community are part of the entire process: 'Proposal', 'Construction', 'Lifetime' and 'Future'. The building employs an optimised design strategy to make it zero-carbon, benefitting not only the community but the surrounding environment as well.

EAD.7 Kaia Wells, Y4 'Water Squatters: Informal self-build settlements'. Living on a boat is an affordable way of life in London. Moorings are, however, increasingly hard to find due to increased demand, their removal and neglected infrastructure. 'Water Squatters' is inspired by conversations with Surge Cooperative, who create community-led moorings. The project uses squatter's rights to bypass permission to occupy space. Tidal land is owned by the Crown and can be rented for 100 years for £0.01. Non-residential property, like that on Channelsea Island in East London, can be legally occupied without permission, providing no damage is caused and utilities are not used. 'Water Squatters' occupies land by straddling it, so as to not disturb it, and harvests rainwater and solar energy to stay off-grid. The architecture is responsive to the user's changing environmental and spatial needs, using moving mechanisms and ad-hoc self-build systems created from waste material. It facilitates decision-making for the people by the people.

EAD.8, EAD.9 Rabia Turemis, Y4 'Urban Farming, Greenwich Power Station'. Greenwich was originally called 'green wic'; 'wic' meaning 'farm' or 'port'. Wics were centres of trade where people sold their produce. The project reimagines Greenwich Power Station as an urban farm and encourages self-sufficiency and food sustainability. The project consists of three key spaces: urban farms where food is grown, a restaurant where the produce is cooked and served, and a marketplace where fresh food is sold. Additional programmes include workshop spaces where clay crockery is made for the restaurant, teaching spaces where local schools learn about urban farming and a library on the existing power station jetty. By 2050, around 68% of the world's population is expected to live in urban areas, leading to an increased demand for food. As we live in a time where produce from around the world is immediately available, we have lost appreciation of the energy needed to produce our food. Several passive design and renewable energy strategies, such as PV panels, have been implemented in the project to achieve net-zero carbon status.

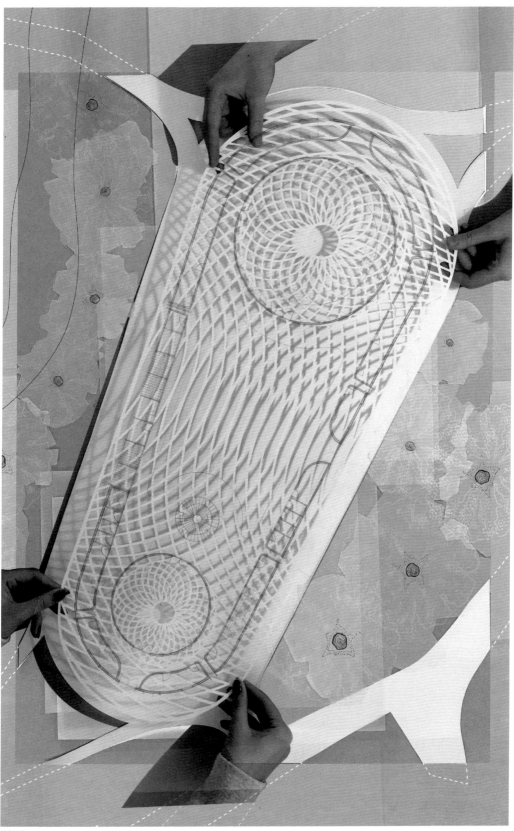

EAD.2

EAD.3

EAD.4

15:22 - 0.57m

EAD.5

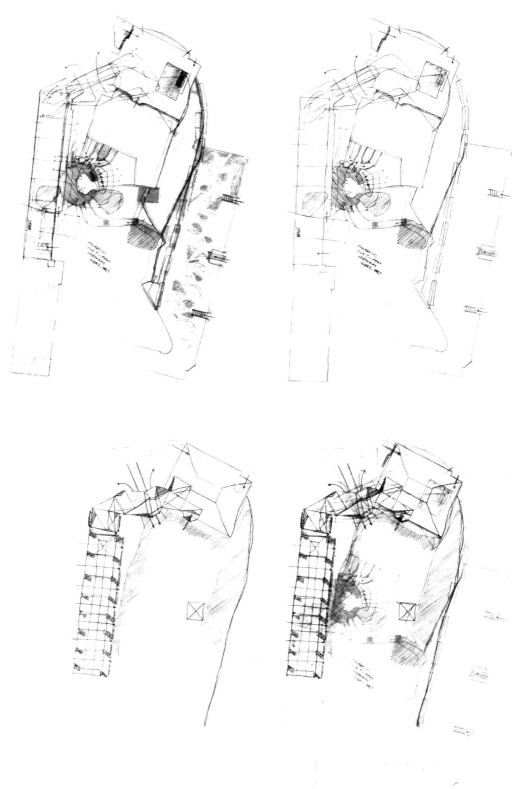

EAD.6

Continuous-Stack-and-Climb Self-Builvd Construction System Made of Waste Material.

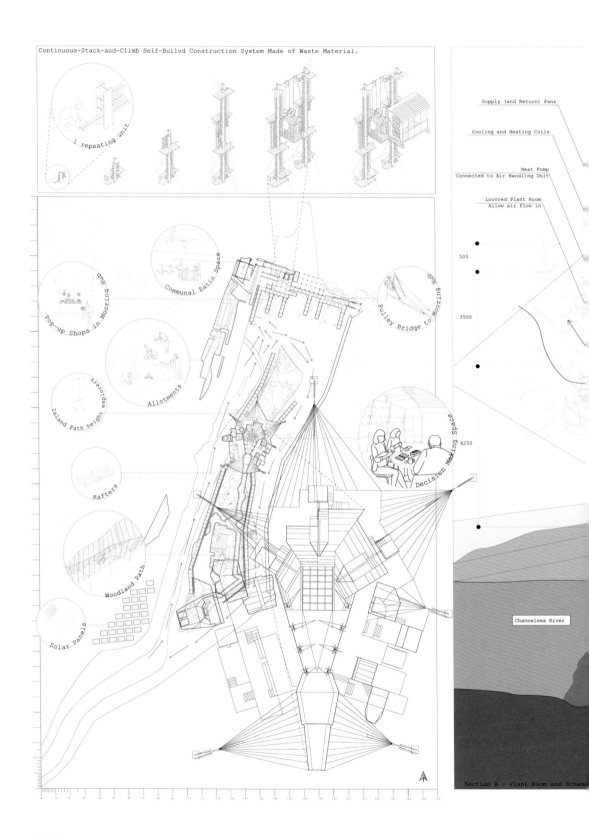

1 repeating unit.

Communal Eatin Space

Pop-up Shops in Mooring Hub

Pulley Bridge to Mooring Hub

Allotments

Island Path height explorers

Decision Making Space

Rafters

Woodland Path

Solar Panels

Supply (and Return) Fans

Cooling and Heating Coils

Heat Pump
Connected to Air Handling Unit

Louvred Plant Room
Allow air flow in

500

3500

4250

Channelsea River

Section A - Plant Room and Schema

EAD.7

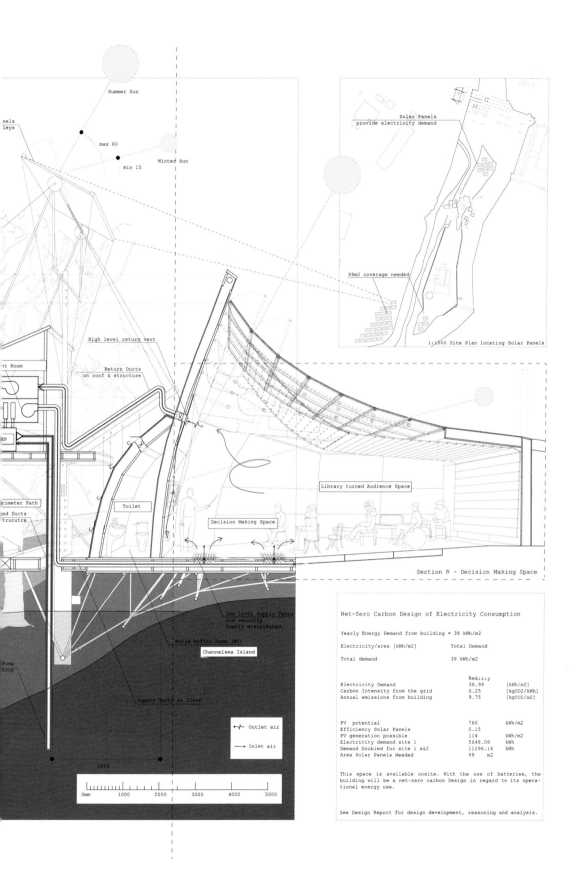

Summer Sun

max 60

min 15

Winter Sun

nels
leys

Solar Panels
provide electricity demand

99m2 coverage needed

1:1500 Site Plan locating Solar Panels

High level return vent

t Room

Return Ducts
on roof & structure

HP

imeter Path
nd Ducts
trucutre

Toilet

Library turned Audience Space

Decision Making Space

Section B - Decision Making Space

Low level Supply Vents
Low velocity
Evenly distributed

Noise buffer Room (WC)

Channelsea Island

Pump
Loop

Supply ducts in floor

←↑→ Outlet air

→ Inlet air

3000

0mm	1000	2000	3000	4000	5000

Net-Zero Carbon Design of Electricity Consumption

Yearly Energy Demand from building = 38 kWh/m2

Electricity/area [kWh/m2]   Total Demand

Total demand   39 kWh/m2

	Reality	
Electricity Demand	38.99	[kWh/m2]
Carbon Intensity from the grid	0.25	[kgCO2/kWh]
Annual emissions from building	9.75	[kgCO2/m2]

PV potential	760	kWh/m2
Efficiency Solar Panels	0.15	
PV generation possible	114	kWh/m2
Electricity demand site 1	5648.08	kWh
Demand Doubled for site 1 &2	11296.16	kWh
Area Solar Panels Needed	99	m2

This space is available onsite. With the use of batteries, the
building will be a net-zero carbon Design in regard to its opera-
tional energy use.

See Design Report for design development, reasoning and analysis.

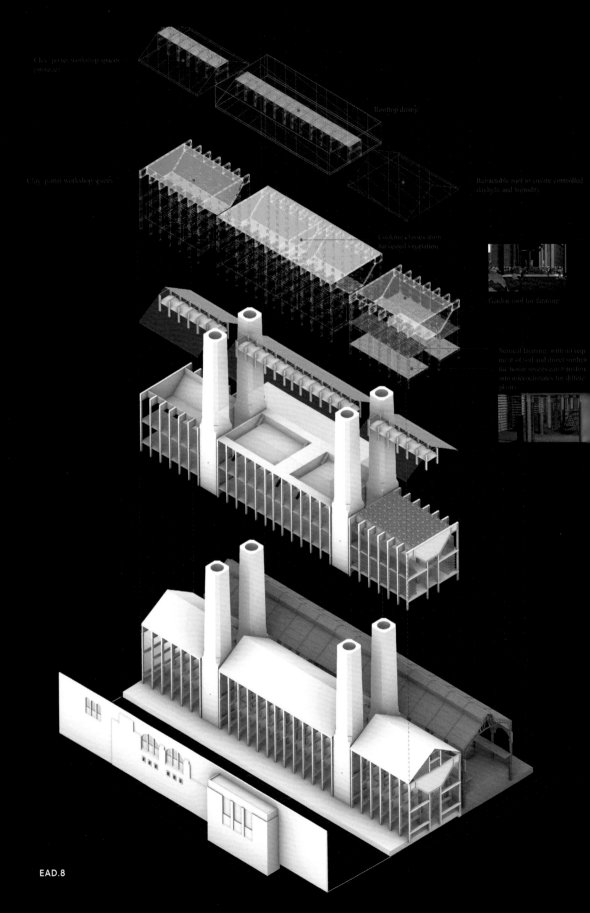

Clay potter workshop spaces (storage)

Rooftop dining

Clay potter workshop spaces

Retractable roof to ensure controlled daylight and humidity

Cooking classes from harvested vegetation

Garden roof for farming

Vertical farming, with no requirement of soil and direct sunlight the boiler spaces can transform into microclimates for different plants

EAD.8

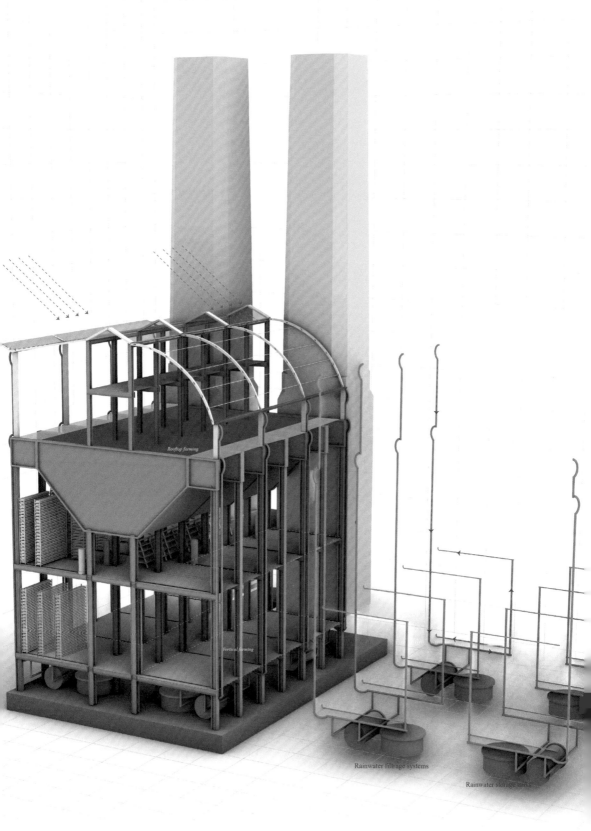

Rooftop farming

Vertical farming

Rainwater filtrage systems

Rainwater storage tanks

EAD.9

Architecture MSci Year 1 students at the
Here East film studio. Photo by Sara Shafiei.

Architecture MSci
(ARB Part 1 and Part 2)

10m

1.1

Architecture MSci (ARB Part 1 and Part 2)

Programme Director: Sara Shafiei

Architecture MSci is a new five-year programme that integrates the undergraduate and postgraduate study of architecture (ARB Part 1 and Part 2) and includes a final year on placement at an architectural practice. During the first four years of study, students explore design and construction challenges facing the future of the built environment and learn how to incorporate specialist disciplinary information with creative, sophisticated design. Students examine relevant world issues through an annual theme that consists of broad architectural and social issues, e.g. health and wellbeing, housing and sustainable cities. These themes extend across the years and modules, and are examined from a local and global perspective that encompasses historical, current and future challenges. The structure of the programme encourages creative research and close ties with practice from early on, while the final-year placement gives students the possibility to test their imaginative ideas in the real world.

As well as defining the relationship between students' learning and their participation in research, the programme offers a holistic approach to education, encouraging connections between disciplines, years of study, staff (practice-based and academic) and students. It promotes interdisciplinary questions and challenges, encouraging both staff and students to critically interrogate the nature of evidence and knowledge production across different subject fields in our digitally mediated world.

This year saw the first cohort of Architecture MSci students welcomed to the school. For both students and staff, it has been an opportunity to start something new and break with traditions often thought of as fixed. The programme challenges preconceived ideas of what architecture is and how we use and inhabit space. It encourages a culture of individual research, through testing and reexamining the fundamental elements of architecture. The students embark on a journey into the unknown and embrace the experimental and forward thinking, as well as the mundane.

This year's work explores the theme of 'Climate Change'. The programme fosters a creative dialogue between design, digital and analogue representation, technology, history and theory to enable students to make informed yet creative decisions that are grounded in a real-life context. This year, students explored architectural interventions in and around Hackney Wick in East London and responded creatively to complex site conditions, addressing the social, historical, technological, political and cultural narratives of the area. They considered the life cycle of materials used in the construction process to make sensitive yet ambitious design proposals.

Year 1 Director
Patrick Weber

Staff
Vasilija Abramovic, Matthew Barnett Howland, Megha Chand Inglis, Sam Coulton, Christina Dahdaleh, Peter Davies, Stelios Giamarelos, Kostas Grigoriadis, Matei Mitrache, Thomas Parker, Danae Polyviou, Guang Yu Ren, Sara Shafiei, Alistair Shaw, Sabine Storp, Barry Wark, Sara Martinez Zamora

Programme Administrator
Kelly Van Hecke

Year 1 Students
Rebeca Allen Tejerina, Maria Paola Barreca, Tabatha Crook, Hanna Eriksson Södergren, Xan Goetzee-Barral, Salyme Gunsaya, Samuel Jackson, Ryan Long, Ming (Leroy) Ma, Ismail Mir, Alannah Nethercott, Dominic Nunn, Toby Prest, Yutong Tang, Shuhan (Hansen) Wang, Anna Williams, Jun Zhang

1.1 **Jun Zhang, Y1** 'Hackney Wick Teahouse'. In this project drinking tea connects people from diverse cultural backgrounds. It attempts to challenge prejudices between cultures by breaking the stereotype of a teahouse. The semi-open structure blurs the boundary between inside and outside to welcome people and celebrate the seasons.

1.2 **Dominic Nunn, Y1** 'The Hackney Lightwell'. Wedged between new and old buildings, 'The Hackney Lightwell' offers commuters a shared experience of merging work and home life during the pandemic. It serves as an interstitial congregation space, which brings commuters together, designed through a temporal connection with sunlight. Acting like a halfway house, it offers shared spaces for relaxation and cooking, and cares for commuters and their wellbeing.

1.3 **Salyme Gunsaya, Y1** 'Light Formulating Space'. Through the process of analysing and inhabiting a staircase, the project investigates the impact light has on the perception of a space. It explores the ways in which light inhabits space, not only revealing surfaces but creating them. The interactive model explores how light can actively reformulate space, with only the surfaces touched by it existing.

1.4–1.5 **Toby Prest, Y1** 'A Social Respiratory System'. A shared residence based in Hackney Wick that accommodates two couples, and acts as a vessel for climate-based experiments and investigations. The proposal negotiates and investigates the relationship between human occupants and environmental inhabitants. It integrates environmental factors into the living space and questions the norm of shutting weather conditions outside.

1.6 **Samuel Jackson, Y1** 'In Conversation with a Garden'. The project responds to the theme of neglect in Hackney Wick and to the emerging mental health crisis across the world. Much of the community that once made-up the area has had their homes demolished or have been priced out. This is the inspiration for an architecture that considers the community above all else. By exercising the idea that nature can act as a therapist, it responds with a garden that considers the needs of both plants and people, with a goal of improving mental health and wellbeing.

1.7 **Ryan Long, Y1** 'The Intangible Volume'. The project responds to the theme of neglect in Hackney Wick and to the emerging global mental health crisis. Following the idea that nature can act as a therapist, a garden is proposed that considers the needs of both plants and people. It serves as a hub for the displaced community, with a goal of improving mental health and wellbeing.

1.8 **Tabatha Crook, Y1** 'Sitopian Hackney Wick'. A space that brings the community together through food. The project is a space to prepare and eat food, and has communal areas for local residents, canal users and people who may find it challenging to find an inexpensive cooked meal. The semi-transparent structure enables the community to see the capacity of the food bank and plant growth.

1.9 **Xan Goetzee-Barral, Y1** 'Sexual Health Centre for the Queer Community'. Hackney Wick's history as a layered edge-land and site of gathering began with industrial manufacture and is now present in the form of a Queer community. A sexual health centre for the community is proposed, which explores what it means to gather on 'the edge'. The centre provides spaces within a protective walled landscape to socialise, interact and engage with the wider community.

1.10 **Shuhan (Hansen) Wang, Y1** 'The Hackney Exchange'. Situated next to a canal lock, the project creates a point of gathering and exchange between the different groups of people who use the canalside daily. The site is defined by datums. Each level has a different atmosphere, and the people that inhabit them exist in parallel to each other without ever really interacting. By creating an inhabitable stepped landscape, the project blurs the boundaries between the datums to foster a new community.

1.11 **Ismail Mir, Y1** 'The Hackney Hydro Forum'. This project investigates a new relationship with the water. It serves as a forum, a gathering space and a place for encouraging community discussions on water pollution. The building investigates how materials may register the environment to become a signal and record of change.

1.12 **Yutong Tang, Y1** 'A Work Cafe During Covid-19'. The 'Work Cafe' explores how Covid-19 has influenced the way people work and study, and how buildings have responded to these changes, by investigating highly ventilated open spaces. In response to climate change, the design tries to maximise the use of sunlight and natural ventilation.

1.13 **Maria Paola Barreca, Y1** 'Encounter House'. The project is a home for the elderly that reimagines the urban model. It creates a space for cross-generational cohesion and encourages a healthy lifestyle. The programme of three residents and two carers allows for shared spaces with artists. It is the threshold moments between the building skins that encourage conversation, sight and sound on various levels. A space for the community, which promotes inclusion rather than segregation, creates a positive environment.

1.14 **Hanna Eriksson Södergren, Y1** 'Narrowing and Opening'. The views from and by the site are unique; from West to East a narrow channel opens up to the Olympic Park in Stratford, London. The buildings on the other side of the canal create a wall, narrowing the space further. Being locked in our homes during the pandemic has changed the way we look at enclosure. We work and sleep in the same room, with very little variation of space, causing irregular sleep patterns and affecting wellbeing.

1.15, 1.17 **Anna Williams, Y1** 'Canal-Side Washhouse'. The washhouse is an investigation into the human relationship with water and atmospheres of immersion. It is an attempt to recombine typologies, such as the bath house, public bathroom and laundrette, to overcome their ecological and economical shortcomings by drawing these activities into a communal space.

1.16 **Alannah Nethercott, Y1** 'The Hackney Agora'. Reimagining the ancient *agora* (public space) in the context of Hackney Wick, this project looks at how a semi open-air building can facilitate communication and public discourse within a community. It aims to encourage and expose conversation around issues pertinent to its diverse population. Interest in this layered porosity, allowing for visual and acoustic entrances, grew from initial observations of the site. Visual density is created by overgrown vegetation.

1.2

1.3

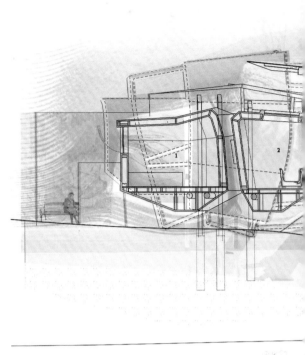

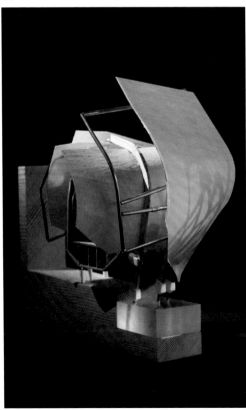

1.4

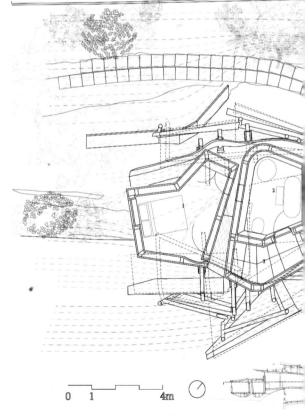

0   1   4m

1.5

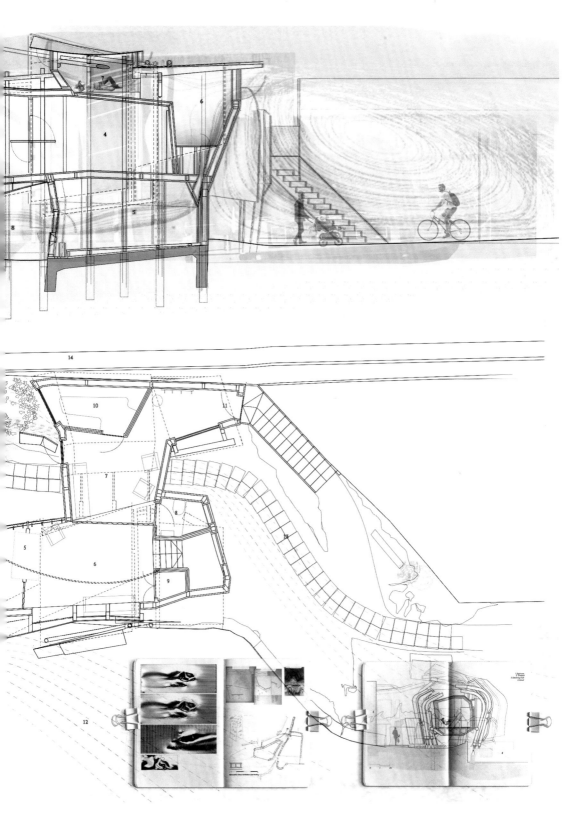

1.6

1.7

230

1.8

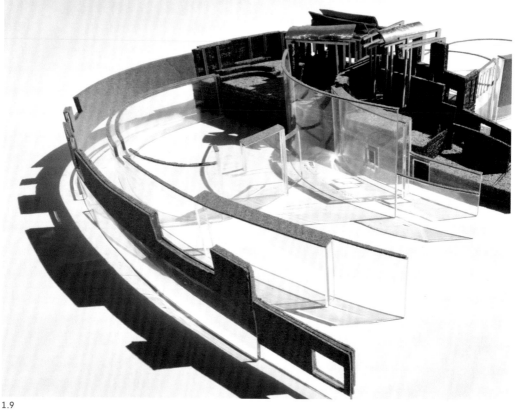

1.9

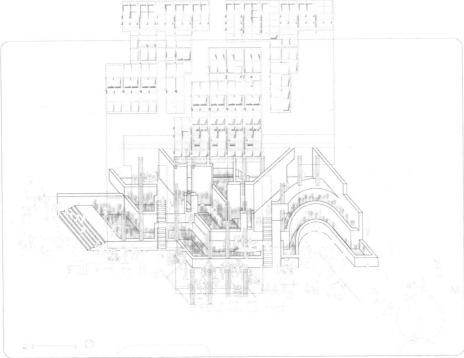

1.10

1.11

1.12

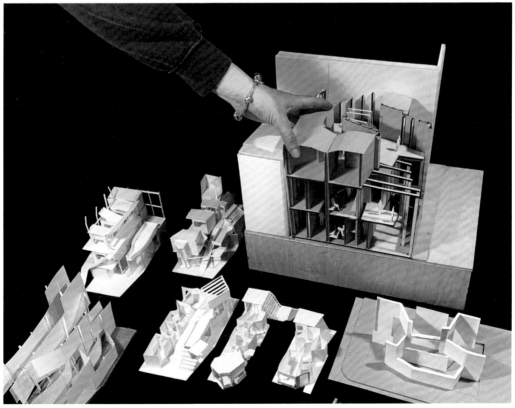

1.13

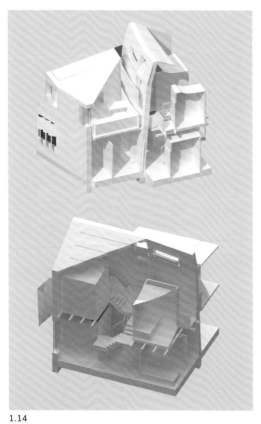

1.14

1.15

1.16

1.17

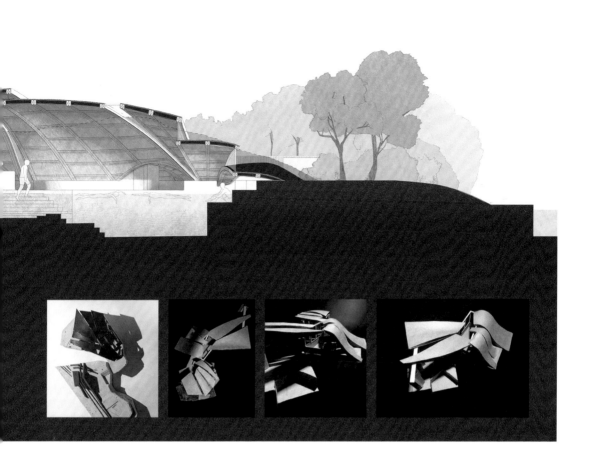

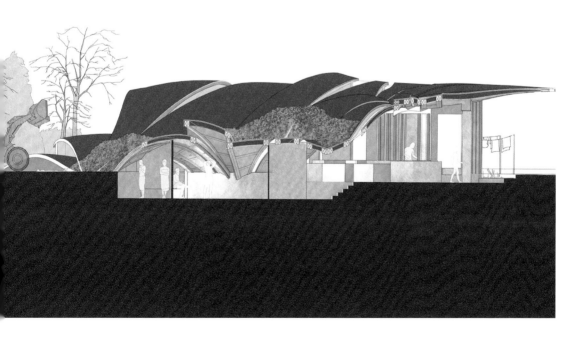

PG17 students assembling a collaborative model.
Photo by Thomas Parker.

Architecture MArch
(ARB/RIBA Part 2)

Architecture MArch (ARB/RIBA Part 2)

Programme Directors: Julia Backhaus, Marjan Colletti

'Keep Calm and Carry On' asserts the wartime slogan devised by the British government in 1939, now a popular meme. This message has, however, rarely been more relevant than in 2020–21. Steadily, decisively and resolutely we carried on from the moment Covid-19 disrupted our lives. Last year we were antagonised by the unexpected, sudden and catastrophic. This year our vibrant school community faced a plethora of challenging and unnerving questions: Would we find the spirit to start the academic year with optimism? Would we have the stamina to cope long-term with the physical and psychological strain? Would we possess the critical ability and resilience to remain positive, agile and proactive? Would the incoming Year 4 students, many of them new to The Bartlett School of Architecture and London, manage to find the necessary momentum to start a postgraduate course, with unknown peers and tutors, and focus their study on the development of a comprehensive building project? Would graduating Year 5 students return to university with the necessary motivation to positively develop their thesis, intellect and career, since our final year – understood as the school's pinnacle in research-based professional education – is driven by rigour, excellence and freedom?

There have been far too many individual and collective crises. Yet, in the midst of enduring constraints – navigating our learning and teaching into abstract space; continuously shifting and rethinking our practices, conventions and pedagogies; endlessly e-conferencing and confined to our homes, mourning the physical space and the tangible instruments so essential to our discipline – we did not give up on our new and profound sense of online community, empathy and generosity. On the contrary, while global mobility, tourism and travel decelerated to unimaginable levels, students propelled themselves from the cockpits of their home offices into a brighter, more equal and diverse future. Together with their tutors, students spelt out new architectural grammars, augmented physical realities with new technologies, provoked established dogmas, set new agendas and extended the realm of architecture way beyond the physical. The students' projects and essays provide indisputable evidence for their resilience as designers and architects.

The endless hours spent in front of the screen, sharing good and bad with local, yet distanced, friends and global audiences across time zones were not in vain. Never has a cohort embraced with more confidence, passion and conviction so many critical issues: old and new normalities, low-tech materials, hi-tech computational processes, affordable domesticity, adaptable building systems, resource efficiency, sustainable communities, environmental strategies, social inequalities, renewable energies, smart cities, cyclical ecologies, entrepreneurial practices, carbon footprints, building lifecycles, air pollution, soil contamination, fire safety and rising sea levels, amongst others. From behind our own walls, whole architectural universes were imagined and dreamt: nothing was too small to deserve our attention or too big to inhibit our design ambitions; no material was too simple to star in intelligent buildings or technology too complex to trigger our curiosity; and no subject matter was too intricate to be elaborated on in depth or hypothesis too ambitious to be rigorously and originally developed.

In the past century the use of the term 'resilience' exponentially increased in popularity and frequency, up 2,370% until 2019 according to Google Books Ngram Viewer; a statistic that will surely be dwarfed in 2021. Our own numbers certainly need to be counted, as they all stand for resilience: One Master's, two year groups, five modules, 14 units, 36 tutors and 229 students. Our infinite gratitude goes to all: Keep Calm and Carry On!

Acts of Kindness

Simon Dickens, CJ Lim

In the age of pandemic, protests and politics, we need to nurture kindness and compassion in the multi-engagements and practices of the built environment. Kindness is not a cure but it can be a tool to help prevent the negative impact of violence, fear and subsequent discriminatory behaviours. Without individual or collective acts of kindness, there is no hope for equity, democracy and diversity. This year PG10 asked, How might kindness from different perspectives – cultures and communities, economies and ecologies, politics and policy – promote social transformations of cities and buildings? How might networks of compassion and forgiveness build resilience and address the challenges posed by climate change?

Protecting our planet is an act of kindness. George Orwell, after witnessing the destruction of London's trees during the Blitz, wrote the essay *A Good Ward for the Vicar of Bray* suggesting that '... every time you commit an antisocial act, make a note of it in your diary, and then, at the appropriate season, push an acorn into the ground. And, if even one in 20 of them came to maturity, you might do quite a lot of harm in your lifetime, and still... end up as a public benefactor after all'.[1]

Patriotism is an act of kindness; contrary to popular perceptions of merely being ornamental melancholic buildings of no useful purpose, follies were mechanisms for maintaining national social good during times of unrest. The construction of Conolly's Folly (1740) in County Kildare, Ireland, was intended to provide employment for starving farmers stricken by successive cold and wet winters, without robbing them of their dignity by issuing unconditional handouts.

Improving quality of life is an act of kindness; by showing kindness towards others, we strengthen our sense of interconnectedness and the wellbeing of our communities. Maggie's centres – a network of drop-in centres across the UK and Hong Kong, which aim to help anyone affected by cancer – are not in any form a substitute for hospital treatment. The network of buildings offers informed advice, therapy and daily practical and emotional support, and are there to improve quality of life for patients and families.

The discourse on kindness started with three workshops on two-and-a-half dimension drawings, animations and speculative narratives. Each student posited a divergent status quo to establish an intellectual position and visionary ideas to address the world in crisis. Whether it is a national campaign, an informal community initiative or simply an individual act, the heart of this year's architecture narrative was where we discovered the true potential of our human condition.

Year 4
Luke Angers, Tu-Ann Dao, Shuwei Du, Leo François-Serafin, Tsun Lee, Thabiso Nyezi, Elliot Pick, Jignesh Pithadia, Shaunee Tan, Roman Tay, Rebeca Thomas, Alexander Venditti

Year 5
Billie Jordan, Hiu Chun Kam, Yongwoo Lee, Jiashi Yu

Technical tutors and consultants: Philip Guthrie, Jon Kaminsky, Christopher Matthews

Workshop consultants: Xiaoliang Deng, David Roberts, Edmund Tan Hong Xiang, Vilius Vizgaudis, Matthew Wells, Eric Wong

Critics: Peter Bishop, Andy Bow, Christine Hawley, Simon Herron, David Roberts

1. George Orwell (1946), 'A Good Ward for the Vicar of Bray', *Fifty Essays*, (Oxford City Press), pp398–401.

10.1 Luke Angers, Y4 'A Columbarium of Dark History'. In John Steinbeck's *Of Mice and Men* (1937), an act of kindness is also an act of grim sacrifice. Just as historical sacrifices of resources have transformed the built environment, so too can personal and symbolic sacrifices reshape our future responsibilities, with a little technological help. The project investigates the decline of oil-producing American states and proposes a specific intervention in the derelict town and oil field of Drumright, Oklahoma. Through a process of disassembly, the disused industrial 'accomplices' of airplanes and automobiles feed the construction of a mechanical landscape to reclaim the oil field. Disassembled materials are painted white using limestone pigment to reflect sunlight, creating a new micro-climate that attracts insects and flora. The operable fuselage roof structures act as large insect-capturing mechanisms that attempt to control rising populations of crop-eating locusts, while providing a sustainable protein source for the nearby population in Oklahoma City.

10.2 Shaunee Tan, Y4 'The Anatomy of Being Chinese'. Kindness is the navigation of love and lies in Lulu Wang's film *The Farewell* (2019), highlighting the differences between Western and Chinese family values, perceptions and prejudices. The Chinese Embassy in London aims to provide a counter-argument in response to the misconception of China, its community and the second generation Chinese-British immigrant. The spatial versatility of a traditional Chinese courtyard house is reimagined as the home of an ambassador, providing a full range of diplomatic and consular services. By rotating the courtyard outwards, the typically personal and vulnerable typology of a home is exposed to welcome all. It no longer faces heaven, but towards humanity. Concepts of care, navigation, transparency and progress are synthesised into an essay of porcelain blue, collectively representing the nation and what it means to be Chinese, by the Chinese, to the British public.

10.3 Rebeca Thomas, Y4 'The Silhouettes of Christmas'. The urban strategy supports the vulnerable, mediates unconscious bias and redefines the act of giving as an act of kindness itself. The inhabitable silhouettes of the first 11 days of Christmas are distributed along the River Thames – the lightweight constructs enable community involvement through donation of tinned food and allotments. Located next to the Houses of Parliament is the 12th day, featuring a piccalilli store with more allotments and a mushroom farm where food is cultivated all year round for the Christmas dinner. Critical thinking is further embedded through the architectural collage of the silhouette structures to form the seasonal building, a metaphoric spatial extension of the Common's Library. Since the UK Parliament is often referred to as the House of Commons, the spatial layout of the project reflects diverse architectural aspects of 'the people's palace'. The architecture of silhouettes is a socio-political commentary on the modern consumerist Christmas and responsibilities of Parliament.

10.4–10.7 Yongwoo Lee, Y5 'Dear My Beloved Mircioiu'. Kindness is patience and with true love, memory and hope we can erase divisions and borders. Inspired by a true story in which North Korean orphans were sent to Eastern Europe in the 1950s as a result of the Korean War, the project explores how kindness and emotions are resources for the built environment. Narrated through the imagined diary of Cho in North Korea and the fragmented information from his wife Mircioiu in Romania, the principle design strategy is to apply the atrocities of the war as a landscape of memory and patience to restore hope, love and humanity. Against the inevitability of time, architecture is regarded as a continuous process, existing through diverse interpretations, incorporating timescales of transformation. The constructed metaphor takes the form of social architecture with communal benefits supported by the authoritarian regime. Cho exploits the constructed reality to make his personal idealism tangible and real. Taking on the idiom 'hidden in plain sight', each tectonic has a dual function and meaning: social benefit and Cho's hope, memory and love for his wife.

10.8–10.9 Jiashi Yu, Y5 'Kindness Is Farewell?'. The accelerating divorce rate in China has become a destabilising force. Can the Great Wall, which once served as a powerful national defence infrastructure, protect familial and social stability? Taking inspiration from Marina Abramović and Ulay's performance *The Lovers* (1988) – over 90 days, the then-lovers walked from opposite sides of the Great Wall and met in the middle to break-up – couples contemplating divorce embark on a journey along the wall to reflect and possibly reconcile their differences. The reimagining of the Great Wall is an homage to Chinese family values, but also a criticism of the wall's history and the feudalistic mindset it represents. The conceptual lines and materiality of the new architecture captures the fragility of marriage and the maintenance required for an enduring one. While a single line might be easily broken, weaving them together creates resilience and strength. This bitter-sweet architectural story of kindness can impact China's future built environment and offers an alternative analysis and appreciation of historical monuments.

10.10–10.13 Hiu Chun Kam, Y5 'A Love Letter to My Childhood Hero'. In Harper Lee's *To Kill a Mockingbird* (1960), an act of kindness is not presented under the scrutiny of light but in its purest form, hidden within the intangible realm of shadows. The project is a love letter to a domestic helper called Sonia, whose day of rest on Sunday may seem mundane but, through the imagination of a child, is a fantastical journey of self-empowerment using shadows. Statue Square in Hong Kong is transformed into an ephemeral garden harvesting shadows for the earthly foolishness of consumerism, which has cultivated an obsession with fair skin in China. In an ironic twist of fate, domestic helpers are the guardians of that sought-after resource. The imaginative retelling of Sunday gatherings is a whimsical and satirical socio-political story of shadow that reaffirms the 'mockingbird' values of care, empathy and kindness.

10.14–10.15 Billie Jordan, Y5 'The Perfect Storm'. Within the magic of literature, kindness is repentance, reconciliation and recuperation: Prospero repents in the last act of Shakespeare's *The Tempest* (1611), just as Britain repents for its past ecological destruction by allowing for the coastline to be given back to the sea; the retreat of the British coastline provides a new zone of international sovereignty that welcomes climate refugees of all nationalities, reconciling a post-Brexit Britain with the international community; the protagonists of the floating city are appointed as environmental warriors to pioneer new sustainable utopian communities, recuperating the damaged British coast. The new community embraces Ariel, the representative of rising sea levels, climate change and the wild spirit of ecology. The two faces of humanity are both practical and romantic, logical yet ideal – Prospero's idealism allows us to venture into the unknown, embracing the fluctuation of ecology and the emancipatory power of Ariel's storm. The poetic and magical tempest in Prospero's books empowers and redeems the citizens. Can the naive fantasies of Prospero recuperate the societies and ecologies which were once destroyed?

10.2

10.3

10.4

10.5

10.6

10.7

10.8

10.9

247

10.10

10.11

10.12

10.13

10.14

10.15

250

11.1

Uncommon Ground

Laura Allen, Mark Smout

This year's brief challenged students to rethink the edges and intersections between landscape and the urban realm, hand-in-hand with those between public and private space. These relationships are fluid, volatile, contested and reciprocal, and challenge the polarised notions that the unit continues to revisit: preservation versus progress and wilderness versus culture.

Situation Abnormal

Our rural environment is substantially cultured as 'wilderness kept in check' or for the production of vast quantities of food – 70% of the UK's land is agricultural.[1] Environmental technologies and nature have become inextricably linked; cutting-edge technologies are increasingly deployed that engineer nature from the micro scale of genetically modified crops to the global scale of GPS agricultural automation. Furthermore, the landscape is crisscrossed with infrastructural networks, inter-urban links of road and rail that also connect cities with their surrounding rural areas and the regions of supply with the centres of demand. We asked, What are the radical outcomes of the synthesis of urban and rural spaces?

A further blurring of the distinction between rural and urban, and private and public is the privatisation of nature. Natural capital – stocks of natural assets, access to and control of material resources, even forests and fields, soil, geology, water, air and all living things – are controlled by property rights where commercial agendas can overturn seemingly common sense. In our cities too, public spaces are being transferred to private ownership – Privately Owned Public Space (POPS) – with byelaws, urban design, surveillance and policing to control perceived misuse. We asked, How can architectural and technical innovations alleviate the pressure of private encroachment on public environments?

Re-Commoning

We can see that the future of the city is inextricably linked to that of the rural. Controversially, some advocate for re-commoning – the application of a 'sharing economy' to urban space, borrowed from archaic rural environments that persist today. Contemporary commons are not only a material resource; they are also a form of social organisation that could be revisited in our urban environment. During lockdown, the use of urban parks soared where commoning laws – the rights of certain individuals to enjoy the property of others – were exploited. The Victorian parkland concept of 'rational recreation' – the ordered and orderly use of landscape – was stretched to breaking point. We asked, How can principles of commoning be applied to urban space?

Year 4
Theo Clarke, Michael Holland, Justin Lau, Kit Lee-Smith, Rory Martin, Iga Świercz, Yun Tam, Annabelle Tan, Zifeng Ye

Year 5
James Cook, Peter Davies, Meiying Hong, Thomas Leggatt, Liam Merrigan, Jack Spence, Sarmad Suhail, Ryan Walsh, Yitao Zhu

Thank you to Rhys Cannon for his invaluable Design Realisation teaching, structural consultant Stephen Foster and environmental consultant Ionnis Rizoz

Thesis supervisors:
Matthew Barnett Howland, Mollie Claypool, Edward Denison, Daisy Froud, Polly Gould, Gary Grant, Jan Kattein, Oliver Wilton

1. Department for Environment, Food & Rural Affairs (2015), *Agriculture in the United Kingdom 2014* (accessed 22 June 2021), gov.uk/government/ statistics/agriculture-in- the-united-kingdom-2014

11.1 Peter Davies, Y5 'The Stone Language Centre'. Sited in the dormant Welsh granite quarries of Nant Gwrtheyrn, the project advocates a revival for low-carbon structural stone construction and demonstrates the whole-life benefits of stone, from extraction to material reuse. Monolithic stone buildings form The Stone Language Centre, creating a space for learning and discovery within the rich Welsh landscape.

11.2 Thomas Leggatt, Y5 'A Corn(ish) Community'. The Cornish coastline is being increasingly appropriated by outsiders, for outsiders, specifically second-home owners. Using a pub(lic) model, a dialogue is established between the architect and community in the design of a new village for second homeowners and local residents. The model encourages collaborative design and an immersive understanding of the project as a whole.

11.3 Annabelle Tan, Y4 'The River, Restoration and its Rituals'. Sited along the River Wensum in Norfolk, the building is a roving restoration scheme that visits rural villages to restore the vulnerable chalk river while engaging and empowering the local community to sustain an intimate relationship with the environment through rituals and beliefs. The building is simultaneously a restorative and ritual machine, marrying ecological values with the process of restoration.

11.4 Kit Lee-Smith, Y4 'Orkney's Udal Energy'. Orkney's foreshore and landscape boundaries, eroded by anthropologically driven climate change, are explored via an infrastructural design for the archipelago's preservation. The design uses archaeological language and materiality alongside stone machining techniques to expose the relationship between the building foreshore and community-centric architecture.

11.5 Rory Martin, Y4 'The Hiker's Retreat'. Situated in the intertidal mudflats off Osea Island in the Blackwater Estuary, the project creates a 'hearth' – a lost historical focal point in the home and a place for people to reconnect and share stories and experiences. The project works in harmony with the surrounding historical vernacular of the Essex coastline by referencing traditional building. The central *kachelöfen* (stove) stands as a beacon of sustainability and efficiency.

11.6 Theo Clarke, Y4 'Floreat Blaenau'. The town of Blaenau Ffestiniog, strewn with glaciers of cascading waste material, is one of seven identified sites to be included within a new UNESCO World Heritage bid. The project challenges the vision of UNESCO by highlighting Wales' historical relationship with Patagonia, resulting in the formation of a Patagonian enclave. Analytical, physical and digital experimentation reveal elemental and man-made forces, exposing the visitor to the uncanny implementation of mechanical installations.

11.7 Zifeng Ye, Y4 'Inhabiting Common's Nature'. The project seeks to establish a woodland common inside an old gravel quarry by the East Tilbury coast in Essex. Facilities allow access to the site and initiate a century-long programme of reforestation. The design aestheticises 'waste' land and materials, in order to rekindle a common interest in living with unappreciated landscapes.

11.8 Yun Tam, Y4 'Percolate Agri(Park)'. Merging agriculture, water and park in a symbiotic relationship, the project brings food currency to the citizens of Hong Kong by bridging the gap between the sensory connection of the public to the origins of food and the enjoyment of the recreational parkscape.

11.9 Iga Świercz, Y4 'Dressing the Scottish Landscape'. The ministry, located in the Cairngorms, has a profound understanding of the Scottish ancestral textile industry by creating soft architecture that also promotes a tourism strategy for the Highlands. The clothed interiors recall domestic rituals, the art of weaving, seasonality and the colours and textures of the Scottish tradition.

11.10 Justin Lau, Y4 'Leigh Frontier'. Extreme changes to global climates are expected to breach over 1,000 historic landfill sites on the British coast, through erosion. The increasing risk poses serious pollution damage to the estuarine landscape and beyond. 'Leigh Frontier' proposes a chained fortification embedded along the eroding edge of Leigh Marshes, allowing time to remediate one of the most toxic old landfill sites in the UK.

11.11 Michael Holland, Y4 'The Commons Community Centre'. The project raises awareness of the growing rate of food poverty throughout the borough of Hackney. It tackles the often negative associations of food banks, through the integration of commoning principles that inspire a sense of 'togetherness' and community expression, celebrating the sharing of culture, food, resources and knowledge.

11.12 Sarmad Suhail, Y5 'Power Palace Park'. The idiosyncratic Crystal Palace is reimagined as the showcase for the 'Green Industrial Revolution', providing a model for parks to become energy generating and carbon-capture resources. Ersatz materials and visual trickeries blur the line between what is 'park' and 'building', to provide a locally sourced, national-facing infrastructure.

11.13 Ryan Walsh, Y5 'Digital Archaic Commons'. How do we build a future where personal digital fabrication is utilised towards the common good? This project explores how users of commons, such as FABLAB, apply sophisticated digital manufacturing and scanning tools to produce decentralised architecture.

11.14 Yitao Zhu, Y5 'Parking Rectory Farm'. Rectory Farm is a derelict site near Heathrow, where a new public park is to be built on top of an underground logistics facility. The project challenges the park typology and envisages an alternative landscape for the site, which addresses potential financial crises. A mixture of housing, industry, infrastructure and landscape encourages richer interactions between domestic and park activities.

11.15–11.16 James Cook, Y5 'Inhabitable Billboard Vernaculars: Brush Park Agrihood'. Set in Detroit, 'Brush Park Agrihood' reimagines the potential for hoardings and billboards. Drawing inspiration from Denise Scott Brown, Robert Venturi and Steven Izenour's book *Learning from Las Vegas* (1972), the hoardings stage moments in the storyline of construction and provide a framework for inhabitable spaces, which inevitably spill out into the backlands of the site. The agrihood's infographics and community messages, embedded within the framework of the building, inform people about Detroit's environmental crises.

11.17 Meiying Hong, Y5 'Productive Landscapes: Food community in Regent's Park'. To counteract food poverty and waste post-pandemic, this project replans a section of Regent's Park as an experimental food community, integrating housing with food production, collection, distribution and disposal. The terraced gardens, roof orchards and growing lands form a productive landscape in an overlooked section of the park.

11.18 Jack Spence, Y5 'The 4th Epoch: Reinhabiting desolate landscapes'. Highlighting the significant climate threat facing the UK's coastline, this proposal looks to reinvigorate Hurst Castle in Hampshire through the siting of a research outpost. Digital inhabitation of the surrounding gamified landscape also enables the immersive engagement of 'virtual researchers' from around the world with the vulnerable coastline.

11.3

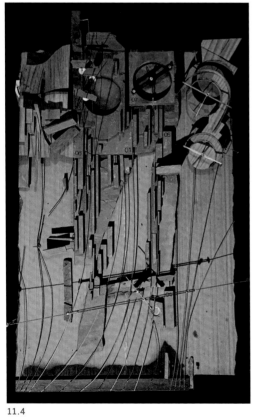

11.4

11.5

11.6

11.7

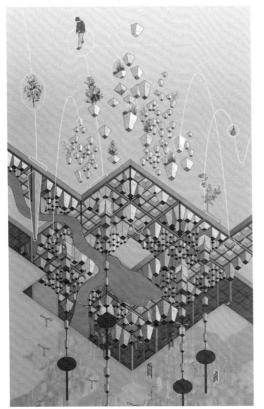

11.8

11.9

11.10

11.11

11.12

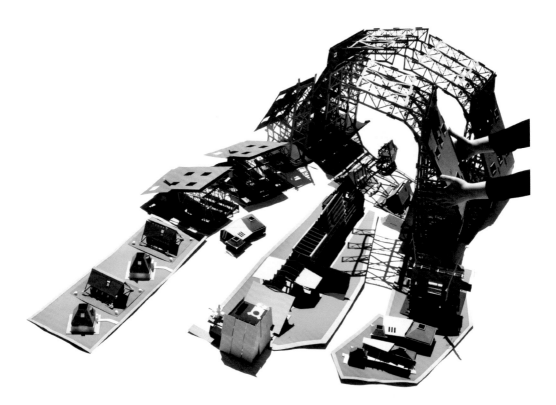

11.13

11.14

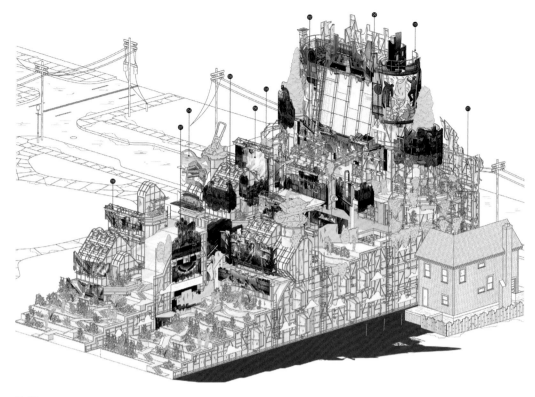

11.15

11.16

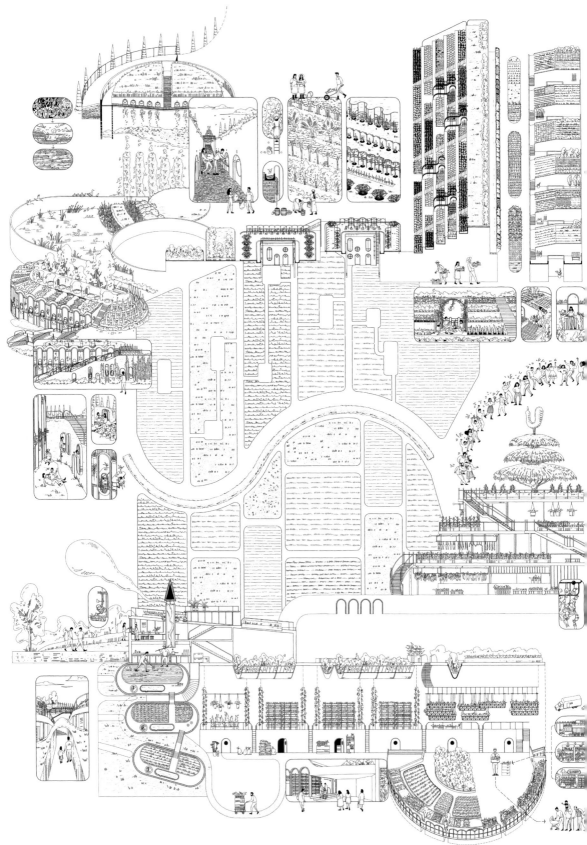

11.17

11.18

12.1

Rewilding London

Elizabeth Dow, Jonathan Hill

Exceptional architects are exceptional storytellers. Such tales have special significance when they resonate back-and-forth between private inspiration and public narrative. When everybody else is looking at one time and place, it is always good to look elsewhere as a discovery may be yours alone, and thus more surprising.

In PG12, we learn from the past and stimulate radical solutions for the future. Our project this year was 'Rewilding London', from which new architectures, landscapes, ways of living and cities emerged. The source of inspiration might be a person, place or event. Equally, it could be a construction technique or material language. The inevitability of change – whether of climate, ethics or architecture – requires us to utilise it, notably as a design may take years to complete. Conceiving design, construction, maintenance and ruination as simultaneous ongoing processes that occur while a building is occupied, we encourage designs that are drawn in multiple times and states. Assembled from materials of diverse ages, from the newly formed to centuries or millennia old, and incorporating varied rates of transformation and decay, a building is a time machine that curates the past and imagines the future.

The last ten years have witnessed significant changes that will influence our education, jobs and national identities: the 2008 worldwide financial crash, 2016 Brexit vote and the target for net-zero carbon emissions by 2050. Furthermore, 2020 and 2021 were momentous years as a result of the Covid-19 pandemic.

Ideas about climate change express wider societal values, including attitudes to nature, governance and design. The dangers of global warming are real and need to be addressed when and where possible, notably because their effects are unequal, often causing greater harm to disadvantaged communities. Awareness of climate change may also encourage cultural, social and environmental innovations and benefits, whether at a local, regional or global scale, stimulating more thoughtful and exciting designs. Architects must have the courage to ask awkward questions. We need to look deeper into the past and further into the future.

Rewilding usually entails transforming land into a self-conserving system with minimal human intervention, but the term has greater relevance when it is applied to the urban as well as the rural. It is understood as a means to acknowledge the interdependent co-production of the human and non-human in all aspects of a shared Earth.

Caitlin Davies, Lola Haines, Theodore Lawless Jones, Jaqlin Lyon, James Robinson, Felix Sagar, Gabrielle Wellon, Tianzhou Yang

Year 5
Sabina Blasiotti, James Bradford, Jean-Baptiste Gilles, Elliot Nash, Callum Rae, Arinjoy Sen, Benjamin Sykes-Thompson, Chuxiao Wang, Yunshu (Chloe) Ye

Technical tutors and consultants: James Hampton, James Nevin

Thesis supervisors: Alesandro Ayuso, Edward Denison, Murray Fraser, Daisy Froud, Stelios Giamarelos, Elise Hunchuck, Zoe Laughlin, Tania Sengupta, Iulia Statica

Critics: Kirsty Badenoch, Carolyn Butterworth, Blanche Cameron, Barbara-Ann Campbell-Lange, Adrian Hawker, Jan Kattein, Toni Kauppila, Constance Lau, Igor Marjanovic, Jason O'Shaughnessy, Franco Pisani, David Shanks, Tim Waterman, Alex Zambelli, Fiona Zisch

12.1 **Callum Rae, Y5** 'The Olive Morris Institute for Drawing, Building and Squatting'. The project provides an alternate proposal for the site formerly occupied by Olive Morris House: the Lambeth Council housing office in Brixton and named after the housing activist Olive Morris. The proposal is a new educational institution that teaches hand-drawing and construction skills as constituent parts of an architectural education that combine in the embodied act of squatting.

12.2–12.4 **Arinjoy Sen, Y5** 'Rituals of Resistance: Narratives of critical inhabitation'. The project addresses the contested inhabitation of fragile ecosystems in the Sundarbans, situated in the borderlands of Bangladesh and India. It proposes a self-sustained productive settlement that fosters a construction of spatial identity, while elevating the significance of indigenous land stewardship. Additionally, the settlement seeks to increase the ritual narrative practices of marginalised and hybridised identities, as a means to resist erasure, through the apparatus of a travelling theatre.

12.5 **Jean-Baptiste Gilles, Y5** 'The Bricks, the Stucco and the Air'. Before we can propose a less-damaging way of living in which isolation of the building is reduced, air must be considered as an architectural material. The project is a series of bedrooms for guests of the Royal Institution. An architecture is created that can be appreciated through the bricks, stucco and the air.

12.6–12.8 **Chuxiao Wang, Y5** 'Lost in London'. The project is an enigmatic book describing the lives of monsters in London. The monsters struggle to adapt to city life and carry out their purpose of freeing the ravens in the Tower of London. By telling their stories and experiences, the book explores a non-anthropocentric city life involving history, mythology, legend and literature, interweaving the real with the unreal and history with the future.

12.9 **Jaqlin Lyon, Y4** 'The Embassy for Dirty Things, Messy Ideas & Unfinished Endeavours'. Dirt denotes difference; using its power to disrupt, the project proposes a reconfiguration of cultural attitudes, bureaucratic order and objective values. Exploring the transgressive potential of programmatic hybrids and formal paradoxes to overcome binaries within social, cultural and political operations, the Embassy combines a laundromat, debate chamber and printing press in London's bureaucratic district. This creates space for public exchange in the margins of hegemonic structures.

12.10 **Felix Sagar, Y4** 'The Aldgate Chalkland School of Special Scientific Interest'. The proposal explores wilding the un-wild city child using chalk as a 'bonding material'. By using atmospheric phenomena, human and non-human occupants establish new urban dialogues. The project explores how an existing building and curriculum might be altered to support a wild and non-didactic learning model. Inspired by biological mutualism, the method links the process of play to biological and geological cycles that create new learning landscapes.

12.11 **Lola Haines, Y4** 'A Theatre for 'Lesser' Creatures'. The theatre addresses urban society's disconnect with nature. Learning from and giving agency to the environment creates a dialogue of exchange with humans. The theatre's function is linked to natural and seasonal events, like insect migration and behaviour, to stimulate greater change across the city. As insects disperse pollen, a wandering theatre festival seeds the ground for future growth.

12.12–12.14 **Sabina Blasiotti, Y5** 'The Village Inside the Nuclear Power Plant'. The design narrates the future of a decommissioned nuclear power plant and the surrounding village Mihama in Japan. The narrative generates and is generated by an interminable dialogue between nuclear forms and heritage, recycled nuclear waste and traditional customs in the coastal town. This dialectic is further reflected in the construction of a Shinto sanctuary, integrating ceremonial and commercial activities such as fishing, rice farming and sake brewing.

12.15 **Benjamin Sykes-Thompson, Y5** 'Barking Sands & Borough Bells: The London sound authority'. The project is informed by Japanese sound culture that does not resonate with architectural acoustics and reintroduces the overlapping aural communities that once made up London's population. Architecturally, spaces mimic the aural spaces of old Whitehall – areas of rumour, declamation and democratic 'transparency' – while also exploring the phantom sounds that exist between ourselves and the perceived built environment.

12.16–12.17 **Theodore Lawless Jones, Y4** 'The New HM Liberty of the Clink'. A contrived shimmering neon microclimate, where darkness reveals lost rhythms in sedentary human existences, stimulates behaviour to rewild London. Condemned prisoners, guilty of environmental wrongdoing by the Court of the Clink, lead a primitive existence in their communal and autonomous garden complex. The objectives are personal desistance, the empowerment of synanthropic birds within their delicate urban-ecosystem and the consequent realisation of mutual fulfilment and natural affinity.

12.18 **James Robinson, Y4** 'Martian Miners of Portland'. Having settled on Mars for the past 30 years, the first Martian miners have come back to Earth. Residing on the Isle of Portland, Dorset, within the Coombefield Quarry, the practice of a New Stone Age is formed. Fabricated from the history of Portland and future Martian regolith mines, the Portland-Martian vernacular is created.

12.19 **Tianzhou Yang, Y4** 'Ode to Life: A natural process'. This project is designed for gradual and pain-soothing organic burials where both fallen leaves and deceased human bodies integrate with nature to nurture new life. Fallen leaves are collected and memorialised through the construction and reconstruction of the cemetery. Human bodies are composted to further contribute to the prosperity of plants, accentuating that life is not linear but circular.

12.20 **Caitlin Davies, Y4** 'The Worshipful Company of Dismantlers'. The 111th guild within the City of London promotes the reuse of the city's architecture through the act of dismantling and remantling. The new guild reflects the role the built environment plays within the environmental crisis and how we might change the practices and reasons for building as we do.

12.21 **Gabrielle Wellon, Y4** 'News from Nowhere'. Rendering the fantastical commons-based world of cooperation, sketched out by William Morris in his utopian novel *News from Nowhere, or, an Epoch of Rest* (1890), the project proposes a community in Gospel Oak, London, that is self-governed, managed and developed by the residents. Morris' conceptualisation still retains the potential to stimulate a democratic dialogue between work, art, nature and society.

12.22 **Elliot Nash, Y5** 'Forgetting Whitehall; Casting Blackhall'. The project proposes a building that subverts methods of physical and non-physical preservation, to fold time through Whitehall in pursuit of a kind of rewilded London. It moves through themes of redaction and transience, and the idea of the counter monument to arrive at an architecture that challenges contemporary thought and practice around conservation.

12.2

12.3

12.4

12.6

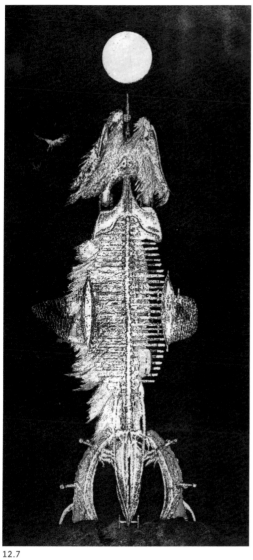

12.7

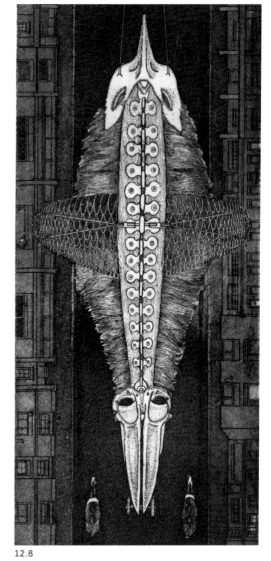

12.8

12.9

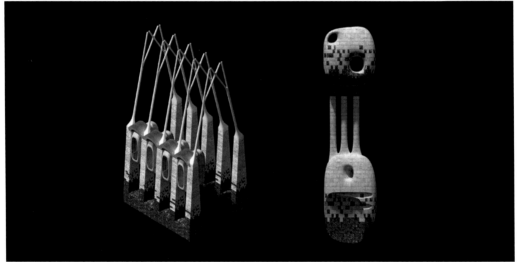

12.10

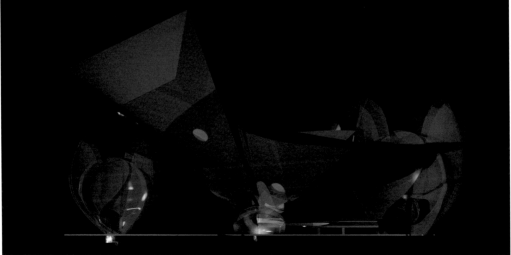

12.11

12.12

12.13

12.14

12.16

12.17

12.18

12.19

12.20

12.21

13.1

The Living Laboratory: Being radical

Sabine Storp, Patrick Weber

The most powerful architectures have been created out of crises, rebellions or clear breaks with the past. In times of great uncertainty radical ideas emerge – a pattern seen throughout architectural history.

The last year has challenged our students and staff. The Covid-19 pandemic is not an isolated event; it sits connected to other crises – most of them manmade and many existential threats to mankind. What is needed is a shift in how we operate and a reconsideration of the basic principles of how we live and treat each other and our planet; it is down to us to be radical.

This year PG13 – the Bartlett Living Laboratory – has been continuing to explore how we live and inhabit our spaces and cities. Our students have been empowering communities and inventing new typologies of living through their work.

The Bata – a Czech footwear manufacturer – company town in East Tilbury, Essex, was our focus site. Our Year 4 students envisaged new radical concepts for how this site could be unlocked and how the vulnerable landscape in the Thames Estuary provided potential rather than risk.

Our Year 5 students developed their own agenda, continuing with the themes of the unit but responding with a range of architectures in a personal way. Projects included an augmented town hall in Somers Town, London; a new aquatic way of living for Hong Kong, guided by the lunar calendar; an architecture fabricated out of universal elements that revives the village of Silver End in Essex; a new vernacular architecture on the Baltic coast of Lithuania that responds to local myths about forests; and a seedbank embedded in a glacier on the Nordic island of Svalbard that pushes the boundaries of architecture into the realm of fragile melting speculation.

Over the last two years we have been participating in a collaborative workshop with students and teachers from Hanyang University, South Korea. Both universities have been radical in questioning the concept of 'refuge', exploring ideas of a resilient city fighting urgent urban issues, climate change and migration. The work of our students will be presented at the Seoul Biennale 2021.

Year 4
Nikhil Isaac Cherian, Agata Malinowska, Jolanta Piotrowska, Muyun Qiu, Callum Richardson, Thomas Smith, Chloe Woodhead

Year 5
Jonas Andresen, Dovile Ciapaite, Luke Draper, Victor Leung, Marjut Lisco, Jarron Tham

Thank you to our technical tutors and consultants: Toby Ronalds and Nick Wood

Thank you to our critics: Rita Adamo, David Bickle, Marc Brossa, Carlos Jiménez Cenamor, Paul Galindo, Alice Hardy, Ophélie Herranz, So Young Kim, Alicia Lazzaroni, Maxwell Mutanda, Inigo Minns, Robert Newcombe, Caspar Rodgers, Marianne Sætre, Antje Steinmuller, Serhan Ahmet Tekbas, Jonas Žukauskas

Partners: Samson Adjei, Tom Budd, Naomi De Barr, Jarrell Goh, Gintare Kapociute, So Young Kim, Emily Priest, Adrian Siu, Yip Siu

13.1 Luke Draper, Y5 'The New Rural: A guide to realising Arcadia'. Radical change is needed to evolve the way in which we inhabit our natural world. 'The New Rural' is a manifesto, guide and proposition for the necessary realisation of Arcadia in Britain. The culmination of 'The New Rural' has been an effort to 'undesign' Essex by providing a guide to a settlement typology that questions the existing separation of dwelling and nature.

13.2 Marjut Lisco, Y5 'Collegio Reborn'. The project looks at a new way of using collectives of materials that, through up-cycling systems, can mirror the interaction of different ethnicities living together in the former ruin site of the Collegio Tommaseo in Brindisi, Italy. The project investigates the new role of the architect as mediator, through three phases: 'Collection', 'Interpretation' and 'Participation'. The city of Brindisi becomes the new European Bauhaus capital, as its scheme best represents the key points of the movement.

13.3 Callum Richardson, Y4 'Emergent Heartland'. A self-build masterplan to facilitate bottom-up, self-directed urbanism. Each building is made from a kit-of-parts constructed in a central workshop and communal space. Over time each cluster grows and adapts to the needs of its inhabitants. Modification, addition and eventual disassembly are central to the approach. The masterplan is a framework to allow the residents maximum flexibility in designing spaces for their own needs and to learn new skills in the process.

13.4 Dovile Ciapaite, Y5 'Crafting a Lithuanian Forest'. Carefully crafted building details highlight industrial forestry practices in the Lithuanian territory of Curonian Spit. The project introduces hand-carved structures that enable people to experience the forest and remind us of our caring responsibilities: to maintain, restore and sustain. Storytelling becomes a form of sharing this craft-based knowledge through intergenerational interactions that create a future for an old growth forest.

13.5 Chloe Woodhead, Y4 'DO (NOT) ERASE: A radical recording and register of intangible heritage'. The project redefines the traditional model of a museum for heritage, which is not physical but intangible. Methods of preserving the intangible involve erosion and mark-making via community interaction with material architecture, specifically chalk – a local building material. Through erosion over time, spaces of rest and pause are revealed that encourage the community to converse and interact and, in doing so, social heritage is recorded and preserved.

13.6 Jolanta Piotrowska, Y4 'Making Bata'. A project based in East Tilbury, Essex, that gives the community the power to create their own future through decision-making for the town. It focusses on providing people with the tools and skills needed to self-build and govern the new community facilities: a ceramics workshop, a wood workshop and a community space. The project explores how governmental streams of funding can focus the build on up-skilling and learning.

13.7 Muyun Qiu, Y4 'Yong'an Fang 2.0'. The project rejects Tabula Rasa planning and proposes an economically viable and socially sustainable alternative to the renewal of Shanghai's *lilong* neighbourhoods, where domestic lives are highly socialised and exteriorised. By moving the residents into a superstructure designed to recreate the same social experience as the original *lilong* complex, and freeing up the existing buildings for commercial development, this proposal preserves the social network, lifestyle and collective memories of these communities and allows for land to adapt to changing market dynamics.

13.8 Nikhil Isaac Cherian, Y4 'Nine Meals from Anarchy'. This project redefines the public house as a community infrastructure. Taking cues from the masonry stove and the centrality of the chimney, the scheme examines the hearth as a potential space for cohesive social praxis. The chimney was explored as both a structural and social component within the scheme.

13.9 Agata Malinowska, Y4 'Stacey's KITSCHen & The Grand BATA Hostel'. The project researches alternative methods of living and building construction. It investigates how emphasising the absurdity and questioning the everyday can evolve into playfulness. The project is inspired by Wes Anderson's film *The Grand Budapest Hotel* (2014). It takes the form of an unconventional megastructure, where the residents benefit from a new approach of bringing back community spaces and helping young homeless adults seek a better future.

13.10 Thomas Smith, Y4 'Bata's Wild Regeneration'. The project questions our contract with nature, within the context of our relationship with the once natural landscape of East Tilbury, Essex. Through the industrialisation of the past 200 years, we have severed our connection with nature, ignored its cyclical processes and, as an act of self-sabotage, abused the environments that benefit our health and wellbeing most. To reverse this damage, we must recognise the rights of nature, adhering to principles of permaculture to change the way we live, design and build.

13.11 Jonas Andresen, Y5 'Embassy of No-land'. Exploring the notion of time and transition, this project speculates an alternative future for the Svalbard Global Seed Vault in Norway. Through six narratives from different scales and perspectives, the project speculates how a stronger symbiosis with the natural environment can be created. It creates an infrastructure built on natural transitions and an architecture that grows and erodes with seasonal and social changes.

13.12–13.13 Victor Leung, Y5 'Isle of Lunar-Sea'. Amidst proposals for construction of a 1,700 ha artificial island within Hong Kong's archipelago, 'Isle of Lunar-Sea' proposes an alternative floating city, establishing connections with the marine surroundings and offering safety to its boat people. The lunisolar calendar, tidal change and maritime geography form the basis of a model masterplan and its comprising modules, which ever-change to suit both seasonal and future climates.

13.14 Jarron Tham, Y5 'Virtually_Public'. The project speculates a public realm with a virtual townhall for the future expiration of Story Garden's tenure. Although the garden physically appears as a public retreat, it is transformed through an augmented reality to become a townhall, taking an integrated form of two parts where one reality suggests the existence of the other. It speculates on how the civic, social and virtual constructs of future 'publicness' alter the nature of who we are, how we interact in public space and how we gather local information and meanings of civic symbolism.

13.2

13.3

13.4

13.5

13.6

13.7

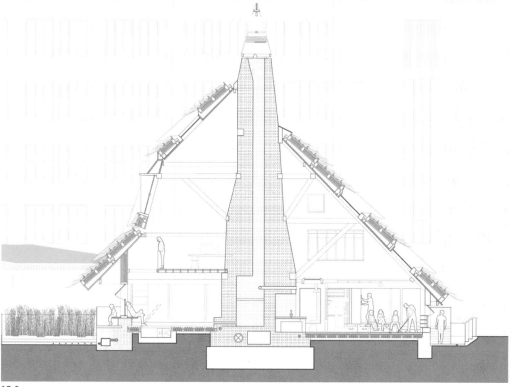

13.8

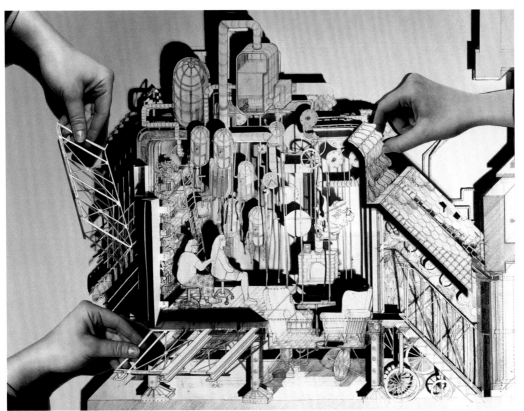

13.9

13.10

13.11

13.12

13.13

13.14

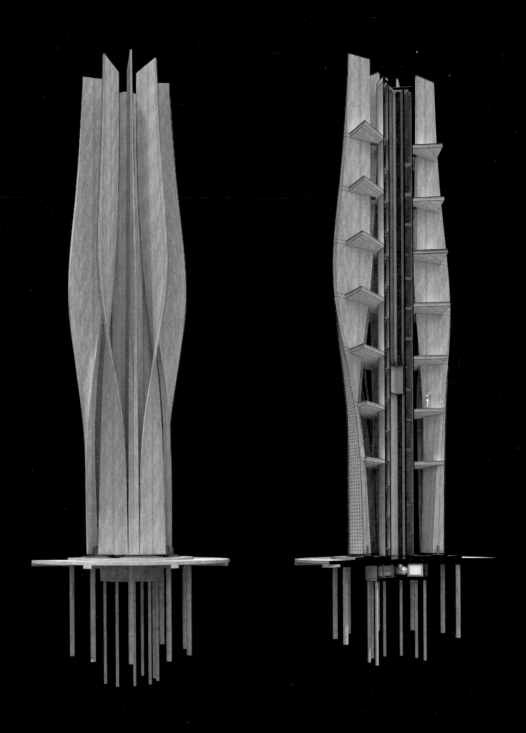

14.1

Inner Form

Jakub Klaska, Dirk Krolikowski

PG14 is a test bed for architectural exploration and innovation. Our students examine the role of the architect in an environment of continuous change. As a unit, we are in search of new leveraging technologies, workflows and modes of production seen in disciplines outside our own. We test ideas systematically by means of digital and physical drawings, models and prototypes. Our work evolves around technological speculation and design research, generating momentum through astute synthesis. Our propositions are ultimately made through the design of buildings and the in-depth consideration of structural formation and tectonic constituents. This, coupled with a strong research ethos, generates new, unprecedented, viable and spectacular proposals.

At the centre of this year's academic exploration was Buckminster Fuller's 'comprehensive designer': a master-builder who follows Renaissance principles and a holistic approach. Like Fuller, PG14 students are opportunists in search of new ideas and architectural synthesis. They explored the concept of 'inner form', referring to the underlying and invisible but existing logic of formalisation, which is only accessible to those who understand the whole system, its constituents and the relationships between.

This year's projects explored the places where culture and technology interrelate to generate constructional systems. Societal, technological, cultural, economic and political developments propelled our investigations and enabled us to project near-future scenarios, for which we designed comprehensive visions. Our methodology employed both bottom-up and top-down strategies in order to build sophisticated architectural systems. Pivotal to this process was practical experimentation and intense exploration using both digital and physical models to assess system performance and application in architectural space.

Year 4
Teodor Andonov, Vegard Elseth, Holly Hearne, Ryan Moss, Benjamin Norris, Alasdair Sheldon, Svenja Siever, Chenru Sung

Year 5
Daniel Boran, Austen Goodman, Ivan Hewitt, Andre Hoelzle de Moraes, Nnenna Itanyi, Connor James, Jack Lettice

Technical tutors and consultants: Damian Eley, Charles Harris, Martin Gsandtner

Thesis supervisors: Andrew Barnett, Carolina Batram, Tania Sengupta, Michael Stacey, Oliver Wilton

Critics: Andrew Abdulezer, Vishu Booshan, Florian Gauss, Thorsten Helbig, Manuel Jiménez Garcia, DaeWha Kang, Xavier de Kastelier, Saman Saffarian, Patrik Schumacher, Charles Walker, Dan Wright

14.1, 14.3 Austen Goodman, Y5 'St'á7mes Microhub'. The project focusses on the performative properties of structurally folded cross-laminated timber for the use of column-free assemblies. It considers the current state of the engineered timber industry and speculates on what future build-ups can achieve with the proposed technological advancements. Located in Squamish, Canada, the proposal speculates that local forest industries, in partnership with the First Nations peoples of Canada, can incentivise growth in the engineered timber industry.

14.2, 14.20 Connor James, Y5 'London Gateway'. The project investigates freeports as a mechanism for post-Brexit and post-Covid-19 economic recovery, while considering the developing global climate crisis. To synthesise these competing narratives into an architectural hybrid speculation, a new urban zone and satellite port, facilitating trade in physical and intangible service assets, sits atop a flood-defence system. A slowdown in the global economy since the financial crisis of 2008 has fed international efforts to provide favourable conditions for economic growth; special economic zones (SEZs) are part of this international incentive strategy. Freeports are situated within a nation's borders but include legislative exemptions; this specific condition allows for speculation towards hyper free-market conditions and their spatial manifestation.

14.4, 14.5 Ryan Moss, Y4 'The Commonwealth Assembly'. Concrete and timber as a material hybrid has unrealised potential, overlooked and restricted by its opposing material sensitivities. The research develops strand-woven bamboo as a concrete reinforcement that can be applied in fully integrated composite construction. The Commonwealth Assembly is formed through the consolidation of colonial outcomes found in Hong Kong society, which remain cherished today, manifesting in a new political structure that serves as a catalyst for citizens to subvert the current governance of the city.

14.6, 14.7 Andre Hoelzle de Moraes, Y5 'New Complexes of the Brazilian Amazônia.' A proposal for using sustainable timber (hardwood), produced within a tropical agroforestry system and applied to build whole communities. Situated within the most deforested regions of the Amazon, the design offers an alternative to current industrial farming practices.

14.8, 14.10 Nnenna Itanyi, Y5 'Wombs in the Desert'. The project reimagines a desert site on the outskirts of Timbuktu, Mali, in 2063. Constructed to achieve the aims of the African Union's Agenda 2063 on inclusive and sustainable development, the infrastructure contains an urban settlement bolstered by the presence of a High-Speed Network and Great Green Wall Scheme.

14.9 Teodor Andonov, Y4 'Folkloria: Reimagining the Bulgarian folk-house'. Situated in the mountains of Bulgaria, the project synthesises a new vernacular based on traditional folk houses. Villages are reactivated by an influx of remote-working professionals, creating a modern worker village lifestyle that is achieved by applying a holistic tectonic system, which draws inspiration from the country's architectural vernacular, and is optimised using local materials, fabrication techniques and labour. 'Folkloria' is a prototype for a hyper-local and hyper-global way of life.

14.11 Chenru Sung, Y4 'Bundling Bamboo'. Explores the structural potential of bundled bamboo in the construction of train stations. Bamboo is a fast-growing, natural and sustainable construction material and the project site in Taiwan has an abundant local supply. Adopting a modular structure that utilises the material's tensile strength and flexibility, the project proposes a lightweight and affordable solution for future train stations.

14.12 Vegard Elseth, Y4 'Equinor Fornebu'. The project follows a meta-driven approach to design and reparametrises a structural system for a traditional stacking method, recognised in Scandinavia as 'lafting'. By scaling a lumber profile linearly and mixing in a range of new wood properties and dimensions, the lafting profile becomes stronger in regions where it previously performed poorly. The new timber composite is tested as a headquarter cross-pollinated with an open-end headquarter, to establish the Norwegian economic model as an architectural proposition.

14.13 Benjamin Norris, Y4 'Nordicloop Nyhavn'. This project explores the potential of a future mixed-modal bicycle and hyperloop pod, and the role this emerging typology could have in our cities. Rather than siloing inter-city transport infrastructure to the outskirts, like the majority of airport terminals around the world, the project highlights the need for a future distributed network of mixed-modal 3D public infrastructures, which are embedded within the central fabric of urban life.

14.14 Holly Hearne, Y4 'Uncharted Waters'. Develops a structural system using high-performance concretes that are both durable and sustainable. To minimise the impact the construction process has on the landscape, the project explores prefabrication and the possibility of creating a fully integrated precast panel system. Situated in a coastal context, it adopts a sinuous curving form to provide structural rigidity, which acts as a defence mechanism to protect against harsh and extreme weather conditions.

14.15 Ivan Hewitt, Y5 'Integrated Urban Stadia'. Typically, sports stadiums stand idle for long periods of time. Sited along the Oslo waterfront in Norway, a new stadium integrates a highly differentiated context to create a frequently used urban space with increased social, cultural and economic activity.

14.16, 14.17 Jack Lettice, Y5 'Luna 2121'. A building on the Moon must be shaped by the hazards of the lunar landscape, which has a surface gravity 1/6th of Earth. The project explores the architecture of a new lunar culture and how it diverges from our preconceptions of what a building should be.

14.18 Svenja Siever, Y4 'The Living Powerhouse'. Explores ways to achieve differentiated spaces in civil construction and makes industrial architecture exciting to explore and inhabit. In line with Energy Strategy 2050, a centralised fish-trading hub on the outskirts of Geneva, Switzerland, is made self-sufficient using a hydroelectric dam. Through the analysis of computational fluid dynamics (CFD), the dam's sheer walls are adapted to the unequal horizontal pressures acting on them. This material distribution method creates cavities within the walls and generates the dam spillway, allowing water to flow through specific programmes.

14.19 Daniel Boran, Y5 'Unorthodox Union'. The project identifies key structural problems of timber used in Russian orthodox churches, and substitutes it with brick while retaining the original construction method. The project is situated in 2050. Putin is no longer in power and infighting about who should be the next president has left the state fragile and unable to effectively govern regions outside the larger cities. In contrast, the Russian Orthodox Church has been growing in power since the last days of the USSR and has stepped in as a temporary governing authority. A single monastery holds regional power in rural areas and aims to instil a positive and spiritual way of life.

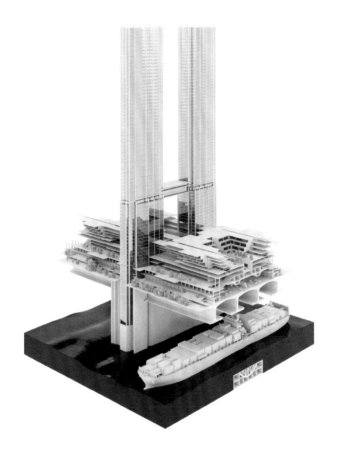

14.2

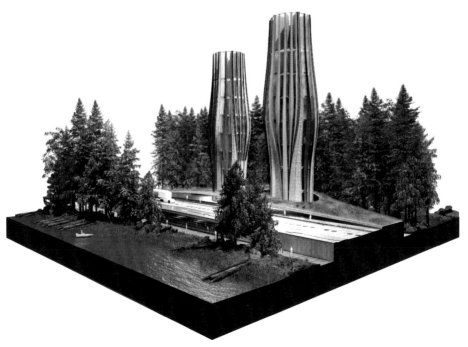

14.3

14.4

14.5

14.6

14.7

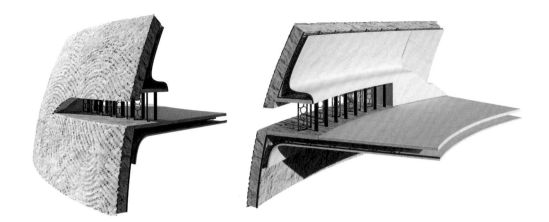

14.8

14.9

14.10

294

14.11

14.12

14.13

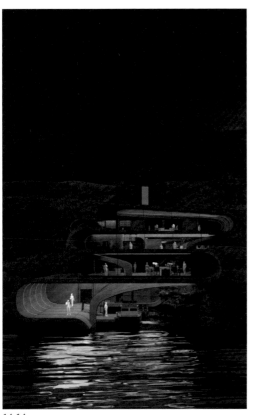

14.14

14.15

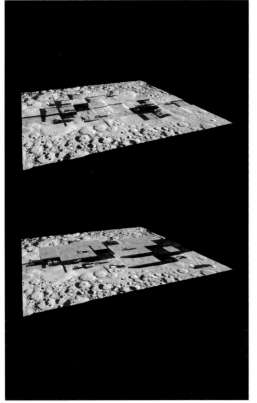

14.16

14.17

297

14.18

14.19

14.20

15.1

Commons

Kate Davies, Susanne Isa

PG15 investigates the hinterlands and transitions of cities operating in between the real and imaginary. We are interested in the transdisciplinary fields of architecture, art, museology, anthropology and geology in order to explore the psychology of place, the narrative of history, mythologies, rituals and magic.

As architecture reinvents itself to remain pertinent in the 21st century, it needs to engage with other disciplines and have an understanding of the past, present and future. More than ever, we need to nurture the collective and protect the things we value for the many, not the few. PG15 examines 'commons' as a collective spatial and intellectual territory: common knowledge and common ground.

The Plot Line
Students conducted focussed research on a collective site: London's Lea Valley, which follows the route of the River Lea from Luton through to the River Thames. Beginning with 'The Plot Line' – a speculative set of explorations of site, involving walking and filmmaking – students walked the site repeatedly and drew a line on a map that connected a set of thematic interests. They then took this line or journey as the site and subject of a short experimental film, forming a catalyst for their architectural designs. By focussing on the line and the film, students questioned static ideas of site and linear time to embrace complexity within the dynamics of the city and to acknowledge multiple points of view. Throughout the year, the unit maintained time as a driving theme in its work.

The Institute for the Commons
We asked students to house the facilities for the production and study of a specific aspect of the 'commons': Something that is, or should be, held in common and not owned privately, e.g. air, water, twilight, data, the electromagnetic spectrum, communication, land, time, public space, biology, chemistry, physics, mineral resources, health, heritage, gravity, light, knowledge, information, language or copyright. In particular, students considered how their work can make social relationships tangible and how a community can be formed through particular practices, actions and shared experiences.

Year 4
Patricia Bob, Xinhao (Eva) Chen, Bryn Davies, Daniel Johnston, Sijie Lyu, Simona Moneva, Polina Morova, Nikoleta Petrova, Gia San Tu, Haoran Wang, Chenwei Ye

Year 5
Jack Cox, Jack Hastie, Nichole Ho, Mei See Leung, Philip Longman

Thank you to our technical tutor Martin Sagar; technical consultants, Kimmy El Dash, Bola Ogunmefun; guest tutors Sebastian Andia, William Gowland

Thank you to our thesis supervisors: Alessandro Ayuso, Polly Gould, Iulia Statica, Ren Guang Yu, Stamatis Zografos

Thank you to our critics: Iris Argyropoulou, Max Dewdney, Nicholas Elias, Naomi Gibson, William Gowland, Simon Herron, Thomas Parker, Ingrid Schroeder, Nathan Su, Jonathan Walker, Graeme Williamson, Simon Withers

15.1, 15.10–15.12 Mei See Leung, Y5 'One Park, Two Meanings'. The KongHong Land (歪) is a theme park proposal that changes sophistries into reality in Hong Kong. It begins with the principle of 'one country, two systems'. Hong Kong's shifting political and social context has raised concerns that the city's autonomy is being suppressed and lost to more tight controls by China. Is there another way to reveal its stories? The attractions are layered with a collage of commentaries that presents the true Hong Kong People's Park. It is an aspiration for a fantasy land that leaves a permanent memory in the hearts of Hong Kong's people.

15.2–15.4 Jack Hastie, Y5 'In the Shadow of the Spectacle'. This project operates across a long span of time and is situated at the mouth of the River Lea in London. The architecture aims to create a new meeting ground; a remnant of events to come. Its goal is to protect the Lea Valley and to represent the value we must place on the long future ahead. The spaces signify the passing of time and act as a frame of reference.

15.5–15.6 Jack Cox, Y5 'House for a Man who Steals Meat'. The project is a house for the hawker. The hawker steals flesh. He takes it from butchers, abattoirs and the streets. He moves through the night in dimly lit pubs, selling the cuts of meat out of his large coat. The city's alleys act as dark cuts into the river, like flesh or architecture that is excised from the building, pulled out in the night market where parts are cut up and displayed to be sold. A strange dancing of flesh and architecture.

15.7–15.9 Nichole Ho, Y5 'Negotiating the Commons'. The project proposes a material line in the form of a cycling path along the periphery of Singapore, which threads together migrant worker communities and residential heartlands, industrial landscapes, cityscapes and the built environment with nature. This 'line' is celebrated through the hosting of an annual 100-mile cycling race, which, in its aftermath, leaves behind a strategic placement of temporary infrastructures that act as a catalyst for spaces of engagement and community support for migrants and locals.

15.13–15.14 Philip Longman, Y5 'On Places Strange and Quiet'. A cultural history of the Deep England Research Unit. This project is an exploration of a decentred and dispersed archive. It understands architecture as an organising system; and a way in which we orient ourselves within the world. Using the existing – and now obsolete – trig point network as both a site and metaphor, the project follows the Deep England Research Unit's work in siting marginalised histories, local curiosities and precarious digital fragments. Oscillating between documentary and conspiratorial fiction, the project follows Robinson as he investigates whether the Deep England Research Unit is already engaging in work to mitigate the problem of the internet.

15.15–15.16, 15.19 Chenwei Ye, Y4 'The Lost, the Abject and the Sacred'. This project proposes to reclaim a field in the Lee Valley to become a temple of grain, a brewery and a local hub, which constructs intimacy and appreciation between people and grain. It ritualises the productive process and collective labour through lunar cycles so that people can be aware of the spirituality of grain as a natural gift. Pragmatically, the project also uses the waste produced on site to nurture the grain field and a moon garden as ways to turn the abject to the sacred. In the end, time may pass and change the project, but the site will remain a pleasant and mysterious place to wander and linger.

15.17–15.18 Xinhao (Eva) Chen, Y4 'Entanglement Of Flora and Stinkiness'. The Victorian flushing toilet brought to London the 1858 'Great Stink', which referred to the smell of the polluted Thames. Construction of London's sewage network started after that. One of the idled pumping stations, Markfield Beam Engine, is now a museum with sewage tanks planted with roses. The architectural proposition is a compost toilet over a rose farm. It produces rose oil and reminds people of the stinky past and ever-present smells. It is not faeces that smell but our fears and imaginations.

15.20 Polina Morova, Y4 'Anima Allegra'. A house manufacturing workshop based on the premises of an IKEA store in London. The project acts against IKEA gamifying capitalist ideas and monopolising design. By integrating community members into all design stages – planning, building and testing – 'Anima Allegra' offers an alternative, more participatory, way of designing and building houses. The workshop interrogates the uniqueness of our preferences and enables designers to share control with users.

15.21, 15.23 Sijie Lyu, Y4 'Water as Ritual'. This project proposes a series of architectural moments that combine modern technologies and mysterious rituals to relate the individual to the collective. The spaces are inspired by traditional rain-making rituals in different cultures. The ritual has a structure and has rules; it repeats things. The project draws on this to form a specific journey through the water. People gain more control over the water by getting involved in the process.

15.22 Gia San Tu, Y4 'Buoyant Vessel'. With the sudden collision of work-life balance, due to the outbreak of Covid-19, 'Buoyant Vessel' is an institution that promotes preventative healthcare and agency in access to health services. It is an outlet space for the individuals affected by the new way of living to let out their suppressed emotions and trauma through vocalisation. In multiple galleries, with enhanced acoustic qualities, users voice their emotions by whispering, singing and screaming. The project aims to release emotional fear, with a final goal of stability.

15.24–15.25 Daniel Johnston, Y4 'The Waiting Room'. The project explores the relationship between the key workers of the city and the act of waiting. The project ritualises the manual act of cleaning to construct a stage revisualising the importance of these workers, and their associated work, while also providing crucial waiting spaces. The project asks, How can the role of the key worker be elevated in the city and how can the ritualised act of cleaning provide reflective spaces of waiting?

15.2

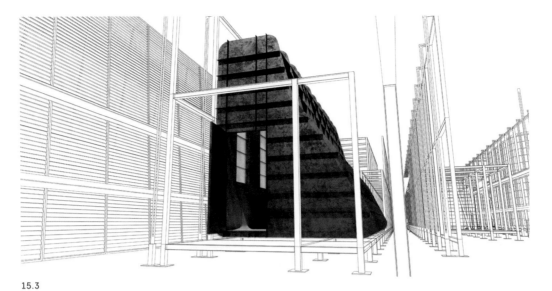

15.3

15.4

15.5

15.6

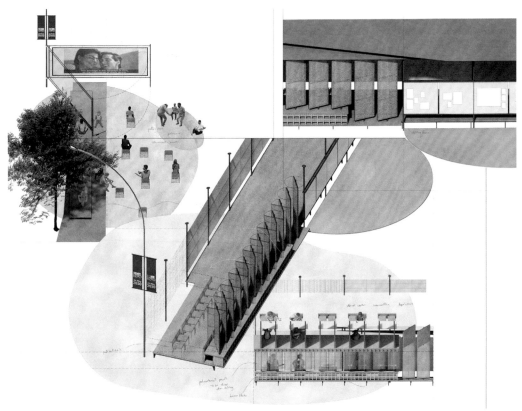

15.7

15.8

15.9

15.10

15.11

15.12

15.13

15.14

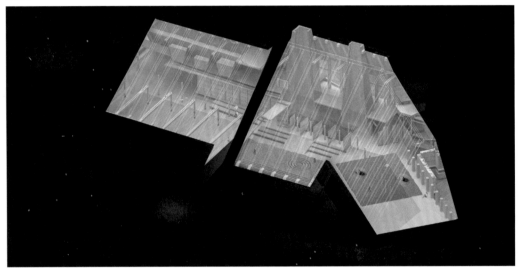

15.15

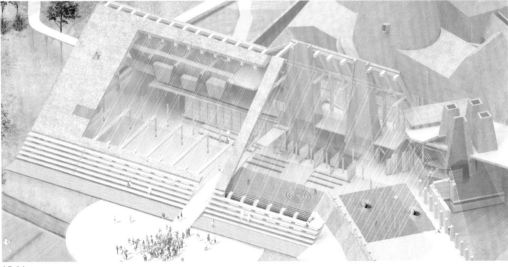

15.16

15.17

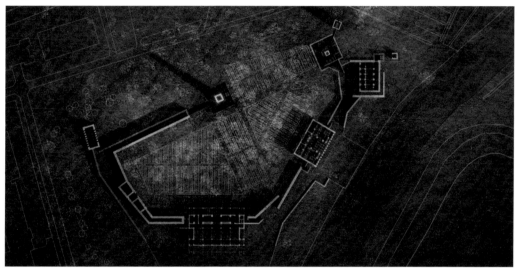

15.18

15.19

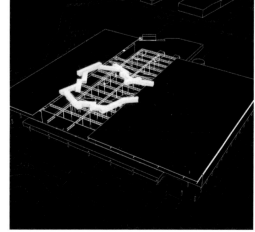

15.20

15.21

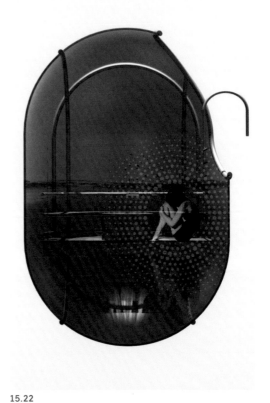

15.22

15.23

15.24

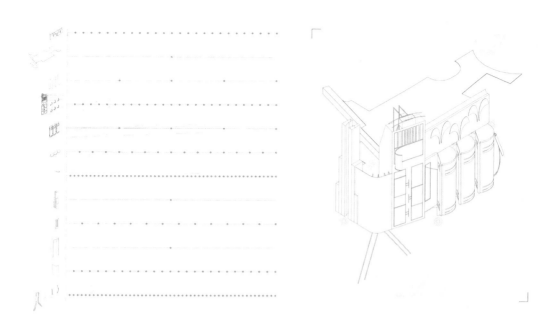

15.25

16.1

A Stationary Body

Matthew Butcher, Ana Monrabal-Cook

PG16 is focussed on the exploration of an architecture that re-emphasises the need to have a physical engagement and relationship with the environments we choose to inhabit. This year we continued our explorations into the meaning of matter and sought to emphasise the human body as the primary site of architectural experience and enquiry. This investigation was framed by two distinct and emerging conditions. Firstly, the effect of the Covid-19 pandemic on the way we experience the objects, materials and ecologies that frame and formulate our daily experiences. Central to this enquiry was the exploration of current circumstances that have forced us to gain a heightened awareness of how we physically interact with the world through our senses, in particular touch, and the way we manifest and develop social relationships through proximities in shared space. Secondly, our investigation was formulated by the desire to find architectures that negate a condition of reduced mobility within an increasingly globalised world.

Our investigations this year started with the human body as a site, looking at contemporary and historical ways to record and measure it, the relationship between our physicality and senses, and the way these affect our understanding of the world. These enquires sought to respond to the opinion that we have entered an era where existing building control and construction standards can be challenged, to consider the senses, character and our new emerging identities. The work then transitioned to proposing inventive and speculative approaches to the act of dwelling and new types of spaces that enhance our relationship with the environment.

Our design outcomes were varied, taking the form of speculative narratives, spatial transformations and material investigations. Students challenged the typology of the terraced house by experimenting with contemporary applications of clay and challenged conventional notions of 'home' through the practice of drag. Students also explored the preservation of environments through the study of existing ecologies, adapting these into building systems such as seed banks to narrate the history of a man-made forest, flood defence mechanisms that address balance in order to stimulate our proprioceptive senses and building structures warning of impending natural disasters, inspired by supernatural beliefs.

Year 4
Jack Barnett, Lauren Childs, Yang Di, Zachariah Harper-Le Petevin Dit Le Roux, Tudor Jitariu, Aleksandra Kugacka, Maria (Tea) Marta, Rupert Woods

Year 5
Ella Caldicott, Hoh Gun Choi, Christina Garbi, George Gil, Hannah Lewis, Przemyslaw Pastor, Daniel Pope, Andrew Riddell

Thank you to our design realisation practice tutor Will Jefferies, structural consultant Ollie Wildman and environmental consultant Sal Wilson

Thesis tutors: Brent Carnell, Stelios Giamarelos, Elise Hunchuck, Shaun Murray, Oliver Wilton, Simon Withers

Critics: Laura Allen, Ana Betancour, Tom Budd, Cristina Candito, Rhys Cannon, John Cruwys, Maria Fedorchenko, David Flook, Will Jefferies, Perry Kulper, Ness Lafoy, TJ Brook Lin, Jason O'Shaughnessy, Mark Smout, Neil Spiller, Dimitar Stoynev, Simon Withers, Carl-Johan Vesterlund

Guest speakers and masterclass hosts: Eddie Blake, Tom Budd, John Cruwys, Sam Davies, Marco Ferrari, Paloma Gormley, Niall Hobhouse, Elise Hunchuck, Summer Islam, Asif Khan, Holly Lewis, Geoff Manaugh, Niall Maxwell, Nicholas de Monchaux, Matthew Page, Nicola Twilley, Marie Walker-Smith, Michael Webb

16.1 Andrew Riddell, Y5 'Lipstick on a Pig'. The project proposes an architecture of a bespoke and new Queer domestic. Questioning traditional domestic spaces that fail to accommodate more fluid definitions of domesticity, it draws on the aesthetic and social attitudes of the drag community. Drag in this context acts as a visual sign of this deconstruction of the wider heteronormative model of living that is held today.

16.2–16.4 Hannah Lewis, Y5 'Four Cities, One Future.' The project imagines a world where polar reversal becomes a reality. In response to this catastrophe, and derived from online user-generated content such as Reddit, a 'cross' of four imaginary cities is proposed at the edge of South Dakota. Each city captures an alternative response to survival and state of mind. Through online presence, the project provides an opportunity to picture a wildly different world with divergent imaginaries for alternate ways of living.

16.5, 16.21 Daniel Pope, Y5 'The Earthen Land Registry'. The project explores the use of clay in contemporary construction methods. Through augmenting extrusion techniques and adopting processes of additive manufacturing technology, the proposal heightens the sensuous relationship between the body and building materials. The project includes a house typology and a retrofit strategy for London's current brick housing stock, supported by a new fabrication facility and a public monument in the heart of the city.

16.6–16.7 Ella Caldicott, Y5 'An Architecture Through an Orchid Sensibility'. The project explores how architecture can enhance a desire for ecological awareness in the limestone district of the Yorkshire Dales, home to one of the rarest orchids in the UK. Balancing the existing conflicts between tourism, the quarrying industry, farmers and locals, the project creates a new appreciation of the protected landscape at both the scale of the orchid as well as the wider ecosystem of the Dales.

16.8 Zachariah Harper-Le Petevin Dit Le Roux, Y4 'After the First Fire'. A proposal for a fire research settlement sited on London's Building Research Establishment (BRE), dedicated to developing two experimental housing typologies. Throughout the two homes, the life of components after fire testing is accounted for; where sacrificial materials might combust to protect occupants. The project explores alternative strategies for risk in the home and suggests how architecture might play a more performative role in fire prevention and safety.

16.9 Przemyslaw Pastor, Y5 'A Society for Abandoned Landscapes'. An architectural intervention to address the negative ecological impact caused by abandoned farmland across the Palo Verde Valley, California. Taking inspiration from the Blythe Intaglios – a group of gigantic prehistoric figures etched on the ground in the Colorado Desert – the proposed structures are carved into the ground to form a satellite desert laboratory for new farming techniques and the creation of 'A Society for Abandoned Landscapes'.

16.10 Aleksandra Kugacka, Y4 'Save the Date'. The project investigates what might constitute a post-pandemic public space. Taking Willesden Junction as a test site, the project considers the railway station as a romantic space of encounter. Speculating on the use of the waiting room and platform as a way to find delight in the everyday commute, the project explores the influence public space has on our mental wellbeing.

16.11 Maria (Tea) Marta, Y4 'A School, a Barn and a House Can Start a Riot'. Situated in the Apuseni Mountains, Romania, the project interrogates the possibilities of ravaged landscapes and forgotten architecture as catalysts for political change. The region suffers from uncontrolled and reckless mining that has led to several major environmental disasters. Three traditional buildings, found in different states of decay,

act as a backdrop for annual activist gatherings, each receiving an architectural costume to protect and augment their presence in the extreme landscape.

16.12 Christina Garbi, Y5 'The Conifer Seed Sanctuary'. Located in Thetford Forest, Norfolk, the proposal speculates on ways to safeguard the future of softwood timber. It attempts to redesign ancestral timber plantation monocultures that show a sensitivity to the ecosystem by diversifying the forest stands. The architecture focusses on providing spaces for storing conifer seeds and preserving their diversity. The spaces, divided by columns of trees, become an extension of the architecture and are reminiscent of forests in the Neolithic period.

16.13 Lauren Childs, Y4 'The Island of Ladies'. The proposal located on Oliver's Island, a narrow island in the River Thames, is a reaction to the self-contained suburban home. It is informed by Leslie Kanes Weisman's research into women's fantasies about the home. The communal dwelling for ten households, each consisting of women and children, proposes a new way of living that provides the conditions for radical kinship, in which everyone 'mothers' each other and domestic labour is shared and visible.

16.14 Tudor Jitariu, Y4 'Prophecy and Exodus'. The project speculates on the future of dwelling and investigates issues relating to 'desertification' in Southern Europe. Firstly, we must learn to accept or reject the relationship between an isolated way of living and increased water scarcity. Through testing the resilience of building materials in conditions of high humidity, moisture content and heat, the project suggests how architecture can act as a material register of this emerging type of environmental ecology.

16.15 Yang Di, Y4 'Non-Place ThinkTank'. Hangzhou, China, is going through an unprecedented process of urbanisation, including the mass development of suburban gated compounds, due to plans to build an international transportation hub in preparation for the 2022 Asian Games. As a response, THINKTANKTM is a replicable and mobile system that acts as an agent to activate communal life, utilising the potential of onsite farming to mobilise the community to participate in local entrepreneurship.

16.16–16.17 Jack Barnett, Y4 'Rewilding Balance'. The project reintroduces balance into our built environment at the scale of buildings and the landscape. Through designed curvatures and geometries, the manipulation of an object's centre of mass informs an architecture no longer comprised of stationary bodies alone. Through rewilding the culverted Pymmes Brook in North London, a seasonal floodplain becomes the site of a lido that choreographs a series of balancing acts to re-engage an individual's physicality and proprioceptive senses.

16.18–16.19 George Gil, Y5 'The Great Reset'. The proposal is a strategy for preparing the isolated, paranoid and mentally numbed architecture student for reintegration into the physical world. The project develops a process to explore and escape the fraught interaction between the body and the computer, which has come to define our consumption of information and the rhythm of existence during successive lockdowns as a result of the Covid-19 pandemic. Topographies of London are relearned to inform a desktop diorama and an inhabitable virtual landscape.

16.20 Hoh Gun Choi, Y5 'The Yokais of Disaster'. The residential project in the suburbs of Tokyo aims to stand as a prototype for rethinking our emotional and physical relationships with natural disaster, using Japanese supernatural beliefs. The introduction of yōkai (supernatural creatures) encourages the idea of catastrophe within a community's imagination and nurtures acceptance for the unavoidable possibility of risk.

16.2

16.3

16.4

16.5

16.6

16.7

16.8

16.9

16.10

16.11

16.12

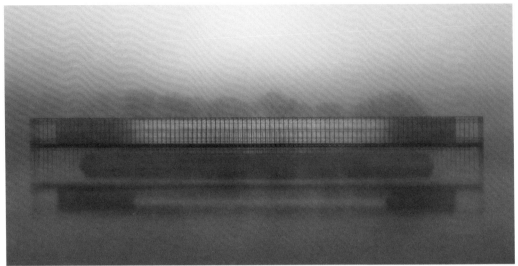

16.13

16.14

16.15

16.16

16.17

16.18

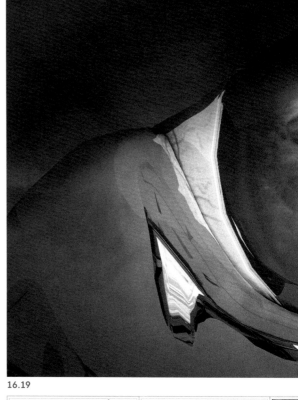

16.19

16.20

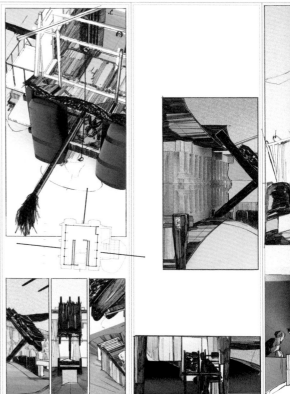

16.21

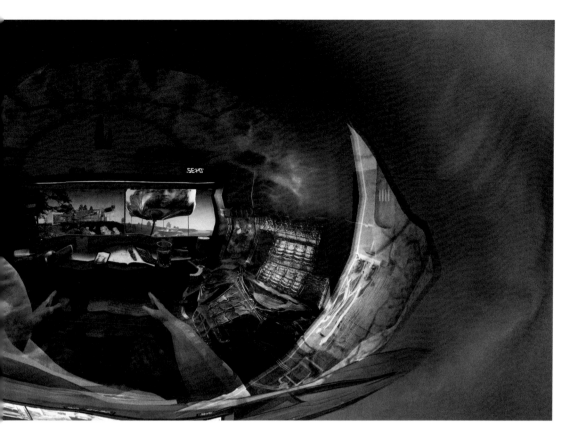

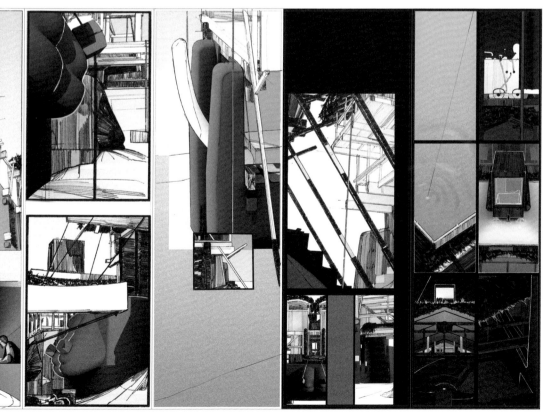

17.1

Extended Mind

Yeoryia Manolopoulou, Thomas Parker

Mind, body and environment is a shared continuum: an integrated reality in which architecture plays a transformative role.

PG17 started the year by visiting the astonishing landscape of Avebury, Wiltshire, with an aim to think about the value of large-scale architectural events, human movement, earthen construction, sustainability and longevity. Avebury physically manifests 5,000 years of continuous human history: it includes the biggest man-made prehistoric mound in Europe and the world's largest prehistoric stone circle, which encompasses a living village. These monumental earthworks were constructed collectively as public theatres for ceremonies. The act of building brought communities together and gave physical expression to their ideas.

PG17 promotes a collaborative understanding of architecture and seeks to nurture future generations of architects who will influence the world differently, precisely because of the pluralistic underpinning of their practices. Creative autonomy is vital but how do we nest it in collective purpose? We seek to amplify the role of the individual in a collective but also the role of collaboration in one's own imagination and critical thought process.

We have a profound interest in the spaces and experiences we create when we become immersed in the act of design. As an embodied and extended action, design is able to diffuse and transform individual thought: it can distribute the mind to body and hands, offload it to tools and materials and, through these, continuously energise itself, making new and reciprocal connections with other minds, actions and technologies in the world. Design, in this way, becomes shared world-building.

Ethical values cannot be separated by aesthetic values. It would be unfortunate if the potential of *mythos* (story and mood) was weakened under the instrumentalism of *logos* (reasoning). In *The Periodic Table* (1975), the chemist and novelist Primo Levi interweaves materials and human events in a sequence of 21 short stories, each one dedicated to a chemical element, including 'Carbon', 'Gold', 'Iron' and 'Uranium'. It is in a similar way that this year we all tried to explore the limits and altering states of different resources and the continual interdependence between material and cultural events in time. In accordance with Herman Hertzberger's view that 'the world is tired of all that architecture on steroids',[1] many of us chose to work purposefully with fewer means.

Year 4
Daeyong Bae, Zhongliang Huang, Rebecca Lim, Kaye Song, Negar Taatizadeh, Ella Thorns, Janet Vutcheva

Year 5
Pravin Abraham, Ross Burns, Ho (Jackie) Cheung, Thomas Dobbins, Naysan Foroudi, Nikolina Georgieva, Yangzi (Cherry) Guo, Hyesung Lee, George Newton, Benedicte Zorde Rahbek

Technical tutors and consultants: James Daykin, Sophia McCracken, Sal Wilson

Critics: Anthony Boulanger, Barbara-Ann Campbell-Lange, Nat Chard, Sandra Coppin, Kate Davies, Beverley Dockray, Elizabeth Dow, Murray Fraser, Maria Fulford, Clara Kraft, Perry Kulper, Chee-Kit Lai, Guan Lee, Anna Liu, Emma-Kate Matthews, Ana Monrabal-Cook, Shaun Murray, Stuart Piercy, Michiko Sumi, Phil Tabor, Peter Thomas, Robert Thum, Sumayya Vally, Victoria Watson, Oliver Wilton, Fiona Zisch

Circle of Friends: Malina Dabrowska, Nefeli Eforakopoulou, Katherine Hegab, Andreas Müllertz, Jack Newton, Danielle Purkiss, Julia Schütz

Guest Speakers: Alice Brownfield, Matthew Barnett Howland, Joshua Pollard, DJERNES & BELL, Local Works Studio, Studio Elements, THISS

B-Made: William Victor Camilleri, Tom Davies, Donat Fatet

1. Herman Hertzberger (17 September 2020), 'Letter to a Young Architect', *The Architectural Review*.

17.1 **PG17** 'Circle'. A collaboration between all 17 students within the unit, where machine-carved oak blocks are brought together to form a single circle. Building upon the idea of community, which has given the Neolithic stones of Avebury, Wiltshire, such presence and importance throughout millennia, each piece denotes the essence and context of our projects. While their sites are scattered across the world, they are all brought together through the act of collaboration, creating a shared continuum. The work embodies our belief that the individual author finds significance and value within a collective purpose, expanded and remembered through time.

17.2 **Hyesung Lee, Y5** 'Extended Heritage'. Exploring a community's relationship with architecture, ritual and fire, the project proposes a festival within the Avebury Stone Circles, held on the summer solstice, at which temporary structures and human activity revive the circle's periphery. Repeated acts of burning and re-building challenge the popular, passive understanding of heritage.

17.3 **Benedicte Zorde Rahbek, Y5** 'Tower of Women'. Bringing a new agenda to the London skyline, the project is shaped and informed by historical and present-day female makers of society, arts and architecture. The design is experienced through shifts in time and light, creating an ever-changing scene where women collaborators continue to evolve and impact the design of the building.

17.4 **Thomas Dobbins, Y5** 'Time in Elmet'. A temporal study of the Upper Calder Valley, West Yorkshire, undertaken across three scales of understanding: human, material and industrial. Using a performative design methodology inspired by the processes of three local artists, a series of scored landscape explorations suggests a new civic infrastructure and writer's retreat along the boundary of a village churchyard.

17.5 **Nikolina Georgieva, Y5** 'Of Fells and Thwaites'. The project develops a deep understanding of the anthropogenic landscape, interrogating its formative human and ecological practices. Located within the glacial, volcanic terrain of the Lake District, a wellness retreat distils qualities of the climatological, geological and worked taskscape and the mentally navigated landscape of the region.

17.6, 17.12 **Negar Taatizadeh & Kaye Song, Y4** 'The Fyfield School of Land'. Advocating for a re-engagement with our land, the project proposes a campus for hands-on-learning set within an area of Wiltshire's farmland, with a 6,000-year history of cultivation. A purposeful system of collaboration creates a dialogue between two designers and their respective buildings, promoting a mindful approach to a landscape and its surroundings.

17.7 **Janet Vutcheva, Y4** 'New Water Meadow'. Responding to the continued ecological degradation of England's chalk streams, due to the climate crisis, the project proposes an infrastructural water network for restoring their health. It does so by harvesting, storing and draining rainwater, which helps support the ecology's intricate webs of life.

17.8 **Zhongliang Huang, Y4** 'Garden Uranus'. Located in Dungeness – a former nuclear site on the coast of Kent – the project seeks to support the area's rich ecology through the establishment of a bird sanctuary. Small buildings and low-rise walls made of local materials establish playful boundaries amongst pools of water and garden equipment, striving to confront the ecological decline caused by human and nuclear power at an architectural level.

17.9 **Daeyong Bae, Y4** 'With the Traces'. The project focusses on how traces of human activity left on built environments commemorate the everyday acts of those who occupy them. Situated in Avebury, Wiltshire, the proposal redevelops an existing park home to accommodate a more social way of living, attuned to the temporal rhythms of life and death that are so present within the stones of its neighbouring Neolithic stone circle.

17.10–17.11 **Ho (Jackie) Cheung, Y5** 'Duologue Between Islands'. Revealing the lost cultural, social and political connections between a small quarrying village and the metropolitan city of Hong Kong, the scheme examines colonial practices of making and incorporates a material history that is found engraved upon its stoney site, it proposes a sculpting school and space for discussion that hopes to empower its local population.

17.13–17.14 **Ross Burns, Y5** 'Re-peating the Highlands'. This project investigates the potential for a system of environmental stewardship through practical and architectural interventions into the Class 5 blanket peat bog surrounding Corrour Station in the Central Highlands. It seeks to maximise the health of the bog by choreographing the relationship between peat, sphagnum moss, water, sound and human occupation.

17.15 **George Newton, Y5** 'The Public House'. Sited in Palmers Green, London, the project suggests an alternative future for The Fox – a now-deserted pub on Green Lanes, one of London's longest and busiest roads. Once a key building within the community, a radical idea for urban living is proposed to break away from cellular systems of housing and work, dissolving the binary conditions of privacy within the suburb.

17.16 **Pravin Abraham, Y5** 'Revitalisation of Wisma Damansara'. Found within an affluent neighbourhood of central Kuala Lumpur, the project repurposes an existing concrete office block to create a series of transient shelters and spaces for teaching that serve the city's marginalised homeless community. The project becomes part of a sustainable solution that promotes public dialogue and interaction.

17.17 **Ella Thorns, Y4** 'Growing Phrontistery'. A transitory space between early learning institutions and the forest, which responds to existing ecological and human cycles in symbiosis with each other. The structure and its population grow as time passes. The building augments the trees' growth and enables inhabitation between branches, a choreography that follows the harmonies of the forest in correspondence with learning.

17.18 **Rebecca Lim, Y4** 'Avebury Seed Barrow'. Set within the Neolithic and agricultural context of Avebury, Wiltshire, the project proposes a seed bank that re-appropriates the preservative notions of the Neolithic long barrow. It uses a dialogue of design practices between human and machine minds to question the generative potentials of drawing and visual media, highlighting the importance of interpretation within architecture.

17.19 **Naysan Foroudi, Y5** 'The Quad'. Positioned in a single field at the intersection of four competing worlds, the project negotiates the often complex, juxtaposed realities of the Salisbury Plain, Wiltshire. The design of a new civic space creates a dialogue between military, historic, residential and agricultural communities, working within the confines of a square to create an integrated approach allowing for the landscape's diverse multiplicity.

17.20 **Yangzi (Cherry) Guo, Y5** 'Snowdonia Nocturne'. The project focusses on the transient journey of ascent from the Welsh town of Blaenau Ffestiniog to the site of slate ruins on the mountaintop plateau within a Dark Sky Reserve. It operates around diurnal and nocturnal cycles, and provides retreats for those who wish to restore their circadian rhythm and sensitivity to natural light.

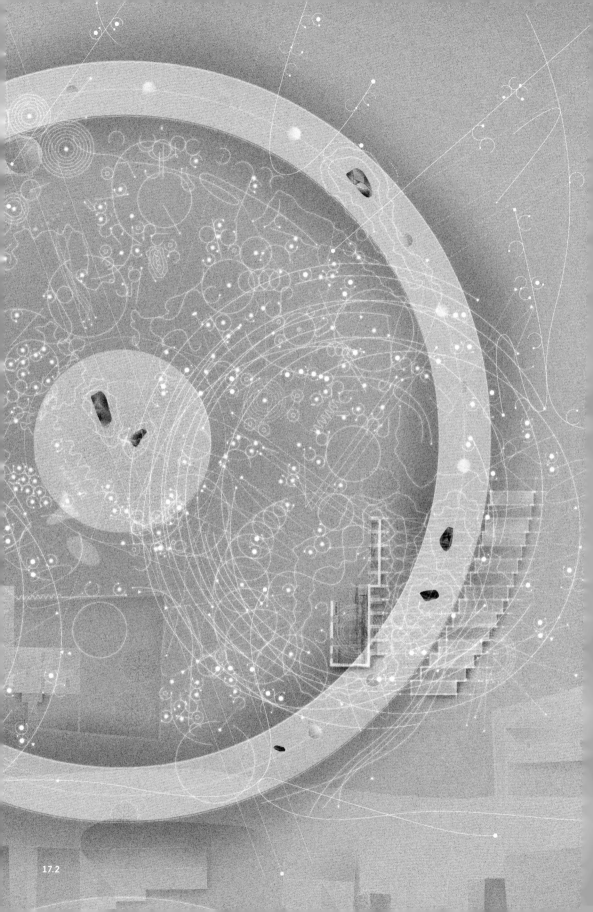

17.2

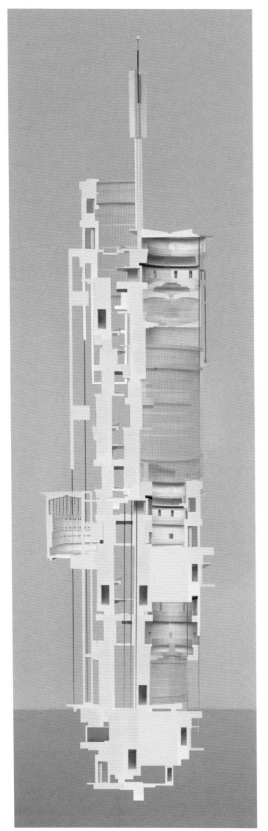

17.3

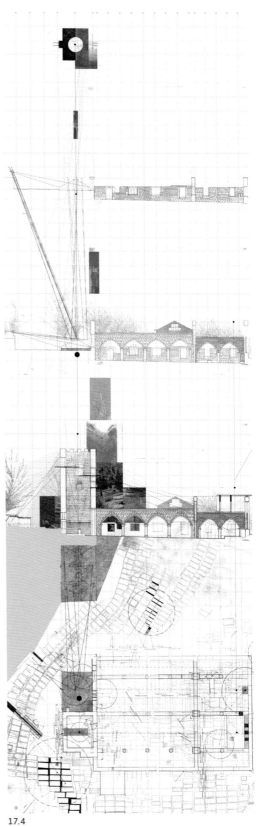

17.4

17.5

17.6

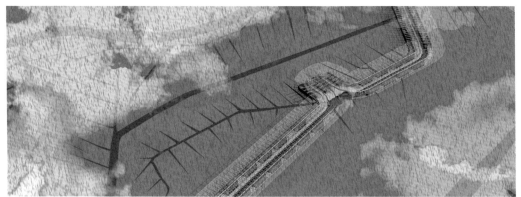

17.7

17.8

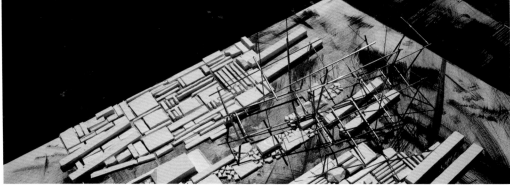

17.9

330

17.10

17.11

17.12

17.13

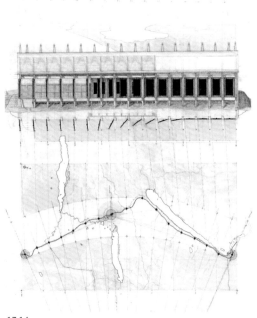

17.14

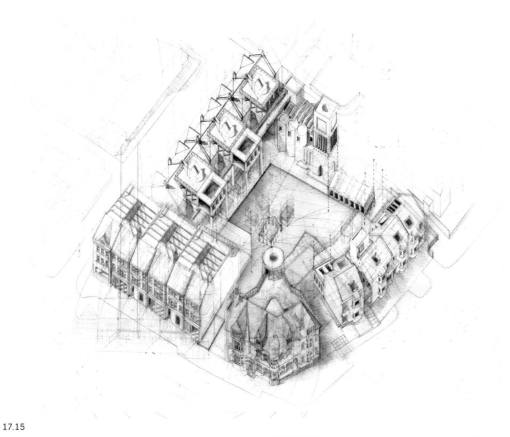

17.15

17.16

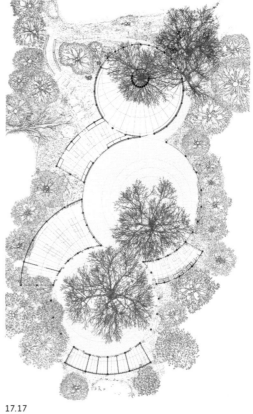

17.17

17.18

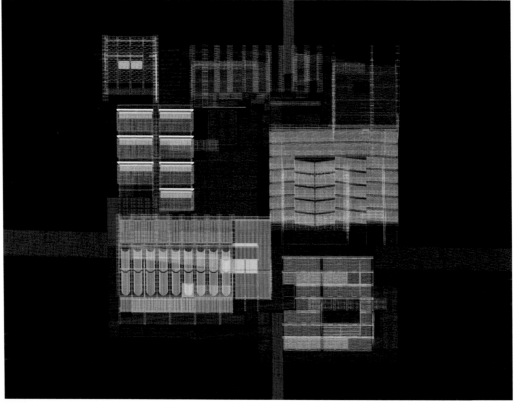

17.19

18.1

Generational Phantoms / Neo-Ecological Myths PG18

Isaïe Bloch, Ricardo Carvalho De Ostos

This year, PG18 studied how to frame ecological urgency by utilising architectural metaphors as arcs of narrative and meaning. Inspired by work on microeconomics, behavioural psychology and environmental sciences, we investigated how metaphors are a powerful tool to visualise and communicate complex ideas. Focussing on the current ecological crisis as the most pressing story of our time, students researched how forest metaphors could be used to reimagine parts of London. From macro to micro metaphors, we looked at how concepts of environmental performance are linked to public perception in London's distinct cultures and physical contexts.

To shape a relevant environmental story into an urban forest metaphor, design proposals had to combine the urban and the natural while navigating the dense woods of knowledge, online activism, fake news and professional bias. PG18 encouraged students to take a position, but never at the expense of learning and questioning. By speculating how London could be transformed via the development of architectures as forest artefacts, students created projects inspired by contemporary topics such as the Covid-19 pandemic, rewilding, technological nature, robotics, conservation and culture wars.

PG18 students developed compelling projects while engaging with today's pressing environmental and cultural topics via well-crafted architectural designs. Most importantly, however, they showed resilience, patience and a will to thrive under adverse circumstances, all of which are key ingredients necessary to write our biggest global story yet: a neo-ecological myth to be inked by us all.

Year 4
Victoria Bocchiotti, Siu Yuk Chu, Grégoire Gagneux, Tobias Himawan, Alvin Lim, Kacper Pach, Sophie Peterson, Raul Rutnam, Michaella Tafalla, Pablo Wheldon

Year 5
Aya Ataya, Yusef Burhanuddin, Alex Desov, Sara Eldeib, Kaizer Hud, Alexander Kolar, Shoakang Li, Rory Noble-Turner, Niall O'Hara

Technical tutors and consultants: Robert Haworth, Bina Nikolova, Anna Woodeson

Critics: Oliver Domeisen, David Hutama, Alice Labourel, Jez Ralph, Yael Reisner, Alisa Silanteva, Nathan Su, Paulo Waisberg, Yeena Yoon

18.1 **Shoakang Li, Y5** 'Under the Mask: Neo dark heritage in the post-pandemic world'. London has experienced economic and social disruption because of the Covid-19 pandemic. In response, the project provides a new form of urban forest architecture for healing and creativity. Using metaphor – the forest as a 'dark' palace of healing and possibility – the design explores the idea of 'dark' heritage. Sited at the ExCeL London, the project is comprised of theatrical space that enables audiences and actors to explore uncanny situations.

18.2–18.3 **Kaizer Hud, Y5** 'Waterlow Hospice: A forest to depart'. In the forest, life and death are trapped in an endless cycle: life turns to death and death feeds life. In UK cities, most people die in hospital – closed-off and often undignified. The project proposes a hospice in Waterlow Park, neighbouring Highgate Cemetery, that incorporates trees as a site of living and dying. The project's design encourages more open conversations about death and dying. After dying, hospice residents are put to rest in a forest park and their bodies turn into trees that shade the living, while dead-matter mycelium provides comfort for the patients.

18.4–18.5 **Rory Noble-Turner, Y5** 'The Forest of Possibility'. Inspired by German Romanticism of the late-18th and early-19th centuries, the project explores the themes of wanderlust and *waldeinsamkeit* (forest loneliness) and applies them to frame the forest adventure as an individual desire for meaning and self-actualisation. Situated in the heart of Tower Hamlets' historic silk district, the project builds on the borough's experimentation with IDEA Stores (educational community centres) as a means of rethinking the public library, proposing the concept of the Knowledge Forest.

18.6, 18.20 **Pablo Wheldon, Y4** 'The Augmented Park'. The project explores parks as open-air living rooms and proposes gathering a variety of park activities into a single building. The building facilitates these activities throughout the year, and during harsh weather conditions, fostering new opportunities for communal interaction. The building is formed using existing paths and landscape, harnessing the sensorial aspects of the forest, with its programmes dependent on the seasons.

18.7 **Raul Rutnam, Y4** 'Rewilding Highgate: London's future urban forest'. It is estimated that UK populations of the most important wildlife have been plummeting for decades. The project investigates this crisis and explores the complex communication between human and non-human life within London's urban forests. It presents a multifaceted understanding of the heterogeneous conditions of Parkland Walk, a 3.1-mile linear green pedestrian and cycle route in North London.

18.8 **Victoria Bocchiotti, Y4** 'Urban Forests: Gateways to new rituals'. Threshold as forest metaphors explores and analyses their influence on our experience of space. The proposal for a market in Castle Square, Elephant Park, introduces a new speed transition in a busy and congested area of London.

18.9 **Yusef Burhanuddin, Y5** 'Land-Fill'. The project is a multifunctional space for marketplaces, performance art, community and business meetings, and retail trading. The building emphasises the critical role of the architect to design collaboratively with the local community, respecting their culture and ambitions, while also anticipating future needs.

18.10 **Alvin Lim, Y4** 'Museum for Slowing Down'. The project is a museum set along the Riverside Walkway, along the South Bank, London. Situated by Gabriel's Pier Park, the project creates an oasis within the fast-paced urban fabric of London. The spaces encourage people to slow down and draw new and unexpected connections with nature.

18.11–18.12 **Alexander Kolar, Y5** 'Sanctuary of the Unloved'. The project develops an unconventional sanctuary architecture, utilising a variety of existing materials arranged to create a plethora of niches, crevices and atmospheres, and allowing certain creatures to flourish within. It includes spaces for the public to understand how nature has taken over these structures and research facilities for ecologists to study wildlife onsite. The project is based in Mill Meads, Bromley-by-Bow, the location of a future Metropolitan Park, according to the All London Green Grid, targeted for completion in 2050.

18.13–18.14 **Sophie Peterson, Y4** 'An Athenaeum for the Unearthed'. Inspired by Lewis Carroll's *Alice's Adventures in Wonderland* (1865), the design explores image distortion and spatial navigation. A local archival display allows a dynamic, non-stop community to access the stillness, surprise and contemplation of the forest. The architecture curates a narrative of local people and objects that would otherwise be hidden, discarded or lost to time.

18.15 **Tobias Himawan, Y4** 'Ephemeral Interconnection'. Beneath the soil participation, communication and nutrient transfer occur as means of maintaining the resilience of the forest, enabled by an underground network formed by fungi. Deep within London, one of the world's most sustainable cities, the project proposes a new social superstructure, a fungus, that reconnects society with energy systems on a social and cultural level, and invites public participation through education and activism.

18.16 **Kacper Pach, Y4** 'Shoreditch Olympia'. Inspired by biophilic concepts and the history of ornament, the project connects symbolic and performative elements through several architectural scales.

18.17 **Aya Ataya, Y5** 'The Future of Human-Nature Relationships'. The project focusses on the role of digital screens in contemporary urban life and explores how digitally mediated nature can become part of architecture.

18.18 **Michaella Tafalla, Y4** 'Canning Town Co-botics'. The project takes inspiration from forest root networks and investigates how they implement collaborative systems to survive in competitive environments. The design accommodates a pilot facility in collaborative robotics and research, which includes apprenticeships and educational programmes, responding to the shift towards digital skills and the digital-skills gap facing our economy.

18.19 **Grégoire Gagneux, Y4** 'UCL Contemplative Centre'. The project explores light pollution and interprets a building's architectural skin as a producer and receiver of light. The building is a place where light pollution can be controlled, used and transformed. Dedicated to UCL students, it offers a multi-sensory relaxing experience.

18.21–18.22 **Niall O'Hara, Y5** 'Through the Eyes of the Forest'. A proposal for a new market typology that integrates contemporary hydroponic systems into its daily programme. The project considers atmosphere and experience as primary motivators for community engagement in the development of urban food production. Agents of change in the forest, inspired by decay and provisions left by the past, facilitate growth and the creation of something new.

18.2

18.3

18.4

18.5

18.6

18.7

18.8

18.9

18.10

18.11

18.12

18.13

18.14

18.15

18.16

18.17

18.18

18.19

18.20

18.21

18.22

TOK(C)CITY (The End Of) PG20

Marjan Colletti, Javier Ruiz Rodriguez

This year, PG20 researched metropolitan, super-urban and hyper-dense megalopolises with increasing populations, buzzing lifestyles, developing infrastructures and huge social, environmental and spatial problems. With the majority of the human population living in towns, new paradigms are required to reinvent the rapport between city and nature, readdress generous civic and private spaces, reinvest in sustainable infrastructure, reintroduce technological and material advances into the built environment and develop objects, buildings and cities that can communicate with each other and us. In line with The Bartlett's 'Build a better future' manifesto[1] – in particular 'Climate Change', 'Nature' and 'Data & Technology' – and the United Nation's 'The 17 Goals'[2] – in particular 'Affordable and Clean Energy', 'Industry, Innovation and Infrastructure' and 'Sustainable Cities and Communities' – students investigated speculative and experimental green, sustainable, diverse and inclusive urbanisation strategies.

As a speculative site for the unit's objective to 'make cities and human settlements inclusive, safe, resilient and sustainable',[3] students researched (remotely) Japan's capital city, Tokyo. Originally a small fishing village named Edo, the Greater Tokyo Area is the world's most populous metropolitan area, with 38 million inhabitants. Tokyo is an Alpha+ city and is regarded as the largest urban economy in the world by gross domestic product. Some of our projects this year reflect on the devastating consequences of climate change on present and future Tokyo, e.g. how floods fully reconfigure the structure of the city, resulting in ambitious propositions and informed speculations where new typologies emerge and old ones adapt or disappear.

Japanese culture provides an extremely rich context in which to revitalise the relationship of architecture and nature. Students invented future scenarios between the poetics of *ukiyo-e*, the 17th to 19th century art form that has profoundly shaped Western perceptions of Japanese art and life; the dynamism of contemporary manga and anime; the animism of the ancient religion of Shinto, in which objects are believed to possess a spirit as much as people and other phenomena; and the country's expertise in and obsession with robotics. A series of skills workshops on procedural design techniques, time-based generative systems and high-resolution hyperreal cinematic videos advanced students' abilities to communicate their ideas in 3D and 4D.

Year 4
Nadya Angelova, James Ballentyne, Michael Brewster, Paul Brooke, Yuqi (Kenneth) Cai, Kar Bo (Thomas) Leung, Carolina Mondragon-Bayarri, Shenton Morgan, Luke Parkhurst, Abigail Yeboah, Zhong Zheng

Year 5
Harry Hinton-Hard, Sze Chun (Kelvin) Hui, Tony Le, Edward Tse, Lukas Virketis, Ning Ye

Thank you to our design realisation practice tutor David Edwards and guest tutors Junichiro Horikawa, Andreas Koerner, Jevgenij Rodionov, Shogo Suzuki

Thank you to our critics: Junichiro Horikawa, Damjan Iliev, Jevgenij Rodionov

1. The Bartlett (2019), 'Build a better future', *The Bartlett*, (accessed 22 June 2021), ucl.ac.uk/bartlett/about-us/our-values/build-better-future
2. United Nations Department of Economic and Social Affairs (2015), 'The 17 Goals', *United Nations*, (accessed 22 June 2021), sdgs.un.org/goals
3. United Nations (2015), 'The 17 Goals'.

20.1, 20.3 Tony Le, Y5 'Neo-Ukiyo'. Tokyo negates hard infrastructural strategies in a speculative wet future. The ground is rejuvenated as the sea takes over and the new city hangs from the sky. The design employs a genetic algorithm to reconfigure the city, as the material of the old city undergoes a metabolic process.

20.2 Harry Hinton-Hard, Y5 'Decay and Deployment'. Time-based decay is embraced within this project through the use of biodegradable matter, such as natural rubber. The rate of decay is programmed to mirror the predicted decrease in Tokyo's population. As organic mass dissipates over time, a transition of occupancy is triggered whereby the remaining structure of previously inhabited flats are retro-fitted as vertical farms.

20.4 Edward Tse, Y5 'Cultivating a Hyphal Urbanism'. Seeking resolve to the global ecological crisis, this project proposes a transverse 'ecologising' of architecture and urbanity for multi-species urban coexistence, where human and non-human modes of living become ever-more intertwined. This is achieved through the use of biological and cultivated materials and reconfigurable generative urban plan and transient surface treatments.

20.5–20.7 Lukas Virketis, Y5 'Neo-Edo: Information age residences'. With the increase of digital culture and technological developments in data and computer science, this project proposes inhabiting environments for the contemporary network society. It explores how big data and machine learning can generate super-site-specific architectural interventions, allowing the urban fabric to become a co-author of a building's design.

20.8 Sze Chun (Kelvin) Hui, Y5 'The Soil-Healing Machine'. This project addresses the issue of contaminated soil in Fukushima, Japan. The proposed long-term decontamination strategy of mycoremediation introduces fungi to remediate the toxic soil. The design provides a system to incorporate mycoremediation over time, at an architectural scale, and integrates itself into the natural landscape.

20.9 James Ballentyne, Y4 '[Bio]Augmentation'. In 2016, the Cabinet Office of Japan published results of an epidemiological survey on *hikikomori*: a phenomenon of social withdrawal where individuals lock themselves away for several months or years without social contact. The design reintegrates *hikikomori* into normal society, providing space to access therapy and education.

20.10 Carolina Mondragon-Bayarri, Y4 'Kyōsei Kawa'. Japanese urbanism is characterised by constant rebuilding, with the current lifespan of timber structures being 21 years. The project challenges this perception by exploring the design of an inhabitable timber megastructure spanning the 500-metre-wide Arakawa River. The architectural strategy combines computational methods of voxelisation with the use of local materials to develop a new housing typology for Tokyo.

20.11 Paul Brooke, Y4 'Symbiocity: The Bloom Network'. Responding to chemical eutrophication – enrichment – of waterways and the resultant hyper-toxic cyanobacterial insurgence in shoreline biomes, The Bloom Network investigates data-driven algal symbiosis as a carbon-negative architectural solution in post-anthropocentric Tokyo. A complex cyanobacterial capillary architecture can bloom de-carbonised microclimates and catalyse the end of toxicity.

20.12 Nadya Angelova, Y4 'Sento'. The project explores the relationship between our spiritual and technological understanding of nature. The design mitigates a climate change-induced disaster: fresh water scarcity. The research studies the role and behaviour of water in Japanese spiritual awakening. A strategy for adaptation is proposed that enhances natural forces using technological solutions.

20.13 Yuqi (Kenneth) Cai, Y4 'Ginza Tera'. Set in Ginza, Tokyo, surrounded by luxury shops, the project is a mixed-use Buddhist temple that reminds people of traditional Japanese philosophies that are under threat from the consumerist values of the West. It is an architecture of thresholds, between perfection and imperfection, permanence and impermanence, contemporary and traditional, secular and religious, and life and death.

20.14 Michael Brewster, Y4 'Fluid(c)ity'. This project focusses on the contemporary office typology and envisions an alternative paradigm that is centred around the needs of the worker. Through the research and digital simulation of Physarum polycephalum, a voxelised building form and performant canopy is generated that utilises site-specific environmental data.

20.15 Abigail Yeboah, Y4 'Nōgyō Vertical Farm'. As of 2019, the food self-sufficiency ratio in Japan has greatly decreased. The ambition of the project is to design and construct an innovative bamboo tower that will be used for vertical farming. The existing farm of Honisshiki 2nd is integrated into the bamboo vertical farm tower, encouraging the local community to produce organic food and promote economic growth.

20.16 Zhong Zheng, Y4 'Hinode Pier Fulfilment Centre'. The Tokyo metropolitan area needs a new form of urban warehouse to accommodate the growth of e-commerce. The project proposes a new vertical retrieval platform, enabling the storage of containers and small parcels in the same space, thus reducing the building's footprint. The BioSkin system regulates the ambient temperature and reduces energy consumption.

20.17 Luke Parkhurst, Y4 'Cyber Rehabilitation'. The project aims to tackle the micro-living of cyber refugees through the integration of landscapes common to many parts of rural Japan. Hokusai's waterfall paintings present an opportunity to explore the representation of nature before Tokyo's urbanity. A symbiosis of digital landscapes and micro-living provides a space to detoxify from the digital and reconnect with nature.

20.18 Shenton Morgan, Y4 '21st Century Hi-Tech'. By exploring the synthesis of the mechanised with the organic, and a Shinto shrine revived for the cyborg human race, the project redefines the anthropocentric relationship of humans and technology, and questions the role of ancient practises in an increasingly digital future. The result is a fully autonomous algorithmic architecture capable of self design and evolution.

20.19 Ning Ye, Y5 'Phygital Housing'. With the development of Industry 4.0, the link between machine, robot, nature and human becomes stronger, while the physical world and cyber space are increasingly blurred. The 'Phygital Housing' project connects physical living space, house ownership, the exchange of digital information and human and high-density urban environments.

20.20 Kar Bo (Thomas) Leung, Y4 'Golden Gai Kabuki Street Theatre: Irezumi architecture'. Exploring the varied histories of *irezumi* (Japanese tattoos) and the red-light district of Tokyo, the project proposes a regeneration of the Golden Gai quarter through the implementation of a kabuki street theatre. It develops a makeshift architectural language that embraces the alley through a gradating series of thresholds, or skins, that compose the journey from street to theatre.

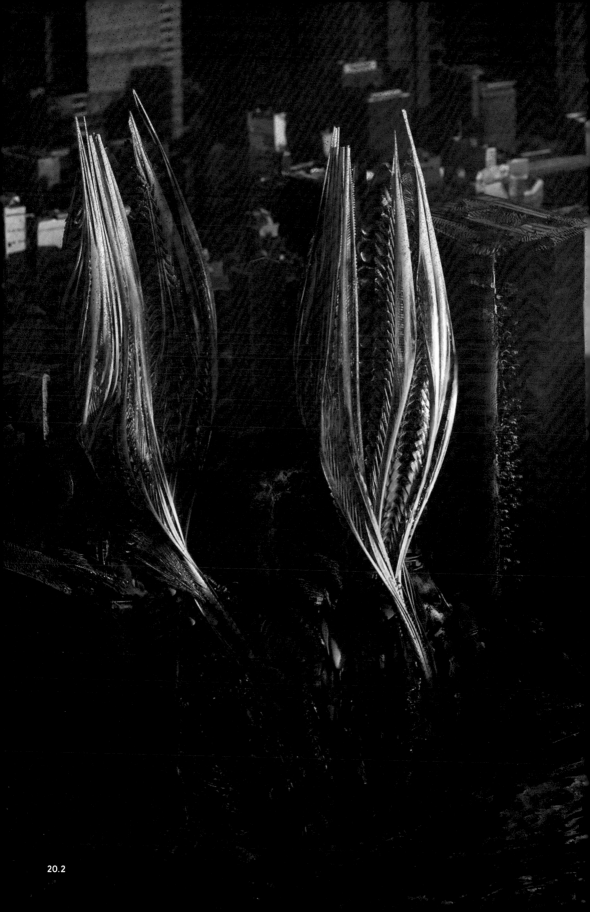

20.2

20.3

20.4

20.5

20.6

20.7

20.8

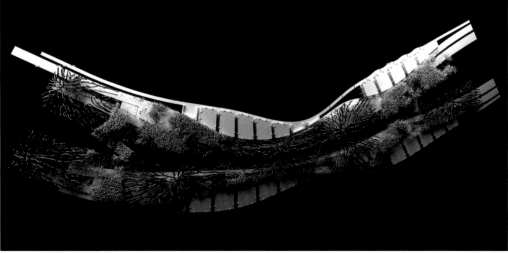

20.9

20.10

20.11

20.12

20.13

20.14

20.15

357

20.16

20.17

20.18

20.19

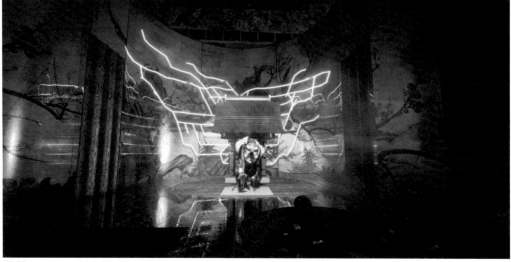

20.20

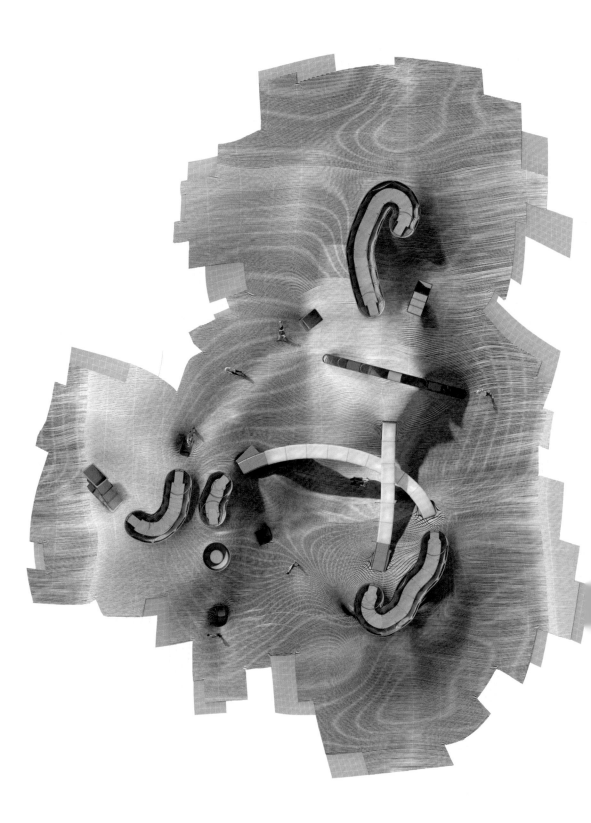

21.1

Uncertainty

PG21

Abigail Ashton, Tom Holberton, Andrew Porter

The mathematician Giovanni Cassini was a pioneer of accurately drawing the universe. In 1679 he produced the first scientific map of the Moon and concealed a tiny figure of a woman in the Bay of Rainbows. No one knows why he hid this fictional maiden within a scientific drawing. Perhaps it was a playful admission of the limits of truth? Despite painstakingly measuring the shadows and smudges of the lunar surface, the drawing still concealed an unknown and uncertain world.

We are living in uncertain times; the Covid-19 pandemic and political instability have shaken our collective sense of the world as relatively predictable. We crave social categories and identities as anchors that make our interactions predictable, surrounding us with shades of certainty. It is easy to live in the echo chamber that is the internet, where algorithms feed false certainty. News and truth are manipulated to group people using confirmation bias, offering the comfort of social categories and a digital environment that reinforces, rather than engaging with, the unfamiliar or ambiguous.

Science offers a different perspective, where the measurement of uncertainty is a vital tool for critical thinking. Quantifying what we do not know is as important as what we do. Artificial Intelligence allows machines to gradually make their dreams converge with reality and create a succinct internal model of a fluctuating world; each iteration creating a new fiction where uncertainties are tested against real data.

Buildings offer the constants of shelter, structure and environment, but architecture often plays and manipulates uncertainties. Every drawing, model and building carries ambiguities through tolerances and translation.

This year PG21 was interested in designs that are not determinate or fixed but are instead uncertain. The unit looked towards the beautiful and eerie landscape of Dungeness on the coast of Kent. Frequently called 'the UK's only desert' – an alternative truth – and 'the fifth continent', Dungeness is home to one third of all plant species found in the UK. 30,000 tonnes of shingle are manually relocated there every year to protect the land from the certainties of longshore drift. Strange buildings and military installations and infrastructure have all been created to confront and watch for the unknown coming over the horizon: smuggling, swamps and atomic fission.

Year 4
Alp Amasya, Kiran Kaur Basi, Lewis Brown, Carmen Kong, Rolandas Markevicius, Ajay Mohan, Maria Eleni Petalidou, Samuel Pierce, Zhi Tam, Yat Shun Tang, Qingyuan Zhou

Year 5
Paul-Andrei Burghelea, Thomas Band, James Carden, Shu Min (Michelle) Hoe, Edward Sear

Thank you to structural engineer Brian Eckersley and environmental engineer Alistair Shaw. Additional Support from Julian Besems, Alex Campbell, Maya Chandler, James Potter, Bethan Ring

Thank you to our critics: Paddi Benson, Julian Besems, Roberto Bottazzi, Luca Dellatorre, Naomi Gibson, Calum MacDonald, Sayan Skandarajah, Kat Scott, Jasmin Sohi, Priscilla Wong

21.1, 21.5–21.6 Thomas Band, Y5 'Rendering the Dungeness Percept'. The iconic image of Dungeness – a totemic object situated within a barren landscape – is synonymous with the mechanistic production of the architectural photograph. Disseminated by websites such as *The Modern House* and *Dezeen*, the imagery shapes our collective understanding of the place, imposing a romanticised fiction upon a working landscape. Dungeness is rendered as a backdrop to the architectural subject: compliant, malleable, representationally inert.

21.2 Edward Sear, Y5 'The Continuous Sea-Wall'. A proposal for an inhabitable section of coastline in Dymchurch, Kent. Bordering land and sea, the scheme includes an esplanade, fish and chip shop, arcades and terrace of almshouses. Generative and analogue design processes are applied to a range of coastal sites and programmes around the UK, with Dymchurch selected as a detailed case study.

21.3 Ajay Mohan, Y4 'The Denge Quarry Co-operative'. The project subverts the contemporary idea of the curated touristic experience; instead, meaning and purpose are derived from a mnemonic and evolving relationship with the ground. Extracted from a quarry, sand and gravel become entities that require repeated manipulation. Scattered urban artefacts in the desolate landscape begin to act as waypoints towards this new decentralised experimental laboratory.

21.4 Lewis Brown, Y4 'Casting Quantum Shingle'. The dynamic shingle landscape of Dungeness is charged with energy, pushed and pulled by geomorphic processes and quantum technologies that populate the flat terrain. An experimental flood-defence architecture is trialled along the coastline, in the shadow of two nuclear power stations. A performative construction sequence utilises uncertainty as a design methodology, harnessing the forces of the ocean and the air to carve inhabitation into the shingle bank.

21.7 Alp Amasya, Y4 'The Blue'. A park of film galleries that also offers filmmaker residencies, it is a place of pilgrimage for Derek Jarman, a filmmaker who lived in Dungeness. The project spatialises 'Jarmanesque' qualities, architecturally and filmically, that capture the relationship between time and landscape, using blue light as a generative sketching tool. The film park offers a biographical filmic museum for Derek Jarman.

21.8 Rolandas Markevicius, Y4 'Parametric Heritage'. By recognising the current preservation and planning policy failures within Dungeness, resulting in growing gentrification and the loss of the local community, new auto-generative methodologies of development are proposed. The project engages with concepts of pattern languages, data mapping and automated architecture towards forming a parametric heritage system for the development of a new regional architecture.

21.9–21.11 James Carden, Y5 'Guerrilla Film Festival'. The project speculates on complex issues of ownership in Dungeness. A guerrilla film festival challenges authorship of the filmic medium, relating film to the physicality of space. A versatile landscape, which projects unlimited opportunities through its physical filmic axis, unites all aspects of a festival into a performative procession through the Dungeness landscape.

21.12 Qingyuan Zhou, Y4 '=?'. A kindergarten located in Aarhus, Denmark, reflects the dynamic signal generated by a nearby anarchist group to keep active. Drawing similarities between kids and anarchist activists helps the group contest territories enforced by the government.

21.13 Yat Shun Tang, Y4 'Duality of Water Systems'. Bathhouse water can be categorised into two types: clean water for bathing and marsh mineral water for hydropower. Waters are carefully arranged with designated routes. The circulation of water is embedded using a heating and cooling feedback system – water enters different bath spaces at a specific temperature to fit various programmes.

21.14 Samuel Pierce, Y4 'The Observer Effect'. In physics, the observer effect is the disturbance of a system through the act of observation. This project explores the potentials of harnessing this disturbance within real-time rendering frameworks that transform measured presence from live Zoom calls and archived footage into form. Conceived as a cultural centre in Brighton, the developed framework presents a unique approach to participatory design through dynamic drawings and models that respond to the user.

21.15 Maria Eleni Petalidou, Y4 'DAP (Dungeness Art Path)'. An artist-residency scheme and creative hub interacts and merges with the landscape. Elements such as screens, façades and revolving platforms make use of light, colour and movement. The building volumes grow alongside a new path that gently curves along the shingle landscape. Dungeness' vast and open terrain make each volume unique in character, creating a continuous, yet ambiguous, spatial experience.

21.16 Kiran Kaur Basi, Y4 'RSPB Experimental Habitat Bank'. A hyper-dense habitat bank designed to increase the populations of red-listed birds. Applying principles from Boids theory, the scheme is designed using flocking algorithms to create landscapes, arranged at specific distances, suitable for much-needed nesting and roosting. Algorithms allow the project to be rolled out across the UK, creating habitat banks specific to the site that target particular species.

21.17 Zhi Tam, Y4 'Dungeness Seed Bank'. The seed bank protects future biodiversity by storing seeds in vaults and carrying out research in the conservation of plants. Located in Dungeness, the seed bank is situated on a nature reserve between a shingle beach and marsh pits. The design spatialises the satellite view through a series of scripts that explore colour and resolution using a pixel block system.

21.18 Carmen Kong, Y4 'Seasonal Museum'. The project translates weather data captured in Dungeness into vectors through digital computation. The museum is calibrated to the seasonal changes of the location and questions conventional linear readings of time within a curated space.

21.19 Paul-Andrei Burghelea, Y5 'End-User Experience'. The project explores how to integrate the by-products of social networks into the design process. It uses social network analysis of Twitter to shape the architecture of a fictitious traditional arts community centre, commissioned by The Prince's Foundation, in the Leamouth Peninsula in London.

21.20 Shu Min (Michelle) Hoe, Y5 'A Bird Watcher's Retreat'. The project is conceived around the idea of framing small precise moments to create a space of timelessness and tranquillity. The design embodies and celebrates the passing of time to offer a place for rich encounters between humans and birds. The humble and low-key activity of birdwatching is transformed into a new experience that pushes the limits of seeing and understanding through its relationship to time.

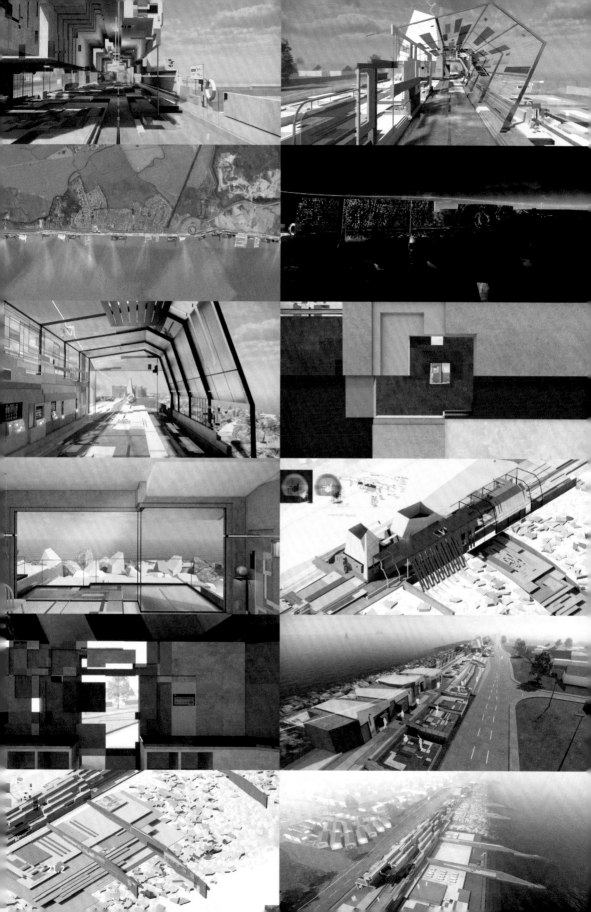

21.3

21.4

21.5

21.6

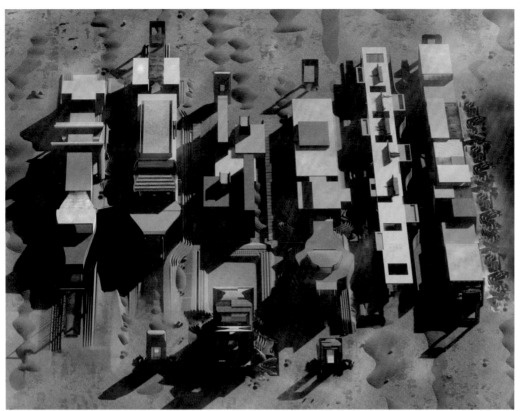

21.7

21.8

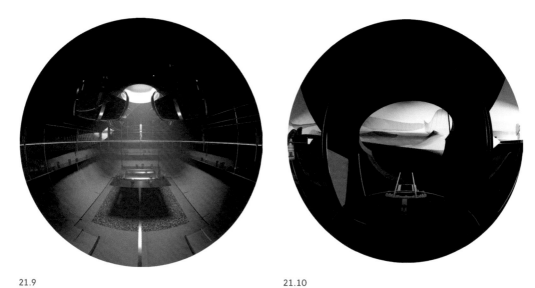

21.9   21.10

21.11

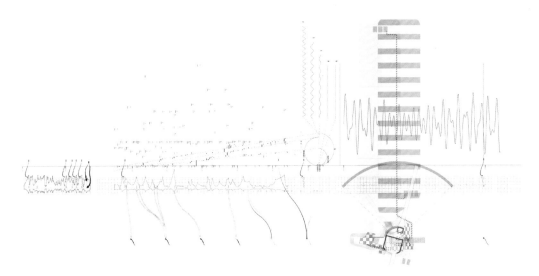

21.12

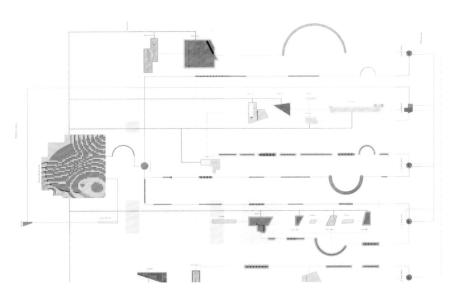

21.13

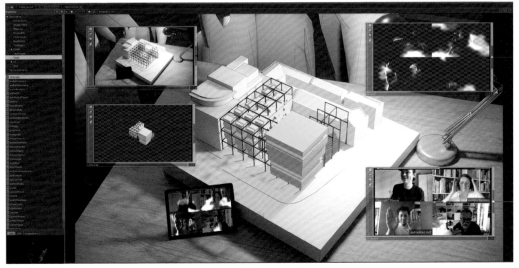

21.14

21.15

21.16

21.17

21.18

21.19

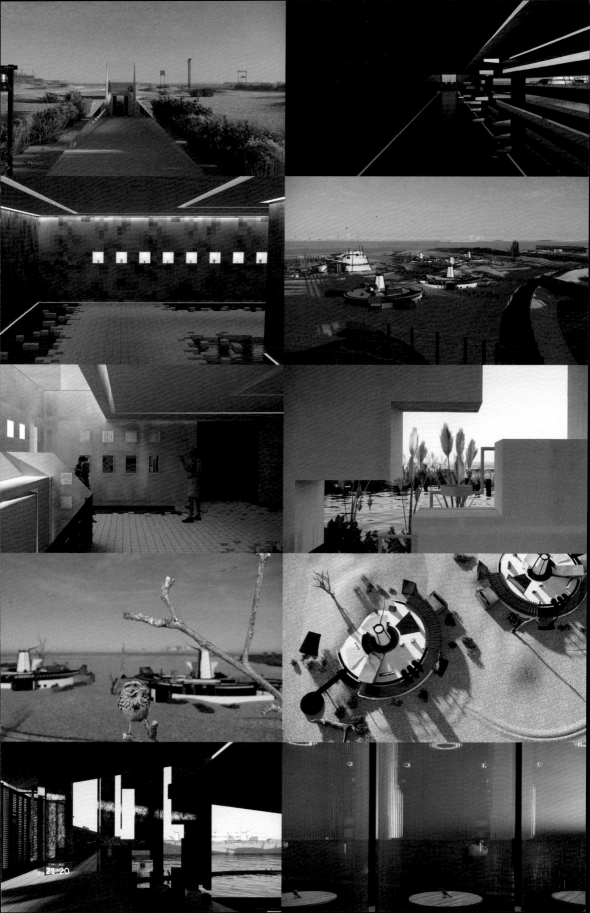

Shaking POPS

PG22

Izaskun Chinchilla Moreno, Daniel Ovalle Costal

In the 1950s, Som and Mies van der Rohe and Philip Johnson dodged Manhattan's strict zoning regulations by building on a small fraction of the sites for Lever House (1952) and the Seagram Building (1957), designating the remaining land as private plazas. Their success triggered a change in New York City's zoning regulations, linking a site's permitted floor area to the provision of open space accessible to the public.

The appearance of Privately Owned Public Spaces (POPS) reversed a trend that had seen the transfer of private open spaces in cities like London and Paris to public hands. POPS have since proliferated in cities across the Americas, Asia and Europe. The provision of POPS has become key to the planning and delivery of large development projects. In the case of London, areas that have undergone large-scale regeneration often feature these spaces, such as around Kings Cross and Tower Bridge.

There is no consensus on the urban value of POPS. Some argue that POPS provide urban equipment at better value for the taxpayer, while others argue that private property goes against the very essence of public space, which should guarantee that any form of social organisation can access the structures of power.

While POPS may generally look and function like public spaces, they are governed by their own rules that tend to benefit and promote a particular lifestyle, namely one based on consumerism. POPS are often found in areas with a high density of retail, with elements of hostile architecture appearing more often. As a result, activities that do not lead to the consumption of goods and services are discouraged or outright banned. The institutions that instigate such bans are often hidden from public scrutiny behind layers of corporate bureaucracy. The lifestyle bias of POPS leads to a degree of discrimination against those who do not fit, follow or cannot afford the prescribed lifestyle.

This year, PG22 researched and critically challenged POPS in multiple contexts around the world, and the lifestyles they promote. Based on this research, students developed design mechanisms to foster diversity and inclusion of different socioeconomic, physical or ethnic subjectivities across discrete public and private spaces and, ultimately, at an urban scale.

Year 4
Asli Aktu, Annabelle Blyton, James Ford, Luba Kuziw, Verena Leung, Hei Tung Michael Ng, Cheuk (Sharon) So, Olivia Trinder, Simon Wong

Year 5
Jason Brooker, Carrie Coningsby, Karin Gunnerek Rinqvist, Megan Makinson, Joseph Poston, Chun Wong

Thank you to our technical tutors and consultants: Gonzalo Coello de Portugal, Pablo Gugel, Nacho López Picasso, Roberto Marín Sampalo

Thesis supervisors: Jan Birksted, Eva Branscome, Gary Grant, Elain Harwood, Luke Lowings, Anna Mavrogianni

Thank you to our critics: Sarina da Costa Gómez, Karen Franck, Faye Greenwood, Alastair Johnson, Maggie Lan, Yuqi Liew, Jonah Luswata, Mireia Luzárraga, Matthieu Mereau, Lucy Moroney, Adam Peacock, Lucía C. Pérez Moreno, Gergana Popova, Guillermo Sánchez Sotés, Stefania Tsigkouni, Kate Woodcock-Fowles

22.1 Jason Brooker, Y5 'The Institute of Lost Craft'. The project seeks to preserve and protect both tangible and intangible cultures, to aid the national identity of heritage sites during redevelopment processes. It takes the stance that traditional Victorian markets should be retained for their social purpose and can be adapted to allow traditional crafts, which once thrived off the market's footfall, to have a permanent home. Smithfield Market in London is used as a testbed to apply this theory.

22.2 Simon Wong, Y4 'Midnight Communes'. London's night-time economy is one of the most vibrant in the UK. Many of its workers, however, have become marginalised, with their wellbeing neglected by employers and public bodies. The 'Midnight Communes' is a pilot programme, located in Marble Arch, initiated by the Night Time Commission. The scheme is designed to provide support and relief to night-time workers between, before and after their shifts.

22.3–22.4 Carrie Coningsby, Y5 'Hydrosocial Cities'. The project utilises the contradictory logic of privately owned public spaces and applies it to London's privately owned water network, arguing that there are elements that should be made available to the public. The result is a multi-scalar design process that aims to 'resocialise' water within the public spaces of the ongoing masterplan for Greenwich Peninsula.

22.5–22.6 James Ford, Y4 'Festival Pier'. The research focusses on the rewilding of the banks of the River Thames and how the seasonality of nature can help to transform the role of transport in people's lives. Developing a more natural system of transition throughout the city, 'Festival Pier' speculates on how Transport for London's annual target of 20 million river bus journeys by 2035 can be achieved. Integrating the historic Thames wetland ecology into the river bus boarding process helps reconnect London with the river.

22.7–22.8 Luba Kuziw, Y4 'The Ciudad Elephante'. An investigation into the redevelopment of the Elephant and Castle shopping centre in South East London. As a result of the development, it came to light that local residents and business owners were being unfairly treated. The project proposes a new home for the local Latin American diaspora. A number of 'hubs' are placed around Elephant and Castle, all within 15-minute proximity of each other, creating a new neighbourhood where the community can converse and thrive without being obstructed by luxury high-rise apartments.

22.9 Joseph Poston, Y5 'Unifying Opulence'. The project is a headquarter building for a new union of finance workers that tackles the working conditions and practices of the high-stress financial industry in Canary Wharf. The programme focusses on three different users: industry workers, union workers and the public. The facilities challenge how each user operates while fostering a mentally engaging environment. Light is a prominent factor in spatial environments, used to challenge the perception of how workspaces engage users.

22.10 Annabelle Blyton, Y4 'Gasholder Theatre'. The project analyses privately owned public spaces in Kings Cross. Inspired by the Edinburgh Festival Fringe, it proposes to transform the outdoor public spaces of Kings Cross for art and performance initiatives. Gasholder No.8 is transformed from an underused park into a multifunctional entertainment space. The structure becomes the main formal art and performance space, sitting alongside the informal festival activities that happen across the site.

22.11–22.12 Megan Makinson, Y5 'Up Down. Back Front. The Now'. The project looks to densify a Victorian terraced street, applying a bottom-up approach. The houses are flipped, disrupting the Victorian typology and

the relationship between the public and private. Domestic labours are no longer forced into small hidden rooms at the back and a new second skin façade creates communal intra-private spaces, both for socialising and economising domestic living and work. Space is unlocked and families can expand and contract into the new streetscape. Shared living spaces are formed to replace underused spaces in private homes.

22.13 Verena Leung, Y4 'The Alley Commons'. The project explores an alternative to top-down urban renewal in Hong Kong. It proposes the regeneration of a street block of *tong laus* (old tenement houses) of multiple ownerships into a co-living complex. It substitutes the undesirable living conditions of subdivided units with refurbished co-living housing that surrounds a communal courtyard. The major move of the project is to re-engage the alleyway that has become an underused backyard space, overshadowed by the tenement's back staircases. Looking at the buildings collectively, redundant fire escape staircases are removed to widen the alleyway.

22.14 Chun Wong, Y5 'Mall City: Urban oasis'. Hong Kong has the highest density of shopping malls in the world. Malls are a major space for public gathering in the city, meaning retail environments play a crucial role in our daily life. The New Town Plaza mall is chosen as a prototype to develop *publicly* owned public spaces into an urban oasis. The project applies biophilic design principles to provide a new shopping experience that can reinvent the mall typology, while enhancing biodiversity across Hong Kong.

22.15 Olivia Trinder, Y4 'A Sitopia in Canary Wharf'. The project takes Jubilee Park in Canary Wharf as a template for an alternate masterplan that redefines corporate life. The existing masterplan and its manicured green spaces are replaced with a space that promotes slowness, employee health and wellbeing, and ecological awareness. The parks are to become inhabited with flora and food-centred biological and cultural diversity.

22.16–22.17 Asli Aktu, Y4 'Spitalfields Rooftoppings'. The project redevelops Fournier Street, formerly the home and workplace of the Spitalfields silk weavers. The scheme explores the ways existing buildings can be repurposed and transformed to better suit the users of today. 'Rooftoppings' creates domesticated community driven spaces, further extending the life span of the 18th-century buildings.

22.18 Karin Gunnerek Ringqvist, Y5 'Torsö Forest Campus'. Forests in Sweden are all subject to the 'right to roam'. Granting everyone equal right to freely enter privately owned land for recreation and exercise, the forest is an important social and cultural space. As a result of urbanisation a larger number of Sweden's forest owners are now urban residents. Living further away from their properties, these owners developed different values and experiences than is traditional. The project investigates what effect this demographic change might have on the forest as a social and cultural space and identifies strategies to bridge knowledge and culture gaps between newly urbanised and traditional forest owners.

22.2

22.3

22.4

22.5

22.6

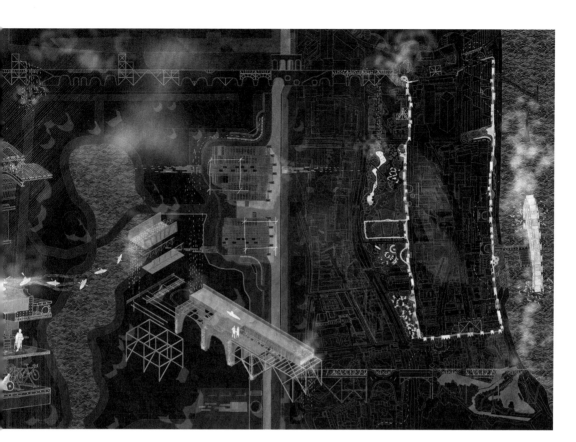

22.7

22.8

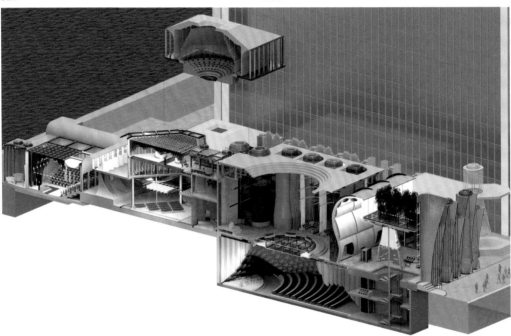

22.9

22.10

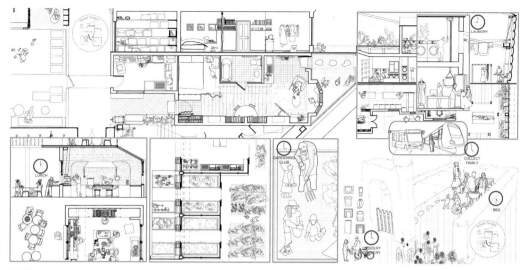

22.11

22.12

22.14

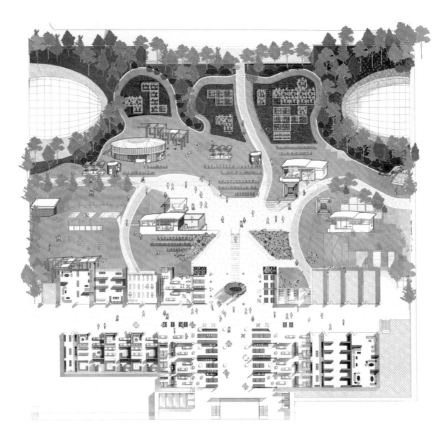

22.15

22.16

22.17

22.18

24.1

Wanderlust

Penelope Haralambidou, Michael Tite

PG24 is a group of architectural storytellers employing film, animation, VR and XR and physical modelling techniques to explore architecture's relationship with time.

This year we continued to address issues of climate change, by reconnecting the body with one of its most basic functions – walking. As the global pandemic upended our lives, we used walking as a primary method of engaging with and reclaiming the city and landscape.

Wanderlust has long been the source of inspiration of many writers and philosophers: Friedrich Nietzsche, Jean-Jacques Rousseau, Virginia Woolf, W.G. Sebald and Rebecca Solnit, amongst others. But, beyond poetry, walking is also linked to abstract mathematical thought, intrinsically related with gauging distance – by measuring units based on the size of the human (male) foot – and the origin of arithmetic calculation itself. Recently, walking itself has become intensely quantified, in number of steps, as an indicator of wellbeing.

We asked, how does wanderlust inform architectural design but also film? Architecture is not experienced as a static contemplation from a single point of view but as a cinematic journey that unfolds in time. A well-designed amble, e.g. the Guggenheim Museum in New York, or the bridging of an impossible passage, e.g. Tintagel Castle Bridge in Cornwall, can be the sole purpose of architecture, which can fulfill dreams of walking on water, e.g. Christo and Jean-Claude's *Floating Piers* (2016), or walking on air, e.g. Tomas Saraceno's *On Space Time Foam* (2012). Architecture itself can be taken out for a walk. In traditional Japanese festivals, Mikoshi shrines are transported within a district, activating collective space. Archigram's influential *Walking City* (c. 1960) can be seen in modern fables such as *Howl's Moving Castle* (2004) and *Mortal Engines* (2018). Furthermore, the representation of walking in the built environment led to inventions such as the dolly system and the Steadicam, which were key to the development of cinema. Advancements in immersive film, VR and XR are allowing this to evolve further; we can now construct a digital spatial overlay around the moving body that can be inhabited in real time.

Between wandering, marching and rambling we questioned issues of mobility, age, gender, race and disability, and studied architecture through the romantic exploratory hike, the habitual daily commute, the purposeful personal quest, the meandering flânerie, the protest, the adventurous expedition and the dedicated pilgrimage.

All of our projects built a new and dynamic design vocabulary, proposing new ecological modes of occupation that can foresee and withstand the needs of our dramatically changing world.

Vitika Agarwal, Jatiphak Boonmun, Kalliopi Bosini, Paris Gazzola, Gabriele Grassi, Holly Harbour, Carlota Nuñez-Barranco Vallejo, Tom Ushakov

Year 5
Camille Dunlop, Viktoria Fenyes, Alexander Fox, Maxim Goldau, Yee (Enoch) Liang, Elissavet Manou, Lingyun Qian, Issui Shioura, Matthew Taylor

Thank you to our design realisation tutor Kairo Baden-Powell

Thank you to our consultants: Krina Christopoulou, John Cruwys, Matt Lucraft, Sonia Magdziarz, Jerome Ng, Kevin Pollard, George Proud

Thesis supervisors: Edward Denison, Stephen Gage, Elise Hunchuck, Richard Martin, Niall McLaughlin, Guang Yu Ren, Oliver Wilton

Thank you to our critics: Kairo Baden-Powell, Nat Chard, Krina Christopoulou, John Cruwys, Kate Davies, Pedro Gil-Quintero, Jessica In, Suzanne Isa, Chee-Kit Lai, Stefan Lengen, Matt Lucraft, Keiichi Matsuda, Kevin Pollard, Sophia Psarra, Nick Shackleton, Sayan Skandarajah, Jasper Stevens, Jerry Tate, Manuel Toledo, Stefania Tsigkouni, Tim Waterman, Fiona Zisch

24.1 Yee (Enoch) Liang, Y5 'A New New Town'. The allegorical film narrates Hong Kong's collective consciousness through the city's New Town Plaza mall. The film follows a boy who enters a surreal parallel dimension of New Town Plaza and wanders through its three spaces. These spaces explore remembering the past, savouring the present and building towards the future. The three spaces act as architectural characters that spatially guide the boy to rediscover his lost childhood and innocence, as a kind of coming-of-age journey in reverse. Allegorically, the boy's journey represents Hong Konger's rediscovery of their love towards the city and their perishing dream to preserve an expiring identity and reclaim a right to the city. Universally, it is a story that encourages one to break free from worldly social expectations and forge a future according to your beliefs.

24.2 Lingyun Qian, Y5 'Hundred Year Forest Wall'. Addressing China's commitment to be carbon neutral by 2060, the project is a radical proposal for Beijing – a slow transformation of the old, now lost, city wall site, from the current ring road into a vibrant 'forest wall'. Conceived as an enormous piece of ecological infrastructure, the proposal reorders the city over a long time period, to send a message of how seriously China takes the environmental crisis. The project's main theme is creating nature through human intervention within a multi-scale, cross-generational planning framework. Adaptable, mobile and elevated structures are designed to allow the forest and the road to morph, and to form a ceremonial architecture that resembles the old gates and city wall. As we stand at the precipice of environmental failure, the project is a call-to-arms that levers political power and the will of the collective, for the benefit of future generations.

24.3–24.5 Issui Shioura, Y5 'Ephemeral Preservation'. The film depicts the world of Sampo, a real-life mobile living unit collective that explores a method for disaster preparation in Japan. The project introduces a series of interconnected interventions that operate on a variety of scales: from the 'Tact' mobile expandable kit to the 'MoC' mobile cell, and the *kura* (storehouse) to the *mikoshi* (portable shrine), each one resists the idea of fixity, drawing on the idea of the void space and historic Japanese architectural modes. Influenced by slacker culture and Mike Figgis' *Timecode* (2000), the film is realised as a lo-fi, countercultural rallying cry, where the collective acts of making, gathering, building, remembering (and partying) try to flow with the natural world, rather than create resistive structures. The film is part documentary, part music video; a freestyle rap drives the form of the film. It takes an optimistic attitude and approach to community, rather than built hardware, and offers a new kind of anticipatory, participatory, free-flowing architecture.

24.6 Matthew Taylor, Y5 'Bathhouse of Spiritual Purity'. Located in and around the Hie Shrine in the Chiyoda ward of Tokyo, the bathhouse is conceived as a bridge between the real and the divine – an ecological realm where time and gravity play to different rules. Influenced through a personal affiliation with Japan and Shintoism, the project seeks out a new eco-animistic inhabitation for the 21st century and beyond. The design lies between architecture and mythical storytelling, utilising the boundless potentials of animistic values to form an alternative architecture of co-existence. The project gives partial design control to procedural software, conceived as 'digital spirits' that guide us on a sacred design journey. From the animations of Studio Ghibli to the paintings of Hieronymus Bosch, and decay simulations to Kami iconography, the final film promotes messages of environmentalism and animistic co-existence.

24.7–24.9 Maxim Goldau, Y5 'Matryoshka Tempelhof'. By applying concepts of 'Shearing Layers' and 'Support & Infills' this housing project inhabits the hangars of the former Tempelhof Airport in Berlin, creating the necessary shelter for a participatory architecture. The project examines how better quality, low-tech, inclusive environments might benefit us all. By questioning the humble functions and elements in our homes, it explores to what extent services and furniture can take on architectural roles by activating a mobile form of construction. The design is realised through a series of inventive installation-like objects that are gradually adapted and changed until they become occupiable interiors. The film gives voice to the disembodied view of the articulated service infrastructure, which together with the occupant become collaborators in a reusable and adaptive architecture.

24.10 Alexander Fox, Y5 'Harbouring the Exoskeleton'. This science fiction allegory calls for the preservation of biodiversity, while challenging human interference. Learning from insect life cycles, the architecture takes three forms. In the first, a land train of experimental laboratories, resembling larva or a caterpillar, roams across terrains before decoupling and expanding into inflated biomes, similar to pupa, creating an idyllic habitat, safe from predators, for the reproduction of insects and providing opportunity for scientists to observe. Secondly, the building's AI system, HIVE (Holistic Insect Vehicular Experiment), controls the architecture to create monolithic structures that house insects, while also tethering the inflatables in place. In the final phase, the building goes through a process of ecdysis – the shedding of old skin – and rebirth. The building rejects the human operators it houses and becomes sentient; a catalyst for environmental regeneration.

24.11–24.14 Camille Dunlop, Y5 'Arboreal'. The project operates at the intersection of body, forest and city. 'Arboreal' has two sites: the dance is digitally recorded in the Swedish Tyresta National Park forest and is then translated into a dedicated dance hall in Stockholm. The body-in-motion conducts an architectural act between the wilderness and the city, and the choreography becomes a constituent part of a performing architecture. The building also performs through an adaptable, dynamic and ever-shifting system controlled by the performers. Sited in the centre of the city, tree-like columns host swaying translucent fabrics that blend the building into the urban environment. Motion-capture technology is a key part of the research methodology and the programme. While mobility entangles all living beings within the Anthropocene, digital measures of movement create architectural dualities that challenge human-centric space.

24.15 Elissavet Manou, Y5 'Not Set in Stone'. The project imagines the establishment of a multi-generational settlement on the windy Greek island of Tinos. 'Not Set in Stone' explores the concept of a 'palindromic' construction process that results in a dual green marble architecture. One is a positive, additive construction that relates to the intimate and humdrum everyday life through the creation of a notional settlement, the other is a negative, subtractive carving-out of a rock temple in the quarry that reflects the 'sublime' essence of Tinos. The dialogue between the two programmes and sites explores an alternative way of living – one that harnesses the wind, and questions the nuclear family typology, the traditional role of women and ideas of the sublime. Exploring ideas of longevity, handcraft, technological advancements and the Tinian vernacular, the scheme creates a tension between the everyday and the extraordinary.

24.2

24.3

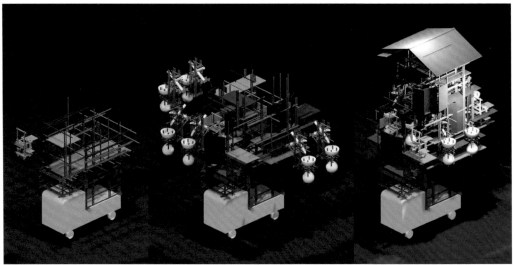

24.4

24.5

24.6

24.7

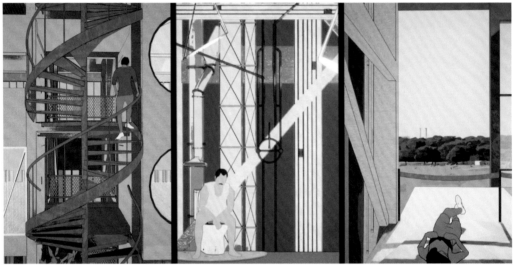

24.8

24.9

24.11

24.12

24.13

24.14

25.1

Decadent Ecologies PG25

Nat Chard, Emma-Kate Matthews

PG25 helps students develop their own methods of practice, concentrating on finding a resonance between the means of representation in design, where the media they invent or appropriate either hold or provide a critical resistance to their architectural ideas. We see this as parallel to the way in which ideas can be made present through the careful and inventive application of materials and processes when building architecture.

Normally, we start the year by building a research project. These range from surveying items to understand a site on the terms of each student to inventions that project an idea onto a site at full scale, or building an instrument that invents or takes possession of a medium. This year, due to the Covid-19 lockdown restrictions and limited access to the workshops, this has not been possible. Despite this, many students developed their own voice through whatever was available at home.

We started the year with the observation that most of the methods used to address climate change operate on the same terms as the actions that caused the difficulties in the first place: reductive systems of problem solving that ignore the larger and more diverse ecologies in which we are intertwined. We therefore did not set out to establish problems and solutions. Rather, we asked about the diverse influences that play on the built environment and how architecture discusses their simultaneous differences. We were interested in how the cessation of activity during lockdown revealed new opportunities, e.g. seismologists listening to the Earth without so much human noise, and aspects of our lives that we had taken for granted, e.g. the accuracy of weather forecasts due to data collected by commercial flights.

Such a broad ecology is synonymous with the way architecture gathers diverse concerns and needs. We embarked on the work by looking at examples that took in the most surprising differences of discipline or need. Our sites were mostly in Brighton and the South Downs, East Sussex. We examined how long-term knowledge of the use of local materials, such as flint and chalk, was built into the vernacular architecture.

As is typical in the unit, each student took the work in their own direction. Projects looked at a range of connections between social groups in the city, issues of trespassing, new landscapes, connecting diverse groups with local knowledge to more disciplinary researchers, and playing out the pleasures of geomorphological movement. Despite the circumstances, students developed their own means of studying their territory.

Year 4
Hannah Anderson, George Barnes, Samuel Beattie, Grant Beaumont, George Brazier, Eleanor Evason, Bessie Holloway Davies, Sindija Skilta, Adam West

Year 5
Conor Clarke, Abigail Cotgrove, Arthur Harmsworth, Zachary David Higson, Emmeline Kos, Louis Peralta, Joel Saldeck, Barry Wong

Thank you to our technical tutors and consultants: Sinéad Conneely, Patch Dobson-Pérez, Egmontas Geras, Jerry Tate, Sal Wilson

Thesis supervisors: Amica Dall, Christophe Gérard, Polly Gould, Thomas Pearce, Simon Withers

Thank you to our critics: Alessandro Ayuso, Kirsty Badenoch, Barbara-Ann Campbell-Lange, Bryan Cantley, Peter Cook, James Craig, Penelope Haralambidou, Florian Köhl, Perry Kulper, Ifigeneia Liangi, Yeoryia Manolopoulou, Ben McDonnell, Rocky, Mark Ruthven, Jerry Tate

25.1–25.3 **Joel Saldeck, Y5** 'Prosthetic Material Realities'.
One of a number of study puppets built to help form an
architecture. Models were built around (and cast off)
the puppets and sets of furniture with various degrees
of specific fit (dimensionally and conceptually).

25.4–25.5 **Zachary David Higson, Y5** 'Sites of Flux'.
The project responds to working in an aggregate quarry
where the lease elapses if a certain amount of material is
not moved each year. It proposes a reconfiguration of the
ground for various events and the architecture provides
the infrastructure.

25.6 **Samuel Beattie, Y4** 'Stowed Away'. A building for
people who, like stowaways, want to belong to another
place. The project was evolved using drawing methods
incorporating a flatbed scanner and geological material
from the site.

25.7–25.9 **Abigail Cotgrove, Y5** 'Amphibious Bodies'.
The project explores the spatial equivalent of
amphibiousness: having two modes of existence of
doubtful nature. The building is situated between the
city and a nudist beach in Brighton and plays out
intermediate sites of belonging to both territories.

25.10–25.11 **Hannah Anderson, Y4** 'Brills Lane Hotel'.
An unfolded elevation of a refurbished seafront hotel
in Brighton. Its interior world is concealed, yet is partly
given away, by the architectural drapery that makes up
the bedrooms and other parts of the hotel, as well as
the way its life is reflected in the walls of the adjacent
buildings. A cutaway drawing depicts two bedrooms
that can be laundered in their entirety between stays.
The folds and thickness of the drapery offers varying
degrees of modesty for the guests.

25.12 **Grant Beaumont, Y4** 'Interloper'. Unfolded section
of a boatyard partly made of reused hulls from old
boats. It is a project thick with displaced attributes
learned from interpolated shadows that were confused
about their origin.

25.13–25.14 **Adam West, Y4** 'Brighton Marina Coastal
Research Facility'. View of the building in a storm.
The project is a multi-programmed building that
entices diverse groups with local knowledge
to organically share their wisdom about the site
with others.

25.15 **Bessie Holloway Davies, Y4** 'Organic Resonance'.
In today's society, time is a precious commodity.
There is a possibility of losing oneself in a moment
of time through the medium of sound. The spatial
qualities of a place change with our perception of
sound and silence. A cymatics device was constructed,
using site-recorded frequencies, quarried chalk and
pigments to investigate and express sonic temporality.

25.16 **Conor Clarke, Y5** 'Institute of Trespassing and
Land Politics'. Stainless steel building shells made on
the English wheel, a metalworking tool that produces
compound curves from flat sheets of metal.

25.17 **George Brazier, Y4** 'A Beacon of Fragility'. An ever
evolving and decaying set of buildings created from
chalk, flint, clay and trees, made in collaboration with
a robot and a group of craftspeople local to the site.

25.18 **George Barnes, Y4** 'The Excavation of the Chalk
Spa'. The project explores how architecture can
propagate plausibility. The chalk stream spa was
designed by painting a premonition of the project in
various thicknesses of paint and then covering this with a
slurry of chalk from the site that is critically excavated to
reveal parts of the premonition.

25.19 **Arthur Harmsworth, Y5** 'Playing Amongst the Wilds'.
The project plays out the space of indifferent acceptance
and partial dependency between godwits, deer, people
fishing and wildlife researchers.

25.20 **Sindija Skilta, Y4** 'An Active Ground'. The project
explores how architecture can work with the
geomorphological shifts in the ground and seasonal
variations, including flooding, rather than resist them.
Various joints were invented and manufactured to play
out these accommodations.

25.21 **Barry Wong, Y5** 'Lost Between Worlds'. The project
asks how spatial and temporal uncertainties can be
created for visitors to a construction on Brighton Beach.

25.22–25.23 **Eleanor Evason, Y4** 'Borrowed Ground'.
An infrastructure for a set of quarry caves built to support
a range of activities and performances. A smaller building
lightly touches the caves.

25.24–25.25 **Emmeline Kos, Y5** 'Quarry the City'.
The project asks how the city can be more like a wild
landscape. It constructs a new ground over Brighton
with interstices that absorb and expand on the existing
programmes within the city. As the new landscape takes
over, it quarries material from parts of the existing city to
expand its reach.

25.2

25.3

25.4

25.5

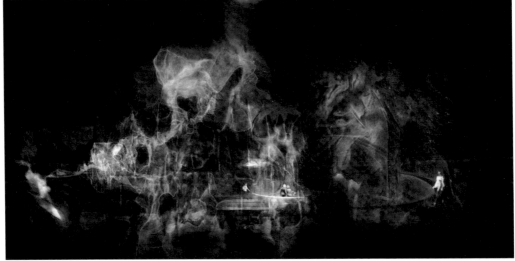

25.6

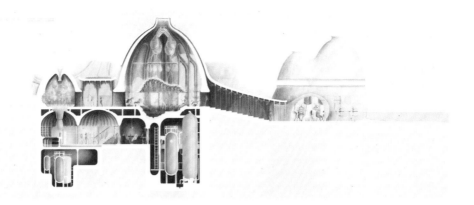

25.7

25.8

25.9

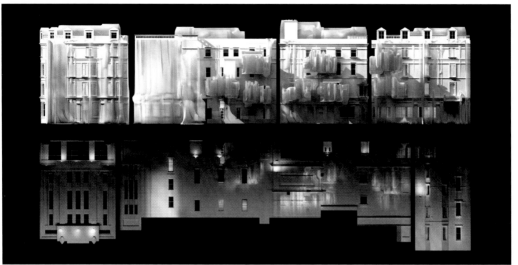

25.10

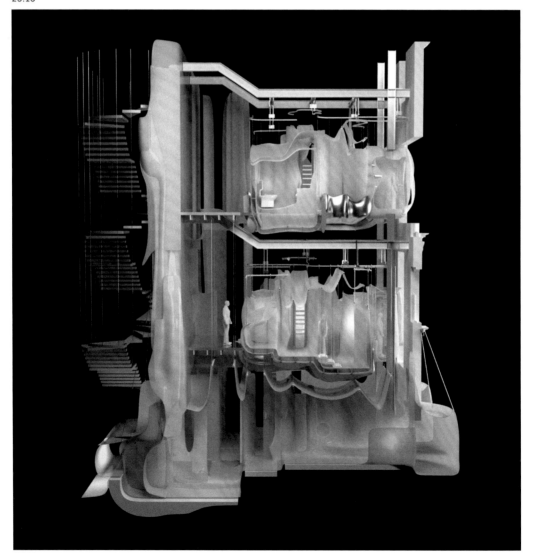

25.11

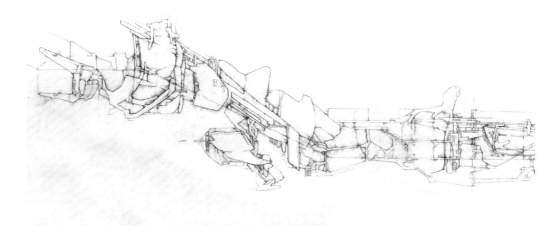

25.12

25.13

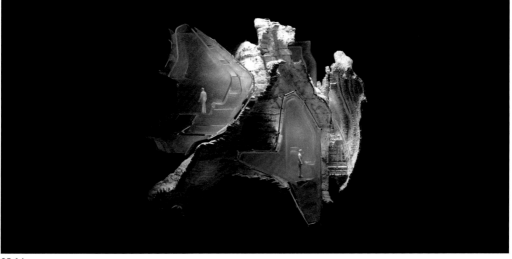

25.14

25.15

25.16

25.17

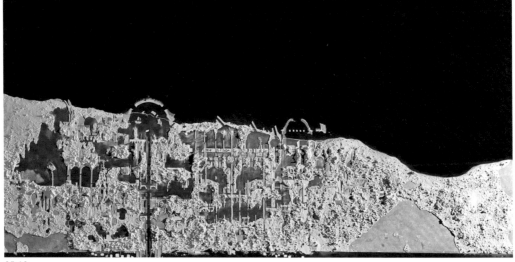

25.18

25.19

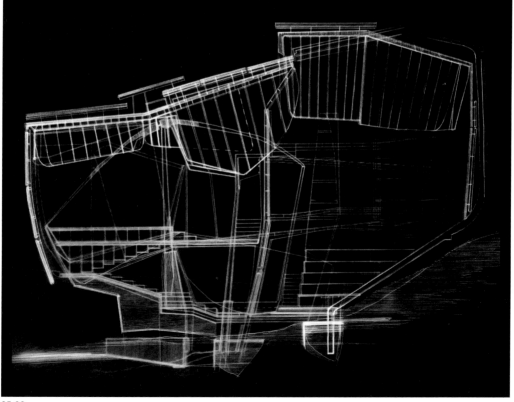

25.20

25.21

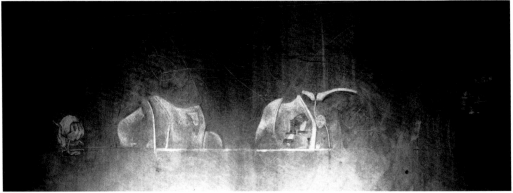

25.22

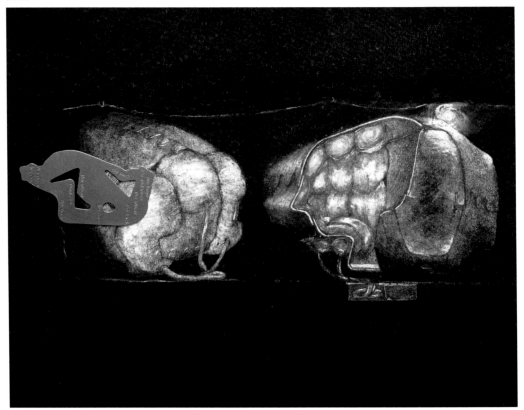

25.23

25.24

25.25

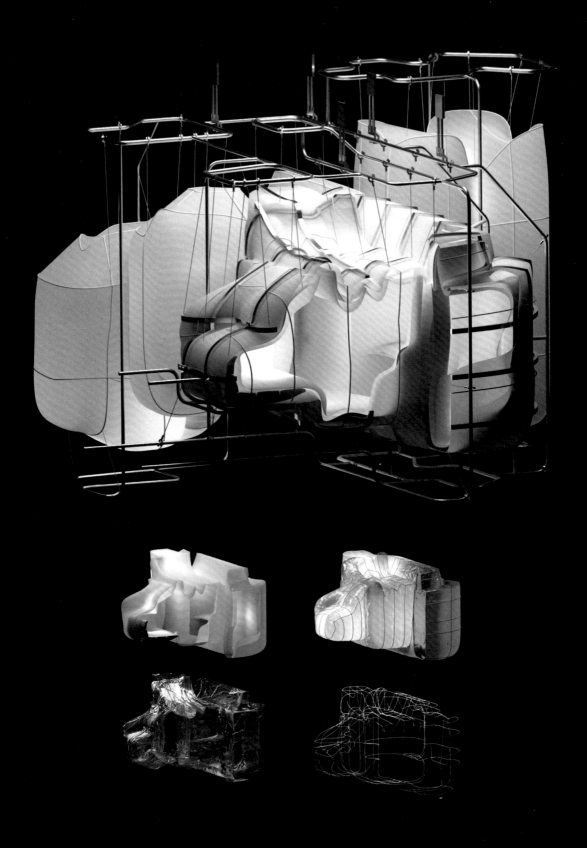

Design Realisation

Year 4

Module Coordinators:
Pedro Gil-Quintero, Stefan Lengen

Design Realisation provides an opportunity for all Year 4 Architecture MArch students to consider how buildings are designed, constructed and delivered. It provides a framework to facilitate experimentation in the design of buildings, and encourages the interrogation and disruption of technical ideas and principles. Students propose their ideas at a variety of scales and represent them using drawings, diagrams, animations, physical models and 3D digital models. They are encouraged to take risks in their design thinking and strategy.

The module bridges the worlds of academia and practice, engaging with many renowned design practices and consultancies. A dedicated practice-based architect, structural engineer and environmental engineer support each design unit, working individually with students to develop their work throughout the module.

This unprecedented year generated a magnificent range of projects that test, explore and innovate across a wide spectrum of principles and mediums. Students embraced the challenges of online learning and produced an array of innovative work that pushes the boundaries of technical and professional practice disciplines. Projects include inventive structural systems, environmental strategies, buildings for challenging sites, community engagement proposals, infrastructure projects and entrepreneurial proposals, to name but a few.

Thanks to our structural consultants Atelier Ten and Max Fordham who have worked with individual students to realise their projects; Sal Wilson, environmental consultant to all design units; and to our practice tutors for their remarkable commitment and dedication.

Lecturers
Matthew Barnett Howland, Klaus Bollinger, Nat Chard, Fenella Collingridge, Robin Cross, Jenna De Leon, Pedro Gil-Quintero, Jan Güell, Jan Kattein, Stefan Lengen, Ho-Yin Ng, Hareth Pochee, Alistair Shaw, Gordon Talbot, Jose Torero Cullen, Bob Treadwell, Emmanuel Vercruysse, Mark West, Rae Whittow-Williams, Oliver Wilton

Practice Tutors
PG10 Jonathan Kaminsky (Hawkins\Brown)
PG11 Rhys Cannon (Gruff Architects)
PG12 James Hampton (New Makers Bureau)
PG13 Nick Wood (How About Studio)
PG14 Jakub Klaska (The Bartlett, UCL)
PG15 Martin Sagar
PG16 Will Jefferies (Rogers Stirk Harbour + Partners)
PG17 James Daykin (Daykin Marshall Studio)
PG18 Robert Haworth (Lineworks Architects), Anna Woodeson (LTS Architects)
PG20 David Edwards (Dave Edwards Design Ltd)
PG21 Tom Holberton (The Bartlett, UCL)
PG22 Gonzalo Coello de Portugal (Binom Architects)
PG24 Kairo Baden-Powell (WilkinsonEyre)
PG25 Jerry Tate (Tate Harmer)

Image: Hannah Anderson, PG25, 'Brills Lane Hotel, Brighton'. The research explores an architecture of negotiated awareness; heightening one's sensitivity to another's presence in space. Taking form as a Hotel on Brighton's seafront, the project uses fabric to investigate the frontstage/backstage relationship between guests and staff – creating a curious spatial mediation between them.

Advanced Architectural Studies

Year 4

Module Coordinator: Tania Sengupta

The Advanced Architectural Studies module in the first year of the MArch Architecture programme focusses on architectural histories and theories. Here we reflect on architecture within a broader, critical, intellectual and contextual field – simultaneously producing and being produced by it. We look at architecture's interfaces with other knowledge fields – from the scientific and technological to the social sciences and the humanities. We straddle empirics and theory, design and history, the iconic and the everyday.

The module seeks to engage students with architectural history and theory as a critical approach to augment design, as a parallel domain to test out approaches or as a discrete or autonomous domain of architectural engagement. It focusses on three key aspects: first, a reflective, critical and analytical approach; second, research instinct and exploratory methods and research as a form of practice; and third, skills of synthesis, writing and articulation. It also acts as foundational ground for the students' final year thesis.

Our lecture series, entitled 'Critical Frames', covered the following themes this year: 'Learning from Disorder', 'Of Naming and Tastemaking', 'The City as Memory', 'Alternative Realities', 'In Other Voices' and 'Two Readings of Materiality'. These lectures were accompanied by the heart of the module, which is a set of themed seminars. The seminars straddle, geographically, the architectural histories and theories of multiple global contexts, and, thematically, buildings, urbanism, landscapes, design, art, ecology and climate crisis, politics, activism, technology, production, representation, spatial and material cultures, public participation, urban regeneration, phenomenology, historiography and feminist and decolonial approaches. At the end, drawing upon the seminars and lectures, the students formulate a critical enquiry around a topic of their choice and produce a 4,500-word essay.

Teaching Assistants
Farbod Afshar Bakeshloo,
Adam Walls

2020–21 Seminars
Insurgent Cities, Sabina Andron
Architecture + Film, Christophe Gérard
U-topographics: Utopic journeys into postmodern culture, Robin Wilson
Architecture and The People, Daisy Froud
Feminist Approaches to Space and Text, Edwina Attlee
Senses and the City, Jacob Paskins
Green New Dialogues, Jon Goodbun
Architecture as Spatial and Cultural Practice, Tania Sengupta
Architecture, Art and the City, Eva Branscome
Architectural Splendour: The history and theory of ornament 1750–2020, Oliver Domeisen
Architecture and the Image of Decay, Paul Dobraszczyk
The Dialogic Imagination: Landship and practices of worlding, Tim Waterman

The Peculiarity of the Chinese: The evolution of the cloud

Kai Farzád Lee
Tutor: Oliver Domeisen

Abstract: In *The Grammar of Ornaments*, Victorian architect and design theorist Owen Jones (1809-74) categorised more than a thousand ornaments of different cultural periods exhibited in the Great Exhibition, to demonstrate that 'certain general laws appear to reign independently of the individual peculiarities of each.'[1] In this taxonomy of ornamental styles, he curiously exclaimed that '... the Chinese are totally unimaginative' and 'had not the power of dealing with conventional ornamental form'.

The British looting of the Qing Empire later gave Jones access to an increased number of art samples from China, which prompted him to dedicate an entire book to the study of Chinese ornaments. Here he retracted his previously unfavourable opinions and declared that Chinese ornaments equally obeyed his universal principles of ornamental forms. Nevertheless, a closer reading of this second book still shows his dissatisfaction with the supra-realistic representation of natural objects, such as the recurring bats, bamboos, peonies, pine and prunes found on artefacts. The first part of this essay, therefore, investigates the figurative characteristic of Chinese ornaments of the Ming and Qing dynasties in particular and attributes it to a predominantly linguistic interpretation of ornaments, which embalms the motifs in a rigid system of symbolism, and renders them incapable for further artistic development.

The Chinese justifiably take pride in the diversity of literary meanings and homophonic allusions associated with these ornamental motifs. However, the propensity of employing a nationalistic art-historical agenda calls for a historical examination of Chinese ornaments. The second part of this essay thus picks up what Austrian art historian Alois Riegl mentioned but avoided discussing in his book *Stilfragen* (1893): the Chinese origins of a particular motif on Persian rugs and other Oriental artefacts, the 'cloudband'.

Utilising Riegl's own methodology of establishing a historical theory of ornament's evolution in an attempt to combat the materialist and symbolist interpretations of his day, this essay traces the dynamic evolution of the cloud motif from Zhou bronzes to Han silk, from a coffin in Hunan to the Buddhist temples of Yungang, Shanxi. What comes to light is the transcultural breeding of ornamental motifs, both among the different Chinese dynasties and between the Chinese and the West.

As ornaments flee the hegemonic persecution of modernism and are torn in the postmodern struggle for idiosyncratic identities in our day, perhaps an appreciation of its transcultural genesis will lead to the next stage of its evolution.

Image: The unmistakable curls of the cloud motif lend any decorated item its 'Chineseness'. Image Source: Plate XXIV from Owen Jones' *Examples of Chinese Ornament* (1867).
1. Owen Jones (2016), *The Grammar of Ornament* (S.I.: Girard & Stewart).

Hermetically Sealed: An analysis of the homogeneous and heterogeneous methods of ecological preservation presented in canned food & Biosphere II
Samuel Pierce
Tutor: Tim Waterman

Abstract: Hermetic seals provide stability to the everyday. Supermarket shelves are stocked with perfectly preserved foods, canned and vacuum-sealed, their contents frozen in an abiotic stasis. Emergence of the air-borne transmission of Covid-19 ignited a need for protective boundaries, the infected quarantined and society disbanded into bubbles filled with panic-bought apocalyptic supplies.

The contemporary built environment relies on specificity to provide comfort and efficiency. Just as canned food relies on perfectly balanced temperature and humidity to prevent natural decay, Le Corbusier believed the machine age could provide stability through 'exact air'.[1] Both present a hermetically sealed utopia of sterile closed air circuits with consistent internal pest-free conditions.

In 1991 an alternative air-tight utopia was enacted. Sealed away for two years in a 3.15-acre greenhouse in the Arizona desert, eight women and men conducted an ecological experiment. The isolated crew survived unaided amongst a maximally biodiverse and self-sufficient ecosystem, designed and named as the spiritual successor to Earth's own heterogeneous life-support system, Biosphere II. In contrast to the sealed tin can's exclusive environment, Biosphere II's biomes were over-packed with flora and fauna beyond their natural capacity, assuming a self-organising ecosystem, a cathedral to Gaia.[2]

My research analyses these two contrasting scales, approaches and utopian responses to ecological preservation, tracing their apocalyptic origins and comparing their technocentric cornucopias through Lyman Tower Sargent's definition of utopianism. Then, following Peter Sloterdijk's description of Western metaphysics as an inherently spatial and immunological project, I explore their methods of sphere-formation, reflecting on the contrasting egos and shared delusions embodied in their controlled interiors. Finally, using Laura Alice Watt's analyses of the conservationist movement in the US National Park Service, I highlight the paradoxical effects of their approach to preservation.

In conclusion my paper begins to make a case for an alternative, 'sympoietic' utopia – one free from self-defined airtight boundaries that deny the reality of an alternative. With porous tissues and open edges, the free passage of air becomes an integral part of its survival. Like the necessity of airflow in the process of fermentation, the utopia should remain 'leaky'.

Image: Model of Biosphere II, assembled from an assortment of tin cans, 2021.

1. Le Corbusier (1967), *The Radiant City: Elements of a doctrine of urbanism to be used as the basis of our machine-age civilization* (New York: Orion Press), p42.
2. Jane Poynter (2006), *The Human Experiment: Two years and twenty minutes inside Biosphere 2* (New York: Thunder's Mouth Press), p75.

Ritual and Space in Modernity: Emergent ecological rituals in the modern everyday
Annabelle Tan Kai Lin
Tutor: Tania Sengupta

Abstract: Ritual study has largely undervalued the significance of modernity and its conditions to ritual practice, especially in reference to architecture as a tool for ritualisation on a mass scale. This has allowed modern architecture's ritual power to go unquestioned while it continues to structure and determine everyday socio-cultural beliefs and practices. This essay traces the evolution of critical 'ritual modes' throughout the modern age, using the frame of everyday life. Through this, I aim to uncover the dialogical relation between architecture, ritual practice and dominant belief systems, traversing the public and private realms.

Fordism catalysed the emergence of a Functionalist mode of ritual, born from the linear rhythms of the assembly line. Factories and machinery regimented bodily movement and gestures in the public realm, while standardised housing design segregated functions of the home in a similarly mechanical way. In our current everyday, most of us still perform our daily rituals in housing arrangements embedded with vestigial remnants of the Functional belief, embodying its beliefs with each 'spontaneous' ritualised action.

The working class resisted the alienation caused by mass production labouring in the domain of the factory with mass consumption in the private domestic realm, creating richly decorated, ornate interiors with a myriad of commodities. Individuals found new agency in transforming their private spaces to pursue the belief of self and identity as constructed by commodity. But again, public spaces like the shopping mall provided the dominant meanings and symbols in this belief system.

Finally, an emerging ecological mode of ritual is investigated in this essay as an evolutionary product of the previous modes, looking particularly at urban ecological rituals like recycling. However, differentiating characteristics between this nascent or emergent mode and its predecessors can be observed when these newly invented rituals are seen as a whole habitus. I have used the case study of the Skip Garden in London to analyse how spatial and ritual practice entwine to promote ecological thinking. In the age of the Anthropocene, modern ritual is reinvestigated here to understand architecture's significance in propagating and nurturing new ecological ritual practices for the future.

Image: Ritual modes of modernity, Oxford Science Archive; Fordist, (post-Fordist) consumerism, *Material World* by Peter Menzel, 1994; and the emergent ecological, author's own.

Thesis

Year 5

Robin Wilson, Oliver Wilton

The thesis enables Year 5 Architecture MArch students to research, develop and define the basis for their work, addressing architecture and relevant related disciplines such as environmental design, humanities, engineering, cultural theory, manufacturing, anthropology, computation, the visual arts, physical or social sciences and urbanism.

   The year starts with a short research methods study. Students then develop individual research proposals which are reviewed and discussed with module coordinators and design tutors. Following review, students proceed to undertake their research in depth, supported by specialist tutors who are individually allocated based on each student's stated research question and proposed methodology. The result is a study of 9,000 words or equivalent, that documents relevant research questions, contexts, activities and outcomes.

   The thesis is an inventive, critical and directed research activity that augments the work students undertake in the design studio. The symbiotic relationship between thesis and design varies from evident and explicit to being situated more broadly in a wider sphere of intellectual interest. The thesis typically includes one or more propositional elements such as discursive argumentation, the development of a design hypothesis or strategy, or the development and testing of a series of design components and assemblies in relation to a specific line of inquiry or interest.

   We anticipate that a number of theses from this year's academic cohort will be developed into external publications or projects.

Thesis Tutors
Hector Altamirano, Alessandro Ayuso, Andy Barnett, Matthew Barnett Howland, Carolina Bartram, Paul Bavister, Jan Birksted, Roberto Bottazzi, Eva Branscome, Brent Carnell, Mollie Claypool, Amica Dall, Gillian Darley, Edward Denison, Paul Dobraszczyk, Oliver Domeisen, Murray Fraser, Daisy Froud, Stephen Gage, Christophe Gérard, Stelios Giamarelos, Polly Gould, Gary Grant, Elain Harwood, Elise Hunchuck, Jan Kattein, Zoe Laughlin, Luke Lowings, Abel Maciel, Richard Martin, Anna Mavrogianni, Claire McAndrew, Niall McLaughlin, Shaun Murray, Thomas Pearce, Guang Yu Ren, David Rudlin, Tania Sengupta, Michael Stacey, Iulia Statica, Robin Wilson, Oliver Wilton, Simon Withers, Stamatis Zografos

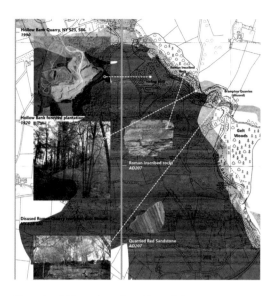

Transient Mapping: An atlas of the anthropogenic landscapes of the Lake District
Nikolina Georgieva
Thesis Tutor: Elise Hunchuck

Abstract: This thesis is concerned with the origins, boundaries, and heterogeneity of the anthropogenic landscape. By developing a deep understanding of these landscapes as dynamic interrelations between ecological patterns and human pursuits, the thesis advances a new approach to analysing the often intangible, temporal relationships that culminate in a place's cultural imagination. Current Western conceptions of landscape as a medium limit its meaning, filtered through the modern desire for scientific objectivity. Ordered around technocratic interests of quantification, categorisation, monitoring and control over natural environments, the terminology around and the representation of nature augmented by humans is often self-referential and uncritical. Environmental psychology, behavioural geography, nature writing and situationist land art are frequently overlooked as credible means of generating knowledge of landscapes due to their perceived subjectivity. The binary between experiential and empirical knowledge is also evident in the predominant visual techniques of landscape imagery, which often result in decontextualised subjects of analysis, flattened, one-dimensional depictions.

The thesis challenges mapping as an active analytical and creative practice. An ecocultural discourse couples mapping and text into new readings of situations and structures in the confluence between human geographies, topographic elements and environmental forces. Multiple disciplines, including landscape architecture, geography, climatology, archaeology and forestry, employ cartographic studies. This thesis positions the agency of these fields in conversation with one another towards a new transdisciplinary methodology of knowledge-making. The Cumbrian Lake District in North West England is a case study, an anthropogenic landscape where agricultural, ecological, cultural and industrial practices collide, and in so doing, have formed the region's identity and role in a collective cultural imagination. Spatial experiences are coupled with scientific knowledge of a place in an effort to remodel and represent the reasoning between the geophysical materials, socio-cultural patterns and economic practices taking place in the landscape determining its future appropriations. A framework for mapping the anthropogenic landscape is developed as a series of landscape readings, emerging from the creative methodology of visual mappings in conversation with writings. From an ecological landscape understanding to cultural, forested, worked and mind landscape readings, this landscape discourse is stretched and thickened with new definitions of the being, ecological timescales, environmental cycles, the development of culture and the complex conditions of their convergence.

Image: Land formations and deformations: the worked landscapes of the quarries. Lake District, Cumbria. Image by the author, 2021.

415

Myth, Identity, Space: The cultural politics of belonging in post-colonial India
Arinjoy Sen
Thesis Tutor: Tania Sengupta

Abstract: The historical and on going tensions between the Indian state and minority groups pertaining to the idea, use and framing of 'nation-space' and physical space have come about through a complex development of conceptions of land, space and identity. These are variously instrumentalised to inscribe, include, exclude or manipulate ideas of citizenship. This thesis explores how specific cultural mythologies and narratives affect such conceptions and are (re)constituted by dominant agents as tools of oppression or persecution of particular groups. Equally, it engages with the persecuted communities' mobilisation of their own mythologies and narratives to resist state dominance as well as to define their own roles, positions, rights and selfhood.

I analyse the cultural politics of India through the conceptual triad of mythology, identity and space. In particular, I reflect on its manifestation in two historical episodes that exemplify the operative capacity of myth, identity and narrative at different scales and temporalities: one affecting national imagination, and the other local, place-based imagination, both of which generate particular conceptions of citizenship and space.

The thesis first problematises the territorial spatiality of the Indian nation-state, exemplified in the strategic deployment of the Hindu religious mythology of a sacred landscape or Ram Rajya. Selectively extracted by India's Hindu right-wing and projected onto the contemporary geopolitical territorial template of the modern Indian nation-state, Ram Rajya reconstitutes a new Hindu spatiality as a mechanism of 'othering' India's non-Hindu minorities.

The notion of a sacred landscape re-emerges in the temporal sacralisation of the forest by the inhabitants of the Sundarbans, in West Bengal, India, through the Bonbibi myth. A means to negotiate identity and territory, here spatial occupation and alternative conceptions of space, also became a mode of resistance for the refugees at Marichjhapi in the 1970s. Similarly, a distinct spatiality of resistance is seen in the recent anti-CAA (Citizenship Amendment Act, 2019) protests of Shaheen Bagh, New Delhi. In their contestations of identity and spatial representations, these episodes problematise the notions of (national) territory, nationhood and citizenship.

The conceptual framework of myth, identity and space posed highlights the deep interrelationships and activates a spatial understanding of narrativised cultural politics. This has wider implications in reading current issues of citizenship, especially in terms of the role space and cultural mythologies play in codifying notions of nationhood, identity and belonging.

Image: The image weaves the rituals, narrative and conceptions of space that inform the negotiated identities of the inhabitants of the Sunderban inhabitants. It draws on the conception of a myth-laden sacred landscape. It also depicts the continued oppression enacted towards this marginalised community, exemplified by the Marichjhapi Massacre of 1979.

Earthen Diversion
Daniel Pope
Thesis Tutor: Oliver Wilton

Abstract: Looking back at the history of building with London Clay, this thesis asks what reasons there might be for renewing this tradition and how current and emerging techniques could contribute to the development of a tailored London Brick architecture, applicable to new and existing buildings.

A history of London Clay is presented, discussing the emergence of brick as the dominant material of London's housing stock and the reasons for its eventual decline. Critical analysis of current London construction methods addresses matters including the harmful trend towards global material sourcing and the way that complex construction assemblies of disparate components can adversely affect building performance and lifecycle. The increasing urgency of addressing the poor energy performance of London's existing brick housing stock is also considered, in the context of the government's current efforts for carbon reduction.

In response, a circular clay resource system, The Earthen Land Registry, is hypothesised. This examines how London Clay from city excavations could be diverted away from landfill and into a new urban material metabolism, facilitating a return to building with London's abundant clay resource. Utilising this system, two architecture propositions are developed: the first is a new-build typology for London, the Earthen House, and the second is a clay-based retrofit strategy for existing brick buildings, the Earthen Blanket. These are developed using a research methodology including design, building surveying, material testing, and physical prototyping.

A real Victorian house is used as a case study to test the Earthen Blanket. Its façade is 3D-scanned and a range of scaled and 1:1 prototype components are made and taken to site, testing the applicability of this approach. The findings are clear: the time-consuming nature of the clay printing process and the bespoke component design stage, as no one brick façade is the same, means further development is needed. Also, the approach has significant potential to give thermal insulation, air tightness and other improvements while honouring the material heritage of the original architecture, and it warrants further development. Future research could develop automated procedural modelling to generate the bespoke clay components using façade 3D scans, consider aesthetic implications in more detail, and also investigate the viability of a mass rollout across London. The thesis contributes to architectural discourse on how emerging technologies can be used to construct clay architecture that meets the standards and responds to the challenges in housing today. A return to building with London clay could offer a sympathetic and innovative response to key challenges, with the longevity to survive for many generations.

Image: Photograph of the anamorphic 3D-printed ceramic Earthen Blanket component tailored to fit the ornate window mullion of this Victorian terraced house.

Voids: Investigating the extraction manoeuvre in 1960s and 1970s art practice and criticism for ecological approaches in contemporary architecture
Emmeline Kos
Thesis Tutor: Polly Gould

Abstract: The thesis questions the dynamic relationships between built and quarried environments and how the extraction manoeuvre is relevant to contemporary architecture's pertinent ecological responsibilities. When architecture is built, material is taken from the earth, displaced, and a void is created in the landscape. This occurs at sites of extraction, such as quarries, that are separated from where we live and build. This unbuilding manoeuvre is a consequence of the intention to build elsewhere, resulting in voids that acknowledge material absences.

The thesis investigates this through projects that foreground extraction. Beginning with the relationships between quarried and built environments of the Isle of Portland and London and investigating further displacement into a photographic medium through the photography of Edward Burtynsky. Continuing to question its potential through theory of the Expanded Field by Rosalind Krauss and her attempt to define postmodern artworks in the 1960s and 1970s between oppositions and negations. Together with the study of artworks of this era, Robert Smithson's *Spiral Jetty* (1970), Michael Heizer's *Double Negative* (1969), Gordon Matta-Clark's *Splitting* (1971), and Mary Miss' *Perimeters/Pavilions/Decoys* (1977–78) I consider operations that challenge and create relational ecologies.

By acknowledging inevitable connections, the thesis highlights that extraction is not exclusive. It is continuous, a transference from one system to another. The manoeuvre reveals relations to systems it was connected to and subsequently becomes a part of. Finally, I propose my own semiotic square that places architecture and landscape between extracted and constructed terms as an attempt to engage with contemporary projects that challenge these binary workflows; David Adjaye's Mass Extinction Monitoring Observatory (2016) and Ensamble Studio's Tippet Rise Art Centre (2016) and Ca'n Terra (2018).

Issues of resource conservation, material limits and our endless quest to build are addressed, but by focussing on the voids the research defers from technological solutions. It considers art in architecture's role in the Anthropocene. It is important for architecture to make connections with the voids it creates to understand how we live and build. Architecture is unpredictable, visceral and how it connects to the wider world is what makes it wonderful. Architects have an ecological responsibility and I imagine them as sculptors. I imagine a practice that incorporates shifting conditions, building and unbuilding sensitively, understanding, negotiating, relating.

Image: Disused Portland stone quarry. Photo by Keith Murray, flickr.com/photos/keithjmurray/28796230050/in/photostream/, CC BY-NC-SA 2.0 https://creativecommons.org/licenses/by-nc-sa/2.0/

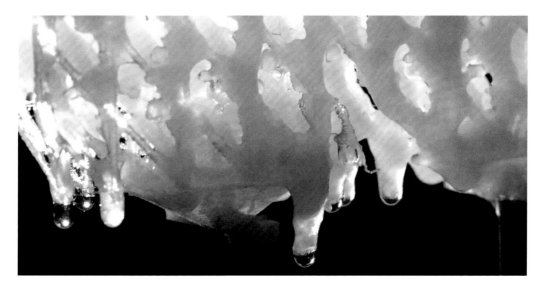

A Melting Light
Jonas Swienty Andresen
Thesis Tutor: Luke Lowings

Abstract: This thesis explores the dynamics of the relationship between ice and light in the High Arctic context of Svalbard. Svalbard is home to the northernmost permanent settlements on earth and is inhabited by a completely foreign architecture borrowed from further south. If the current climate change predictions hold, Svalbard will only become more accessible in the near future. Thus, the debate on how we inhabit the region is more relevant than ever. This thesis is critical of current discourses on building in the region and instead draws on indigenous practices found at similar altitudes. Working with the relationship between ice, light and time this thesis seeks to create an alternative, more organic, and responsive architecture for the High Arctic.

In order to approach a more environmentally responsive architecture, the first part of this thesis begins with a contextual and comparative analysis of the arctic region. The natural low light conditions of the arctic lead to an evaluation and discussion of the psychological impact of low light conditions. This forms a context for an in-depth, speculative and iterative experiment on augmenting low light levels through the architectural use of ice. This work is undertaken using physical prototyping and photography, as a vital method to better understand the fluid materiality. Questions include, How can moulds, surface manipulations, reinforcements, freezing processes, and various types of water alter the appearance of ice, and its transparency and ability to transmit and manipulate light? From phenomenological observations to digital light simulations, this thesis develops a methodology to develop an architectural language that can sculpt, augment, contain, and expose light using the materiality of ice.

The findings are synthesised into a comprehensive proposal and applied to an auditorium design mainly constructed of ice. The auditorium utilises the fluctuating properties of ice to sculpt natural and artificial light into an atmosphere of low illumination levels. Responding to both the dark winters and bright summers, the space integrates both low levels of illumination and darkness adaptation. The auditorium is a showcase for how a space can manipulate ice using lenses, transparent creases and translucent surfaces in order to achieve the desired atmosphere.

This research concludes that ice is a viable material to (re)consider using in remote locations in the High Arctic by rethinking a way of building with the environment. Ice can provide inhabitants with spaces more suitable for the local conditions and allow for a new, more experiential and fluid inhabitation.

Image: Close-up photograph of a structurally reinforced ice wall prototype showing ice sculpting and filtering the light.

Year 1 Architecture BSc studio work. Photo by Jinyi (Athena) Li.

Foster + Partners
fosterandpartners.com

Family crit at home. Photo by Guiming He, UG9.

Our Programmes

The Bartlett School of Architecture currently teaches undergraduate and graduate students across 25 programmes of study and one professional course.

Across the school's portfolio of teaching, research and professional programmes, our rigorous, creative and innovative approach to architecture remains integral. You will find below a list of our current programmes, their duration when taken full time (typical for MPhil/PhDs) and the directors. More information, including details on open days, is available on our website.

Undergraduate
Architecture BSc (ARB/RIBA Part 1)
Three-year programme, directed by
Ana Monrabal-Cook & Dr Luke Pearson
Architecture MSci (ARB Part 1 &2)
Five-year programme, directed by Sara Shafiei
Architectural & Interdisciplinary Studies BSc
Three or four-year programme,
directed by Elizabeth Dow
Engineering & Architectural Design MEng
Four-year programme, directed by Luke Olsen

Postgraduate
Architecture MArch (ARB/RIBA Part 2)
Two-year programme, directed by
Julia Backhaus & Professor Marjan Colletti
Architectural Computation MSc/MRes
12-month programmes,
directed by Manuel Jiménez Garcia
Architectural Design MArch
12-month programme,
directed by Gilles Retsin
Architectural History MA
One-year programme,
directed by Professor Peg Rawes
Architecture & Digital Theory MRes
One-year programme, directed by Professor
Mario Carpo & Professor Frédéric Migayrou
Architecture & Historic Urban Environments MA
One-year programme,
directed by Professor Edward Denison
Bio-Integrated Design MSc/MArch
Two-year programmes, directed by Professor
Marcos Cruz & Dr Brenda Parker (MSc only)

Design for Manufacture MArch
15-month programme,
directed by Emmanuel Vercruysse
Design for Performance & Interaction MArch
15-month programme,
directed by Dr Ruairi Glynn
Landscape Architecture MA/MLA
One (MA) and two-year (MLA) programmes,
directed by Professor Laura Allen &
Professor Mark Smout
Situated Practice MA
15-month programme,
directed by James O'Leary
Space Syntax: Architecture & Cities MSc/MRes
One-year programmes,
directed by Dr Kayvan Karimi
Urban Design MArch
12-month programme,
directed by Roberto Bottazzi

Advanced Architectural Research PG Cert
Six-month programme,
directed by Professor Stephen Gage

Architectural Design MPhil/PhD
Three to four-year programme,
directed by Professor Jonathan Hill
Architectural & Urban History & Theory MPhil/PhD
Three to four-year programme,
directed by Professor Sophia Psarra
Architectural Space & Computation MPhil/PhD
Three to four-year programme,
directed by Ava Fatah gen Schieck
Architecture & Digital Theory MPhil/PhD
Three to four-year programme,
directed by Professor Mario Carpo
& Professor Frédéric Migayrou

Professional
Professional Practice & Management in Architecture PGDip (ARB/RIBA Part 3)
7, 12, 18 or 24-month course,
directed by Professor Susan Ware

Public Lectures

Visit our Vimeo and YouTube channels to watch this year's recorded lectures – search 'Bartlett School of Architecture' to find us.

<u>The Bartlett International Lecture Series</u>
Attracting guests from across the world, our International Lecture Series has featured over 500 distinguished speakers since its inception in 1996. Lectures in this series are open to the public and free to attend.

Due to the extraordinary nature of this year, the series was held live on The Bartlett YouTube channel with a change in tone and format, moving away from 'lecturing' to 'conversing'. Each event was curated and co-hosted by a student and tutor from the school, and guests included diverse groups of thinkers, practitioners and activists from within and around the architectural sphere. Lectures this year featured:

— **Intersectional Architecture**
  Ben Campkin (The Bartlett), Esther Fox (Accentuate), Clare Murray (Levitt Bernstein), Akil Scafe-Smith (RESOLVE), Danna Walker (Built By Us), Sarah Wigglesworth (Sarah Wigglesworth Architects)
— **Can Architecture Be More Horizontal?**
  Pooja Agrawal (Homes England), Antonia Blege (Feilden Clegg Bradley Studios)
— **The Artists' Drawing**
  The Singh Twins
— **Nightclubbing**
  Catherine Rossi (Kingston School of Art), Mykaell Riley (University of Westminster)
— **Built Environments and the Lives of Children**
  Eddie Nutall (Felix Road Adventure Playground), Penny Wilson (Mudchute City Farm)
— **Exchanging Parcels**
  Eva Prats (Flores & Prats Arquitectes), Soraya Smithson (Artist)

— **Defining Diversity Through Lived Experience**
  Adam Furman (Architectural Association), Vinesh Pomal (TateHindle), Sumita Singha (Ecologic)
— **Sitopia: How Food Can Save the World**
  Carolyn Steel (Kilburn Nightingale Architects)
— **Advocating Architecture in Kampala**
  Doreen Adengo, Nina Peters, Franklin Kasumba (Adengo Architects)
— **No Such Place as Away – Creative Ways to Deal with Waste**
  Julia Christensen (Oberlin College)
— **Taking Back Power: Working at the Intersection of Communities, Arts, Design & Technology**
  Melissa Mean & John Bennett (Knowle West Media Centre), Amahra Spence & Amber Caldwell (MAIA)
— **Exploring Feminist Design Practices Then and Now**
  Torange Khonsari (Public Works), Jenny Richards, Sophie Hope (Birkbeck, University of London) and Lesley Lokko (University of Johannesburg)
— **Distance**
  Phil Ayres (CITA, Royal Danish Academy), Irene Cheng (California College of the Arts), Amy Kulper (Rhode Island School of Design), Ayona Datta (UCL), Huda Tayob (University of Johannesburg)
— **Female Imagination and the Production of Space**
  Izaskun Chinchilla Moreno, Penelope Haralambidou (The Bartlett) with John Cruwys, Faye Greenwood, Paula Strunden, Lewis Williams (Bartlett Alumni)
— **Intensive Care**
  Joshua Bolchover & John Lin (Rural Urban Framework and University of Hong Kong)
— **Inaugural Lecture: Winged Words and Weighty Number: 3½ Books on Architecture**
  Professor Sophia Psarra (The Bartlett)

Prospectives
The Bartlett's B-Pro history and theory lecture series continued to offer a platform for the presentation, discussion and theoretical reflection on the links between digital thought, architecture and urban design. Speakers included:

— **Vera Bühlmann (Vienna University of Technology)**
— **Bradley Cantrell (University of Virginia)**
— **Tessa Leach (Accenture)**
— **Anna-Maria Meister (TU Darmstadt)**
— **Kas Oosterhuis (ONL)**
— **Jose Sanchez (Plethora Project)**
— **Kostas Terzidis (Tongji University and ShangXiang Lab)**
— **Theodora Vardouli (McGill University)**
— **Andrew Witt (Certain Measures and Harvard GSD)**

Work in Progress
A new public lecture series from Landscape Architecture programmes, the series comprised curated but informal talks from practitioners and academics. Speakers from a range of disciplines were invited to reflect on their work in progress, working methods and the process of working with landscape. Speakers included:

— **Phil Askew (Peabody)**
— **Ceylan Belek Ombregt (Martha Schwartz Partners)**
— **Devin Dobrowolski (Somatic Collaborative and University of Virginia)**
— **Johanna Gibbons (J & L Gibbons and Landscape Learn)**
— **Meaghan Kombol (University of Greenwich)**

Bartlett Research Conversations
The Bartlett Research Conversations series featured presentations of research from students undertaking the Architectural Design or Architectural and Urban History and Theory MPhil/PhD programmes. Students were joined by senior academics from across the school, including PhD programme directors and supervisors, alongside members of the wider Bartlett and UCL community. This year research was presented by:

— **Alena Agafonova**
— **Atheer Al Mulla**
— **Sebastian Buser**
— **William Victor Camilleri**
— **Kerri Culhane**
— **Elin Eyborg Lund**
— **Stephannie Fell Contreras**
— **Clemency Gibbs**
— **Zoë Quick**
— **Ramandeep Shergill**
— **Anna Wild**
— **Katerina Zacharopoulou**

Space Syntax Laboratory Research Seminars
This academic seminar series featured researchers sharing their findings, discussing their ideas and showing work in progress from The Bartlett's Space Syntax Laboratory. Seminars were moderated by PhD candidate Sepehr Zhand. They were open to the public and attended by The Bartlett's staff and students. Guests included:

— **Liam Bolton (The Bartlett)**
— **Howard Davies (University of Oregon)**
— **Stella Fox (The Bartlett)**
— **Yuhan Ji (The Bartlett)**
— **Sam McElhinney (UCA Canterbury School of Architecture)**
— **Vinicius M. Netto (Fluminense Federal University)**
— **Ermal Shpuza (Kennesaw State University)**
— **Gianna Stavroulaki (Chalmers University of Technology)**
— **Alice Vialard (Northumbria University)**

Conferences & Events

The past year has seen a dramatic change in the usual schedule of Bartlett events as the school moved to an online environment, due to the Covid-19 pandemic. A full programme of conferences was held virtually, exploring innovative ideas and current issues, with inspiring speakers from across the globe.

Fabricate, 9–12 September 2020 was co-organised by The Bartlett School of Architecture, Swinburne University of Technology and Cornell University's College of Architecture, Art and Planning. The triennial conference brought together pioneers in design and making to explore how digital fabrication impacts the future of architecture, engineering and construction.

The poignant **Homework: Lived Experience Through Architectural Histories – Architectural History Symposium, 5–6 November 2020** examined what was afforded and lost to us online during the Covid-19 pandemic.

The **Parliament Buildings International Conference** spanned four days across **12–13 November 2020 and 18–19 February 2021** exploring architecture of power, accountability and democracy in Europe, supported by UCL's Grand Challenges of Cultural Understanding.

A range of performances were given over three days for **Situated Practice: Perform, Screen, Exchange, 18 November– 2 December 2020** exploring issues of injustice, displacement, exhaustion and care.

The 15th annual **PhD Research Projects Conference 23 and 25 February 2021** included two days of intense debate and discussion between students, staff, invited guests, critics and the public on doctoral work in development and drawing to conclusion.

Over 900 people attended **Gender and Infrastructure: Intersections between Postsocialist and Postcolonial Geographies, 4–5 March 2021** to investigate the relationship between gender, subjectivity and space, specifically the ways in which this is experienced and theorised in post-socialist and postcolonial contexts.

This online international symposium **Intersectional Climate: Conversations Towards COP26, 16 and 18 March 2021** celebrated climate practices that prioritise ecological, political and poetic engagement with communities, places and disciplines.

Young architects and activists joined academics in the roundtable discussion **How Can I Build Change? Architectural Activism Against the Status Quo, 22 March 2021** to question how designers can interrupt architectural dogma and challenge the status quo.

Finally, **Automated Architecture (AUAR) Lab**, a research laboratory at The Bartlett, presented a series of takeovers in Spring 2021 to showcase a new housing prototype, **House Block**.

Bartlett Shows Website

In September 2020, the school launched its bespoke digital exhibition environment, presenting The Summer Show 2020. Since then, four further student shows have been shared digitally: The B-Pro Show 2020, The Autumn Show 2020, Fifteen 2020 and PhD Research Projects 2021. The school's digital exhibitions have been visited by over 90,000 users from across the globe.

The digital exhibition space was designed by creative agency Hello Monday, working together with the school's exhibitions and communications teams, to create a unique online experience for the visitor. Hello Monday delivered a virtual show space that allows the user to explore the work spatially, within exhibition rooms, and in detail, on student project pages. Students have the opportunity to display their work using video, high-definition imagery and 3D models alongside detailed narratives.

With each exhibition, the digital environment is being refined to improve the visitor experience and to encourage greater engagement with the student work displayed. New for The Summer Show 2021, projects will be searchable by thematic concern and all previous shows will be available to browse from one single landing page.

The Bartlett's digital show environment has won web design awards at both the Awwwards and Favourite Website Awards and has been shortlisted for the prestigious Archiboo and D&AD Awards in the Digital Design category. Within the UCL community, the virtual shows team, specifically Chee-Kit Lai, Director of Exhibitions, Professor Penelope Haralambidou, Director of Communications, and David Shanks, Project Manager, have been recognised for their outstanding contribution to the learning experience with a UCL Education Award in the student-staff partnership category.

www.bartlettarchucl.com

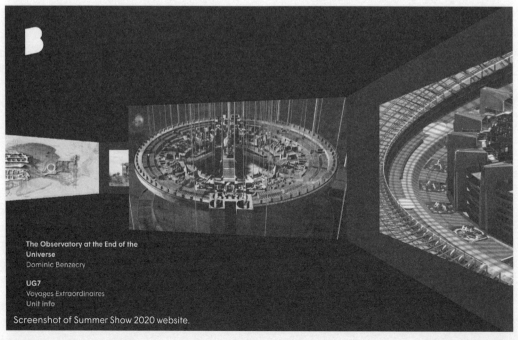

The Observatory at the End of the Universe
Dominic Benzecry

UG7
Voyages Extraordinaires
Unit info

Screenshot of Summer Show 2020 website.

Alumni

The Bartlett's diverse and vibrant alumni play a vital role in the life of the school, as staff, visiting lecturers, mentors, sponsors, donors and participants.

Each year we organise several alumni events, including an 'R&V' evening, founded by and for alumni as the 'Rogues and Vagabonds' over 60 years ago. Usually taking the format of a dinner, during this exceptional year we moved to a virtual platform for an evening to celebrate the ten Bartlett alumni practices featured in the 2020 *Architects' Journal* '40 under 40' list, renowned for highlighting emerging architectural talent.

Each practice presented their work in fast-paced PechaKucha format to an audience of alumni, staff and students. The audience enjoyed inspiring presentations from **Alma-nac** (Caspar Rodgers, Chris Bryant and Tristan Wigfall), **Archio** (Kyle Buchanan), **Assemble** (Amica Dall), **Freehaus** (Jonathan Hagos), **McCloy + Muchemwa** (Steve McCloy and Bo Muchemwa), **Nooma** (Ramsey Yassa), **Office S&M** (Hugh McEwan and Catrina Stewart),

Nudge (Shanks Raj), **TDO** (Doug Hodgson and Tom Lewith) and **We Made That** (Holly Lewis). The event was chaired by Paul Monaghan, Director at Allford Hall Monaghan Morris.

We also invite alumni to join us at The Bartlett Summer Show at an exclusive Alumni Late.

All Bartlett School of Architecture alumni are invited to join UCL's Alumni Online Community to keep in touch with the school and receive benefits including special discounts, UCL's *Portico* magazine and more.

Registered alumni have access to:
— Thousands of e-journals available through UCL Library
— A global network of old and new friends in the worldwide alumni community
— Free mentoring and the opportunity to become a mentor yourself
— Jobs boards for the exclusive alumni community

aoc.ucl.ac.uk/alumni

Illustration by Simon Hayes for the *Architects' Journal* '40 under 40' list.

The Bartlett Promise

Across higher education and in industry, the built environment sector is not diverse enough. Here at The Bartlett, we promise to do better.

The Bartlett Promise Scholarship has been launched to enable UK/EU students from backgrounds under-represented in The Bartlett Faculty to pursue their studies with us, with the aim of diversifying the student body and ultimately the built environment sector. We want a Bartlett education to be open to all, regardless of means.

The scholarship covers full tuition fees for the degree programme, plus an annual allowance to cover living and study expenses. All Promise scholars will also receive ongoing academic and career support during their study.

Professor Christoph Lindner, Dean of The Bartlett Faculty of the Built Environment says:

Society works for everyone when it is shaped by everyone, but right now that's not happening. We know that the cost of education is a very real barrier for many – The Bartlett Promise Scholarship will help to address that by removing this barrier to entry whilst providing additional support.

Prospective students who are offered a place on a degree at The Bartlett are invited to apply to the scholarship in the summer before they begin with us.

When selecting scholars, we consider the educational, personal and financial circumstances of the applicant, and how these relate to the eligibility criteria. Details of the application process and eligibility criteria can be found on our website.

ucl.ac.uk/bartlett/bartlett-promise

Students at 22 Gordon Street, The Bartlett's Bloomsbury home.

Architecture Education Declares

Architecture Education Declares was formed in June 2019 by architecture students from leading schools, including The Bartlett School of Architecture, in response to global scientific predictions of catastrophic climate change and biodiversity loss.

Architecture Education Declares calls for a radical overhaul of architectural education – not just what we do, but how and why we do it. The aim is to move towards a collaborative culture of care to address the climate and ecological emergency and social and environmental justice issues. The declaration calls for a move from Western-centric narratives to a more holistic education that respects diverse cultures, history and heritage. In response, The Bartlett School of Architecture declared a climate and ecological emergency. Through citizens' assemblies and workshops, students started to explore how design briefs, assessment criteria, tutorials and crits could change.

This year, in the midst of the pandemic, the main goal has been to establish a framework of ideas and systems for future students and committee members to use. The Bartlett School of Architecture Society launched a podcast series interviewing alumni on their views and experiences, while further initiatives are planned for summer 2021. In April, students from the society co-chaired a public UCL event, 'Healthy, Biodiverse, Equitable Cities', opened by the new President & Provost, Dr Michael Spence. The event was used as a platform for diverse practitioners to present ideas on how architects and built environment professionals can respond to the climate and ecological emergency.

Architecture students joined campaigns such as the London Energy Transformation Initiative against lowering UK building energy standards; the *Architects' Journal*'s RetroFirst campaign, promoting the refurbishment of buildings instead of demolishing them to make space for new-builds; and the Architects Climate Action Network (ACAN), who have produced an Education Toolkit to help drive curriculum and culture change in architecture schools. ACAN also founded the Student Climate Action Network (StuCAN), with Bartlett students forming a StuCAN group.

The determination of the school's students to make a better world is inspiring, especially during such a challenging year. We look forward to supporting their efforts for a progressive education and a strong student voice in 2021–22.

The Bartlett School of Architecture Society
President: Tyler Ebanja
Treasurer: Siobhan Obi
Vice-President: Jatin Naru
Social Secretary: Tochi Itanyi
Equity & Diversity Officer: Hao Zhang
Media & Communications Officers:
Isabella Shen, Maggie Chao

www.architectureeducationdeclares.com

Staff, Visitors & Consultants

A
Ana Abram
Vasilija Abramovic
George Adamopoulos
Visiting Prof Robert Aish
Rezwana Akhter
Prof Laura Allen
Dr Rahil Alipour
Sabina Andron
Arveen Appadoo
Azadeh Asgharzadeh
    Zaferani
Abigail Ashton
Edwina Attlee

B
Julia Backhaus
Kirsty Badenoch
Beth Barnett-Sanders
Stefan Bassing
Paul Bavister
Simon Beames
Richard Beckett
Ruth Bernatek
Bastian Beyer
Shajay Bhooshan
Vishu Bhooshan
Jan Birksted
Prof Peter Bishop
Isaïe Bloch
Eleanor Boiling
William Bondin
Prof Iain Borden
Roberto Bottazzi
Visiting Prof Andy Bow
Matthew Bowles
Dr Eva Branscome
Pascal Bronner
Alastair Browning
Tom Budd
Mark Burrows
Bim Burton
Matthew Butcher

C
Joel Cady
Thomas Callan
Blanche Cameron
William Victor Camilleri
Barbara-Ann
    Campbell-Lange
Dr Ben Campkin
Alice Carman
Dr Brent Carnell
Prof Mario Carpo
Dan Carter

Martyn Carter
Ricardo Carvalho De Ostos
Tomasso Casucci
Dr Megha Chand Inglis
Frosso Charalambous
Haden Charbel
Prof Nat Chard
Po-Nien Chen
Prof Izaskun
    Chinchilla Moreno
Sandra Ciampone
Ed Clark
Mollie Claypool
Jason Coe
Gonzalo Coello
    de Portugal
Prof Marjan Colletti
Emeritus Prof
    Sir Peter Cook
Marc-Olivier Coppens
Hannah Corlett
Miranda Critchley
Prof Marcos Cruz
Lisa Cumming

D
Christina Dahdaleh
Amica Dall
Gareth Damian Martin
Satyajit Das
Kate Davies
Tom Davies
James Daykin
Klaas de Rycke
Luca Dellatorre
Prof Edward Denison
Pradeep Devadass
Max Dewdney
Dr Ashley Dhanani
Ilaria Di Carlo
David Di Duca
Simon Dickens
Visiting Prof Elizabeth Diller
Katerina Dionysopoulou
Paul Dobraszczyk
Patch Dobson-Pérez
Oliver Domeisen
Elizabeth Dow
Georgios Drakontaeidis
Tom Dyckhoff

E
David Edwards
Fatma Ergin
Sam Esses
Ruth Evison

F
Pani Fanai-Danesh
Ava Fatah gen. Schieck
Donat Fatet
Timothy Fielder
Lucy Flanders
Zachary Fluker
Emeritus Prof
    Adrian Forty
Emeritus Prof
    Colin Fournier
Prof Murray Fraser
Daisy Froud
Maria Fulford

G
Emeritus Prof Stephen Gage
Laura Gaskell
Christophe Gérard
Egmontas Geras
Alexis Germanos
Octavian Gheorghiu
Dr Stelios Giamarelos
Pedro Gil-Quintero
Agnieszka Glowacka
Dr Ruairi Glynn
Alicia Gonzalez-Lafita
    Perez
Dr Jon Goodbun
Dr Polly Gould
Niamh Grace
Marta Granda Nistal
Emmy Green
James Green
Kevin Green
Sienna Griffin-Shaw
Dr Sam Griffiths
Dr Kostas Grigoriadis
Peter Guillery
Seth Guy

H
Soomeen Hahm
James Hampton
Tamsin Hanke
Prof Sean Hanna
Prof Penelope
    Haralambidou
Jack Hardy
Visiting Prof
    Itsuko Hasegawa
Emeritus Prof
    Christine Hawley
Robert Haworth
Ben Hayes
Thea Heintz

Jose Hernandez
Colin Herperger
Simon Herron
Parker Heyl
Prof Jonathan Hill
Thomas Hillier
Ashley Hinchcliffe
Mark Hines
Bill Hodgson
Tom Holberton
Adam Holloway
Tyson Hosmer
Delwar Hossain
Oliver Houchell
William Huang
Elise Hunchuck
Vincent Huyghe
Johan Hybschmann

I
Jessica In
Anderson Inge
Susanne Isa
Cannon Ivers

J
Clara Jaschke
Will Jefferies
Manuel Jiménez Garcia
Steve Johnson
Helen Jones
Nina Jotanovic

K
Jon Kaminsky
Dr Kayvan Karimi
Dr Jan Kattein
Anja Kempa
Jonathan Kendall
Tom Kendall
Maren Klasing
Jakub Klaska
Fergus Knox
Maria Knutsson-Hall
Kimon Krenz
Dirk Krolikowski
Dragana Krsic
Sir Banister Fletcher Visiting
    Prof Perry Kulper
Diony Kypraiou

L
Chee-Kit Lai
Elie Lakin
Lo Lanfear
Ruby Law

Jeremy Lecomte
Roberto Ledda
Dr Guan Lee
Benjamin Lee
Stefan Lengen
Dr Christopher Leung
Sarah Lever
Visiting Prof
    Amanda Levete
Ifigeneia Liangi
Prof CJ Lim
Prof Christoph Lindner
Enriqueta Llabres-Valls
Alvaro Lopez
Deborah Lopez
Tim Lucas
Genevieve Lum
Abi Luter
Samantha Lynch

M

Abel Maciel
Sonia Magdziarz
Nazila Maghzian
Alexandru Malaescu
Shneel Malik
Prof Yeoryia
    Manolopoulou
Robin Mather
Emma-Kate Matthews
Billy Mavropoulos
Claire McAndrew
Hugh McEwen
Prof Niall McLaughlin
Dr Clare Melhuish
Visiting Prof Jeremy Melvin
Prof Josep Miás Gifre
Bartlett Prof
    Frédéric Migayrou
Doug Miller
Sarah Milne
Tom Mole
Ana Monrabal-Cook
Philippe Morel
Shaun Murray

N

Tetsuro Nagata
Elliot Nash
Filippo Nassetti
Rasa Navasaityte
Chi Nguyen

O

Kyrstyn Oberholster
Toby O'Connor

James O'Leary
Luke Olsen
Andy O'Reilly
Visiting Prof Raf Orlowski
Daniel Ovalle Costal

P

Yael Padan
Igor Pantic
Marie-Eleni Papandreou
Annarita Papeschi
Dr Brenda Parker
Ralph Parker
Thomas Parker
Claudia Pasquero
Jane Patterson
Thomas Pearce
Dr Luke Pearson
Prof Alan Penn
Prof Barbara Penner
Drew Pessoa
Frosso Pimenides
Alicia Pivaro
Maj Plemenitas
Danae Polyviou
Andrew Porter
Alan Powers
Arthur Prior
Prof Sophia Psarra
James Purkiss

R

Carolina Ramirez Figueroa
Robert Randall
Prof Peg Rawes
Dr Sophie Read
Dr Aileen Reid
Guang Yu Ren
Prof Jane Rendell
Gilles Retsin
Farlie Reynolds
Julie Richardson
Sam Riley
Dr David Roberts
Felix Roberts
Gavin Robotham
Daniel Rodriguez Garcia
Martina Rosati
Javier Ruiz Rodriguez

S

Martin Sagar
Dr Kerstin Sailer
Prof Andrew Saint
Dr Shahed Saleem
Anete Salmane

Tan Sapsaman
Sanyal Saptarshi
Ned Scott
Peter Scully
Dr Tania Sengupta
Alan Sentongo
Sara Shafiei
David Shanks
Alistair Shaw
Prof Bob Sheil
Don Shillingburg
Naz Siddique
Maya Simkin
Colin Smith
Paul Smoothy
Prof Mark Smout
Valentina Soana
Jasmin Sohi
James Solly
Harmit Soora
Amy Spencer
Ben Spong
Matthew Springett
Prof Michael Stacey
Brian Stater
Iulia Statica
Emmanouil Stavrakakis
Tijana Stevanovic
Rachel Stevenson
Sabine Storp
Greg Storrar
David Storring
Kay Stratton
Michiko Sumi
Tom Svilans

T

Jerry Tate
Sam Taylor Baldwin
Philip Temple
Colin Thom
Michael Tite
Claudia Toma
Martha Tsigkari
Freddy Tuppen

V

Melis Van Den Berg
Kelly Van Hecke
Kim Van Poeteren
Afra Van't Land
Dr Tasos Varoudis
Prof Laura Vaughan
Hamish Veitch
Emmanuel Vercruysse
Viktoria Viktorija

Amilea Vilaplana de Miguel
Jordi Vivaldi Piera
Dr Nina Vollenbroker

W

Michael Wagner
Andrew Walker
Adam Walls
Prof Susan Ware
Barry Wark
Gabriel Warshafsky
Tim Waterman
Visiting Prof Bill Watts
Patrick Weber
Paul Weston
Alice Whewell
Amy White
Andy Whiting
Alex Whitley
Rae Whittow-Williams
Daniel Widrig
Freya Wigzell
Dan Wilkinson
Gen Williams
Henrietta Williams
Graeme Williamson
James Williamson
Dr Robin Wilson
Oliver Wilton
Nick Winnard
Simon Withers
Katy Wood
Anna Woodeson

Y

Sandra Youkhana
Michelle Young

Z

Emmanouil Zaroukas
Sepher Zhand
Dominik Zisch
Fiona Zisch
Stamatis Zografos

ucl.ac.uk/architecture
bartlettarchucl.com
Find us on

Publisher
The Bartlett School of Architecture, UCL

Editors
Phoebe Adler, Penelope Haralambidou

Proofreader
Thomas Abbs

Graphic Design
Patrick Morrissey, Unlimited
weareunlimited.co.uk

Executive Editors
Barbara-Ann Campbell-Lange, Bob Sheil

ISBN 978-1-8383185-2-9

The Bartlett School of Architecture, UCL
22 Gordon Street
London WC1H 0QB

+44 (0)20 3108 9646
architecture@ucl.ac.uk

Summer Show Main Title Supporter 2021

**ALLFORD
HALL
MONAGHAN
MORRIS**

Summer Show Sponsor

Foster + Partners